ISLAND GIRL
TO AIRLINE
PILOT

ISLAND GIRL
TO AIRLINE PILOT

A story of love, sacrifice and taking flight

SILVA MCLEOD

PUBLISHING

First published 2023

Exisle Publishing Pty Ltd
PO Box 864, Chatswood, NSW 2057, Australia
226 High Street, Dunedin, 9016, New Zealand
www.exislepublishing.com

A CiP record for this book is available from the National Library of Australia.

ISBN 978-1-922539-61-8

Cover photograph of Silva in pilot uniform by Jacki Starr
Designed by Enni Tuomisalo
Maps courtesy of Vectorstock
Typeset in PT Serif, 10pt
Printed in China

This book uses paper sourced under ISO 14001 guidelines from well-managed forests and other controlled sources.

10 9 8 7 6 5 4 3 2 1

*To the love of my life, Kenneth Neil, the wind
beneath my wings. I have shared our journey
with the world and I hope you would be proud.
You saw no colour, no status and no difference
in culture, you only saw me, and for that, I thank
you for the life I have and the love we shared.*

> *Ken, I've lived as you lived.*
> *There was no more living left to do.*
> *We'd done so much living together.*
> *I am happy and contented.*
> *I would be glad if I could close my eyes tonight,*
> *And wake up in your arms so tight.*

*To my two beautiful girls, Lizzie and
Tema, the unsung heroines, thank you
for your sacrifice. With all my love.*

CONTENTS

Part 2

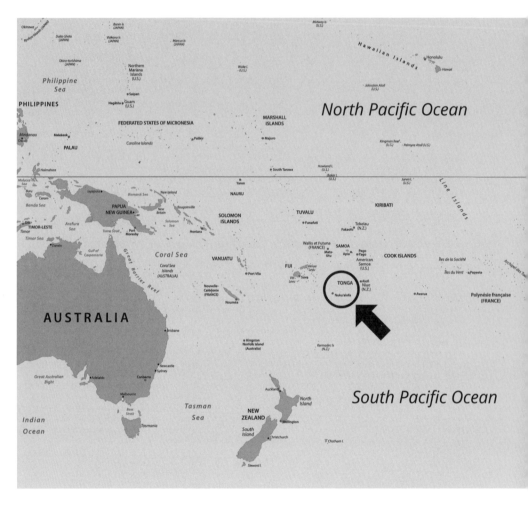

Tonga is a small archipelago in the South Pacific. It consists of 169 islands but only 36 are inhabited. Its total size is 757 square kilometres (288 square miles). Vava'u, where I come from, lies in the northern group of islands. Latitude 18.6505°S, longitude 173.99765°W.

Niuafo'ou

Niua Group

Tafahi
Niuatoputapu

SOUTH

PACIFIC

Fonualei

Toku

Vava'u Group

Hunga

Vava'u

Late

OCEAN

Kao

Muitoa

Tofua

Foa

Lifuka

Uiha

Ha'apai Group

Nomuka

Hunga
Ha'apai

NUKU'ALOFA

Tongatapu

'Eua

Tongatapu Group

Tonga Trench

0   25   50   100 km

'Atū

0   25   50   100 mi

PART 1

Prologue:
Be my voice

Saturday morning, 6 June 2020. Ken's voice pleaded with me during our video call from the hospital. The look of despair on his ashen face was made worse by the white hospital gown he was wearing as he stared back from the telephone screen. He looked lost, scared and so vulnerable.

'Liva, can I come home please? I've had enough of hospital. I've told them a thousand times, but they don't listen.'

'Oh, baby.' Tears streamed down my face. 'Stay right there, I'm coming to get you, but you have to tell them exactly what you've just told me. I can't fight them alone.'

'They don't listen, darl. You're more forceful than I am. Please, darl. You can be my voice! Please.' His voice trailed off like a child asking a mother. If only he could have seen what his words did to my heart.

Partial lockdown and restrictions had been put in place due to Covid, and hospitals were no exception. Ken had been admitted with vomiting and a slight temperature. I hadn't been allowed to enter the emergency department with him so had sat outside the waiting room from 9.30 a.m. until 3 p.m. I'd finally decided to go home as it was hopeless trying to get in.

Ken had complex, ongoing health issues and I had only wanted help to stabilize and get him comfortable, then take him home. But it hadn't happened that way.

On my way home I'd got a call from the doctor at the emergency department. 'Ken has a chest infection,' he told me. 'We're treating him with antibiotics and he's having a blood transfusion as well because his haemoglobin is very low. If he doesn't respond to the antibiotics, he may only last a couple of days.'

'No! no! no! What the fuck are you saying? This can't be happening,' I screamed uncontrollably as I pulled over to the side of the road. *Not the ideal time to deliver such news.* I thought. *Okay, control yourself, Liva.*

'Can I see him?' I said.

'Sorry, but hospital Covid policy is strictly no visitors,' the stoic voice said.

'Fuck your hospital policy.'

He sounded shocked by my reaction. 'What do you want from us?'

I didn't care whether I offended him as I screamed down the phone. 'Simple — stabilize him and I'll take him home. This is the cruellest thing you could do to a human being. Are you saying I could lose my Ken without saying goodbye and he'll be facing his maker all alone in hospital? That's not acceptable. You'd better pray that's not going to happen.'

'I'm sorry. I'll see what I can do.'

'Oh, you better,' I said, but he'd hung up.

I realized I was shaking. Sweat dripped off my forehead but I was cold. *Breathe, breathe, Liva.* I took a few deep breaths, mopped my face, and drove home.

I felt as if I'd lost Ken already and yet he was still here. Our bedroom felt cold and empty as I took ownership of our bed, sobbing my eyes out. 'What have I done? Please Lord, help me. Ken, I'm so sorry, I'm so sorry.'

Within ten minutes or so, I received another phone call. I wiped away my tears as I put on my official voice. 'Hello?'

'Mrs McLeod? I'm the head nurse from the emergency department.'

'Yes?' I braced for impact.

'We have a dispensation for you to visit your husband. We will hold onto Ken for as long as it takes you to get here. You can have a bit of time with him before he's transferred to the Covid ward.'

'Oh! Thank you. I'll be right over.' I exhaled. I'd thought she would deliver different news.

'As I said, no need to rush. Ken will be here until you get in. Drive safely.'

I jumped out of bed and straightened myself on my way out. It was like I was falling in love all over again.

When I got to the hospital the doctor helped me into a protective gown, hat, surgical mask and gloves. He looked at me with calm, kind eyes, with no accusation for my earlier outburst. He was black like me and with that common ground I hope he saw my pain was crippling me.

I seized the moment and pushed him a little. 'With all these bullshit gowns on, will I be able to give Ken a kiss?'

'Let's put it this way. Once I shut the door behind you, I won't know what's going on in there.'

I entered the room and saw Ken lying there, all alone, looking so vulnerable. Fresh tears rolled out. I didn't know if they were tears of relief that Ken was still with me or guilt that I'd put him in hospital.

Ken looked up but he didn't recognize me with all my protective gear on until I pulled my mask off. The look on his face was not something I will forget in a hurry — sheer relief and happiness to see me. Only a few hours earlier, I'd thought I'd never see him alive again and now I was staring at him in the flesh. I gave him a big bear hug and a long hard kiss, savouring the moment.

His poor battered body was hooked up to lots of medical contraptions that branched out everywhere. I was shocked when I realized he was lying on his pillow from home. It had a vomit stain and was saturated with his perspiration.

I got a face-washer and sponged him down, then I lifted his head and turned the pillow over. At least that was the dry side and I didn't have to look at the stain any more. I was aware that doctors and nurses had more serious things to worry about than a stained pillow; it was a small thing but meant so much to me.

Soon it was time to transfer Ken to the Covid ward for isolation, awaiting the results of his test. From then on, I wasn't allowed to see him. It would take 24 hours to get the results. I went up to the ward with him but had to say goodbye when he was wheeled out of the lift. As we hugged, I whispered into his ear. 'Remember our plan — stabilized then come home.'

'Yes. I love you, darl. Drive carefully,' he whispered in his faint voice.

'And I love you more. Just remember that. I'll call you in the morning.'

How we crossed paths

How wrong I was to think I had the world at my fingertips after graduating with my high school certificate, dux of Saint Peter Chanel College, the only Catholic high school in the island of Vava'u, Tonga. I was turning eighteen.

When I couldn't find a job as quickly as I'd thought, I realized that zero experience with only a high school certificate didn't amount to anything. Growing up in the small village of Pangaimotu on the island of Vava'u, there was an expectation that I would be married off, have dozens of kids and ensure the cycle of island living would continue.

'Don't forget, if you lose your virginity before marriage you'll be left on the shelf. No one will want you unless you're needed for a punching bag,' Grandma said, her finger working overtime with the pointing. My sister Selai and I had been reared by Grandma Nane and Grandpa Tai from a very young age. They were my mum's parents.

Mum and Dad had gone their separate ways and each had their own family. Mum moved to the main island of Tongatapu, while Dad lived only a few doors away from my grandparents. In my eyes, Grandma and Grandpa *were* my mum and dad. They fed me when I was hungry, wiped my tears when I was hurt, rejoiced with me when I was victorious.

Well, that's not going to happen to me, Grandma, I thought. I was determined to break the island cycle. Domestic violence was part of normal life, but I'd rather stay celibate than be subjected to that. I had no desire to rush into marriage.

The only way I could delay the inevitable was to find a paid job. After a few months of rejection, I reached a point where I didn't care what type of job it was, as long as I didn't have to stay at home. *Please Lord, please get me out of here*, I prayed.

I landed my first job as a waitress at Port of Refuge, the only hotel in Vava'u. It was owned and managed by an Australian couple, Bill and Wendy. I was ecstatic that not only would I get paid, but I would meet and mingle with palangi — white people or 'man from the sky'.

My desire for a better position and more money saw me confront Bill, my boss, one day. It was an arrogant move, but I had nothing to lose. 'Bill, I've been here a couple of months now. I think I deserve better.'

'What makes you think that?' Bill said with mocking eyes.

'Well, I didn't spend twelve years at school to be a waitress. I'm better than that and worth much more.' I had no idea how to negotiate.

Bill rolled his eyes as if appealing to the heavens above. 'You have balls, I'll give you that, but you know what? I'll think about it.'

I felt so hot with embarrassment that I couldn't wait to get out of his office.

A few weeks after that conversation, I was promoted to the position of bartender. It wasn't what I'd had in mind, but it paid more than waitressing. *It will have to do for now*, I thought.

This was where I first came into contact with three Australians who'd been sent to Vava'u on Commonwealth aid projects, fully funded by the Australian government. They were working on a much-needed hospital and a fuel depot. Tonga relied heavily on foreign handouts as there was no main revenue to support such essential services.

Leo, the builder/project manager, Ken the electrician and Joe the plumber came to the bar at the Port of Refuge Hotel at 5 p.m. every day. They each had three beers, then left. My boss joined them every day and kept reminding me to keep them happy. 'The Australians love their beers cold, so you better make sure they are,' he said in his condescending nasal voice.

'How cold?' I asked, rolling my eyes to the wall so he couldn't see.

'Kiddo, if you don't know by now, you'd better start learning. We can't lose these boys.'

Bloody hell! They should get a life if all they worry about is that the beer is cold. They'd better take a long hard look around. And by the way, where else can they have a beer in Vava'u?

Bill picked up a can of Foster's beer to give me a demonstration. 'If droplets run down the side of either a glass or bottle like this, then it's too warm. Too cold and you'll freeze the beer.'

Whatever!

I managed to keep those VIPs happy and their beer and glasses cold. These Australians were like gods — whatever they wanted, they got. Their routine never changed: once they arrived at the bar, they put their money on the counter to pay for a round of beer. They always had three beers and I helped myself to the money without having to ask.

Ken the electrician always sat at the end of the bar closest to the wall, which happened to be where my bar stool sat. *He's handsome and hot*, I thought. The good Old Spice aftershave smelled great, too.

In the beginning, Ken and I didn't talk much. I was attracted to his white skin first. *How cool would it be to fall in love with this palangi? I* thought, as I danced with the idea in my head.

Maybe Ken sensed my awkwardness (there was no way he could see me blush with my dark skin), but his eyes started playing with me, then he slowly moved to physical touch. We played this game day after day.

After a while, he didn't put his money on the counter any more. He preferred to hand it to me and put his hand out to receive the change. Every time he handed out his money, he scratched my hand while slowly releasing the money onto mine. I knew he was watching my face for a reaction.

This simple form of connection sent electricity through my body. I was sure Ken knew how it affected me and he made it worse by holding my hand a bit longer when I gave back the change. *Am I imagining things or is he teasing me?* I thought. *Why would this handsome young man be interested in me, a barmaid, a nobody? He could have any Tongan girl he wanted.*

I told myself what I was feeling was a teenage infatuation, but his teasing continued. *Don't lose focus on the plan for a better job*, my inner self screamed at me. This job was only an interim one while I was on the prowl for another. While I was enjoying my newfound friend in Ken, I knew I had to move on.

1 HOW WE CROSSED PATHS

A new department store had been completed and they were hiring. I didn't think I'd have too much trouble getting one of the sales positions. I was sure a job in a shop was better than a job at a pub.

I queued for the interview on a typical tropical morning — the sun had been long up and it was hot and humid. Shortly after 9 a.m., there was a commotion. I looked up towards where the rustling was coming from.

'Oh, dear!' I mumbled under my breath. The two people conducting the interview (both palangis) were staying at the hotel. They'd been at the bar the night before and I'd been unfortunate enough to serve them. *Hopefully, they weren't too drunk and they will recognize me*, I thought. As they walked past where I stood, I made a bold move and said, 'Good morning, Mike.'

Mike was the leader of the two. He turned around and, thank god, acknowledged me. I wasn't sure whether he recognized me or if he was just being polite. If nothing came of it, at least I made an impact on my fellow interviewees.

Not long after they'd gone in, I was called. 'Silva? Next.'

I was summoned to the front of the queue. The nervousness quickly washed away as I entered the spacious office with these two gods I'd only met the night before.

Mike took the lead. 'Well, Silva. It was a surprise to see you here this morning.'

'Hopefully not in a bad way,' I said.

'No, not at all.' He glanced at his companion. 'In fact, we were wondering if you'd be interested in coming out for a drink with us after your shift tonight?'

I recognized the look in his eye all too well. This wasn't about my suitability for the job.

I left the interview feeling gross instead of victorious and didn't know whether I'd got a job or not. But instead of saying no to the drink invitation, I'd found myself saying yes.

As I walked back to the hotel, I scolded myself. *I did what women in domestic violence do. They know they should say no yet they continue to go back to the abuse, to the control, saying yes!*

I hated being powerless, poor and unattractive. In my mind, being black meant being primitive. *I wish I was white like Ken, so people didn't look down on me.*

Back at the hotel, the ordeal of the morning faded away and was replaced by work mode. The Aussie boys arrived right on cue at 5 p.m. and I knew that once I saw Ken and felt his teasing touch, I would be okay. I would deal with the sleazebags afterwards.

Ken had known I was going for the interview, but he didn't ask how it went. I was disappointed that he didn't seem to care but when they were leaving, he stopped and turned to me. 'Could I come back later for a chat?'

Is he asking me on a date? My heart flipped with excitement but mostly relief that I could ask Ken to join me and the sleazebags. I had a plan without jeopardizing my chance for a 'better' job. I didn't know what made me think that a shop cashier was going to be better than a bartender.

While the sleazebags were having dinner, I was summoned to the table for their wine order. No sooner had I arrived than I felt an uninvited arm around my hips. I wished I knew whether I'd got a job so I could tell them to piss off. If not, I could still tell them to piss off.

I would play their game if that was what they wanted. Maybe I would enjoy the attention. I knew that Ken was coming back so I purposely put out an empty beer can with loose change to reserve the end of the bar where he usually sat.

When Ken arrived at 8 p.m., the bar was not very busy and we had a bit of quiet time to ourselves.

He finally asked. 'How did the interview go? Have you got a new job?'

'They didn't ask me any questions, so I don't know whether I have a job or not. However, they invited me for a drink afterwards.'

'Oh! That's an interview with a difference. If you like, I'll hang around with you.'

'Are you jealous, Ken?' I teased.

But his eyes darkened. 'Huh! You have no freaking idea, Liva. These men prey on naive girls like you and it shits me. I'll hang around.'

Whoa! and that is an order. Yes sir. My inner self danced. 'Thank you,' I said, trying not to sound too excited as I tried to make light of the situation.

The sleazebags finished their dinner and moved to the bar. They were loud and acted as if they owned the place. They bragged to Ken about how I'd smashed the interview and got the job as a wholesale supervisor.

Who's intoxicated now? That's news to me.

I served the last round and joined them with Ken by my side. I was grateful for his possessive arm around me.

'Congratulations, looks like you have a new job. We'll miss you.' Ken said, squeezing me.

'Yes thank you, it's very exciting but I'll miss you more.'

'You can't get rid of me that easily. I still need building materials from the store for the project. I'll see you more than you think.'

I wasn't so sure about that.

With Ken paying so much attention to me the two gods from the shop quickly lost interest and left before him. It was 11 p.m. when I started to pack up and lock the bar. Ken and I walked out of the bar/restaurant, past the reception where his Mini Moke was parked.

He turned and asked me, 'Can I give you a kiss goodnight?'

Yes, please! I wanted to yell, but instead, I pointed to my cheek. The Tongan way. Ken was much taller than me, so he bent over and kissed me on both cheeks. 'Good night,' he said. 'I'll see you tomorrow.'

I ran to my room, not wanting to wash his kiss off my face — ever. *Oh my god, I've kissed a palangi. That could complicate things.* If that was my first date, then I had also had my first kiss, with a white man, on the cheek. I smiled before I drifted off to sleep.

It was another month before I started my new job, and during that time I fell more in love with Ken. I was saddened by the thought of losing our rendezvous. It was a feeling I'd never experienced before but I continued to remind myself to stay focused.

On my first day at the store, it was buzzing with people and the first-week opening sales were crazy. I was caught up in the excitement of the new job.

Ken came by the shop every day, but it wasn't the same. My new job didn't allow me to chitchat. The following weeks I only saw him once except for weekends. In the meantime, Bill, my ex-boss from the hotel, kept stopping by. 'The bar made so much profit during your time there, would you consider coming back?' he asked.

'Maybe the bartender is drinking the profit,' I laughed.

'I miss you. The Aussie boys miss you,' he said, ignoring my comment.

Little did he know that it was probably all Ken's money as he didn't go back at night after I left. But Bill's proposition empowered me with enough confidence to re-enter a new bargaining agreement with him.

I truly missed seeing Ken every day and wanted to go back to my old job. But there was the question of money versus seeing Ken. I was being paid a lot more at my new job than I had been at the hotel. Nonetheless, I struck a deal with Bill and got my old job back. He agreed to match my salary from the shop and I got to see Ken and hopefully rekindle our friendship.

A few months later, an audit of the office found discrepancies in the books with unexplained missing funds. I volunteered to go over the books and see if I could come up with a solution.

'Well, this is your time to shine, Silva. I give you two weeks if you think you're up for the challenge,' Bill said.

'Yes, sir.'

I combed through the books day and night, and two weeks later I came up with a comprehensive report. Further investigations confirmed that the assistant manager and the head administrator were embezzling funds. They were both dismissed. With the vacancy of these two positions, I was promoted to assistant manager. At last, I got the job and remuneration I was seeking.

With my new position, I no longer served Ken and his mates at the bar. However, Ken and I saw one another every day and sometimes he dropped in at the hotel in the middle of the day to say hi in between jobs. He had to oversee both the projects he was working on — the hospital, which was situated in town, and the fuel depot in the outer village. The hotel was halfway between the two. I loved it when he dropped by as a surprise but it always drew unwanted attention. However, by this time my feelings towards Ken had grown and I didn't care about the critical eyes.

One afternoon, Bill was helping an engineer with a repair on our air conditioning system when he slipped and fell through the roof, breaking four ribs and his pelvis. Ironically, he finished up at the very hospital Ken was working on. It meant that for the next six months, I took over the management of the hotel. I had no idea how I was going to manage it. In addition to overseeing the bar, restaurant and keeping the books, I was expected to run the hotel accommodation, which meant transporting guests to and from the airport. I felt very inexperienced at my age, especially with the enormous responsibility forced upon me.

I offloaded it all on Ken one night. 'How can I run the hotel? I can't drive. Picking up and dropping off guests will be challenging.'

'If what you need is a driver, I can help you with that,' he said. 'I'll see Leo about getting some time off, but that shouldn't be an issue as I'm ahead of my schedule.'

So Ken became my much-needed courier. He picked up and dropped off guests at the airport, as well as picking up stock for me. Without his help, I wouldn't have been able to run the hotel efficiently. Leo was flexible with Ken's times, which enabled him to render assistance whenever I needed it.

Cruise ships came to Vavaʻu regularly. During these visits, Ken continued to help me with shuttling tourists from the wharf to the hotel. The influx of tourists generated much-needed funds not only for the hotel but for the locals, too. I had the privilege of allowing villagers to set up stalls within the hotel premises to sell their handicrafts. I was grateful for a job that enabled me to employ some of my village people.

Bill's recovery was slow, but he was finally discharged from hospital. He was cared for by the hotel staff and his wife, Wendy. Even though he was back, he was in no position to return to work, so I continued to run the hotel with Ken's help. I thoroughly enjoyed the challenge of the job, but more so, it brought Ken and me even closer. *If this is what married life is like,* I thought, *I kind of like it. I don't want Bill to get better because my rendezvous with this white man will come to an end.* I felt terrible for thinking like that, but I truly loved how we worked together.

The half-year report for the hotel was pleasing and I was rewarded handsomely, not only in my salary but also with free accommodation and a meal package with no alcohol. That worked perfectly for me, as I didn't drink anyway.

Throughout all this, Ken continued to support me in whatever I needed to fulfil my job. Bill recovered enough to put in half-days in the office, but I still maintained control. The hotel was always booked out on Friday nights, with our live band attracting lots of people. It required me to be on deck ensuring the three bars were always stocked.

Ken and I formed a close friendship with a local couple, Lenny and Anni. One Friday night, the band was playing and Lenny, Anni and Ken were settling in at the beer garden near the swimming pool. From there, they had a full view of the band. The atmosphere was vibrant and the dance floor crowded. I was on duty but occasionally stopped by Ken's table. 'What the heck are you drinking?' I asked, looking at a strange bottle under the table.

'I don't know but it tastes good. Lenny made it,' Ken said, tugging at me to sit on his lap.

'I think you're pissed, Ken. If I were you, I wouldn't trust anything Lenny made,' I laughed.

'It's like a tropical punch.'

'I think you should stick to white people's drink. It's called beer.' I picked up the bottle and had a sniff. It smelled fruity, but I suspected it wasn't all fruit. Ken looked a bit too tipsy for my liking.

I left them again and a while later I saw Ken walking towards the bathroom, but he didn't see me. He collided with a post just as I walked past. 'Excuse me,' he said and patted the post.

I burst out laughing. *Seriously? He's the man I'm falling for? There's nothing attractive about apologizing to a post blind drunk.*

I was laughing so loud he came out of his stupor. 'Lenny had this juice in a bottle and I had too much of it. I don't think it's good for me.'

'It's mushroom, you idiot,' I said, no longer laughing at his stupidity.

The good thing about the Friday night dance was that you could get drunk then spend Saturday being sick, then Sunday recuperating before Monday.

Tonga is a religious island; Sunday is a day of rest. Everyone went to church and those who didn't found a quiet beach far from the watchful eyes of the police.

Swimming on Sunday is an offence. Ken and I were the worst offenders. I went to the morning service to beg for forgiveness, then went to the beach with Ken in the afternoon.

'You such a hypocrite, Liva,' he said one Sunday. 'Why bother going to church only to come out and do the opposite of what you've pledged not to do?'

'Since when you become a judge, Ken? For your information, I asked for your forgiveness too.'

'Whatever!' he sneered, but he knew he couldn't stop me from going to church. That's what my people do.

We both enjoyed our free time snorkelling at different beaches every Sunday. Sometimes we just enjoyed the coolness of the sea breeze — a welcome relief from the heat.

One Sunday, Ken turned to me. 'Did you ever have a dream, Liva?'

'Yes, but it's too embarrassing to tell,' I said coyly.

'Tell me. I won't tell.'

'Only if you tell me yours first.'

'Okay. I dreamed of buying my own house and I now have that.'

'Is that all?'

'Maybe to have a family one day.'

We both went quiet before he said, 'Now it's your turn.'

I didn't want to say it. 'You promise me you're not going to laugh or tell anyone.'

'Cross my heart, I promise.'

'Well, I've always wanted to be a doctor so I can help my family and my people. We're in desperate need of doctors here on the island, but I think it's a farfetched dream. But ... I have a fantasy.' I winked at him mischievously. 'Not like that. Since I was a kid, I've been fascinated with aeroplanes. I fantasized about being a pilot and seeing the world. There you go, Ken. You're the first one to know of my innermost.'

I waited for the mocking laugh, but it never came. Instead, I faced a very serious Ken. 'You never want to have a family?' He sounded sad.

'Maybe, but you asked me of my dreams. Family comes naturally, doesn't it?'

'You could still have those dreams. There shouldn't be a timeframe if you want it bad enough. I wanted to be a pilot, had a couple of lessons and ran out of money and never went again. Maybe I didn't want it bad enough,' he said. 'Come on, let's go for a dip. It's hot.'

Courtship

Ken and I went from friendship to courtship in a matter of months. We'd been enjoying each other's company so much we were inseparable. He found excuses throughout the day to drop in and see me.

To see this strong, handsome white man oblivious to our differences sent shockwaves through my body every time he stopped by at the hotel. I often wondered what he saw in me. *I'm black, unattractive, come from a poor family in the village and I have nothing to offer,* I thought. But Ken saw none of that; he only saw me. I was a lot darker in comparison to other Tongans, which is why I was dubbed an ugly duckling. Ken could have been excused if he thought of me that way because my own people did.

These feelings continued to haunt me, even though I knew I was falling for this Australian bachelor. I couldn't stop the crushing feeling that possessed me. I knew I could be hurt, yet I shut down my subconscious. I knew that once the hospital project and the fuel depot were completed, our courtship would be a distant memory. All common sense was buried as I bathed in the thought that Ken might feel what I felt.

It wasn't easy to discreetly date a white person in Vava'u. Wherever we went, we attracted unwanted attention. A lot of onlookers eyed us critically. I could almost hear what they were thinking.

What's that palangi boy doing with that black girl?

If that black girl thinks he's going to marry her, she'd better think again.

Once he gets into her pants it'll be bye, bye, señorita.

I was walking with Ken one day when I heard a woman whisper, 'Look at how she walks. She's already a whore.'

I tried not to react but Ken must have seen something on my face as he leaned closer. 'What are they saying?' he asked.

'Nothing important.' I couldn't bring myself to tell him the hurtful truth.

On one of our disobedient Sundays, we were on our way back from the beach when we got a flat tyre. We were in the Mini Moke in the middle of nowhere, bush all around us, the nearest town about 5 kilometres away. We had another Australian diplomat with us. He was from the Australian High Commissioner's office in Nuku'alofa, the capital of Tonga.

Ken left me and his colleague with the Mini Moke while he walked to town seeking help. He arrived back a couple of hours later with an engineer from the Ministry of Works, armed with a new tyre. Once it was fixed, we dropped the guest at the hotel and Ken took me home to my village, where I told Grandma what had happened.

She was the wrong person to tell. 'Serves you bloody right! That was your punishment for going to the beach on a Sunday.'

'Whatever, Grandma,' I said.

'I'm telling you, nothing good will come from this courtship.'

I pretended I was taking it all in.

Even though I had my accommodation at the hotel, I still liked to come home when able. Ken often hung out with me in my village until late at night. One night when he went to leave, we found his tyres slashed and his rear-view mirror bent.

'Please darl,' I said, 'I don't want you to come back here to the village any more. We'll see each other at the hotel.'

I feared this kind of behaviour would drive Ken away. But he must have guessed what I was thinking, and what this meant.

'They're not going to win,' he replied. 'I'm a big boy. I can look after myself.'

I didn't want to be the reason he got hurt. My mum's younger brother, Uncle Lopeti, always accompanied Ken until he was a safe distance from my village.

One night he had a stone thrown at him while driving back in the Mini Moke, barely missing his head. That was the last straw, so the town officer announced a meeting with the village elders and put a stop to this feral behaviour.

Ken continued to visit and eventually gained the trust and respect of my village.

In my culture, when a couple goes on a date, they sit at the girl's house and chat under the watchful eyes of Mum, Grandma or Aunty as a chaperone. It was hard to make Ken understand this at first, but eventually we managed to get through that barrier. I was scared of losing him, not by our own doing, but through our cultural differences. For that, I often resented this cultural restriction.

Screw them, I thought. *I have feelings for this man. I want to kiss him. I want to touch him. But how?*

I rebelled against my family, my culture and my religion. *If Ken takes me to hell,* I reasoned, *then to hell I'll go to be with him. It's my life, my future and my destiny.*

Ken would pick me up for dinner or a dance night. Although it was forbidden for a single girl to go out on a date unchaperoned, I tried. I resented the fact that I wasn't trusted, so I continued to resist. But Grandma was having none of that. On this particular day she raced down and jumped in the back seat of the Mini Moke before me.

I looked at her angrily. 'What do you think you're doing?'

She folded her arms defiantly. 'You need a chaperone.'

I looked at Ken, but he just shrugged. 'If that's the only way I can take you out, then the whole family can come if they want.'

'Shh, keep your voice down or you'll regret saying that,' I said, as if Grandma understood.

I'd had enough of her beating me to the car, so I hopped in and said to Ken, 'Kiss me.' He looked at me, baffled. He shifted uncomfortably. We weren't allowed to publicly display love or affection. It was one of my rare invitations, and of course, Ken was drooling for a kiss, I think — but he wasn't budging.

I had to repeat myself. 'Are you going to kiss me or have Grandma between us all night while we dance? For god's sake, Grandma doesn't speak English, so she has no idea what I'm saying.'

No sooner had Ken leaned over, Grandma Nane couldn't get out fast enough. 'Disgusting! You're going to get pregnant and no one will ever have you. You're acting like a whore. Mark my words, your disobedience will get you nowhere.'

Thank god Ken didn't understand a word. He would have been horrified. 'Good riddance, Grandma,' I said in Tongan, before turning to Ken. 'You'd better not kiss me again or I might get pregnant.'

Grandma was being ridiculous. I had no plan of getting pregnant until I had a ring on my finger. There were some things from my cultural upbringing that I valued and treasured. One of them was to keep myself chaste for the man who would ultimately become my husband. Whether it was Ken or someone else, it was something I wanted to preserve.

When the hospital project was half-finished, Ken was asked to extend his stay for the fuel depot project. He was delighted to tell me he was staying on.

Six Australian welders were sent over for the project. They were married, but that didn't stop them from eyeing the young Tongan girls. Their behaviour embarrassed Ken greatly, as he watched them promise these girls a life in Australia. There were a few unwanted pregnancies, and the worst part was those little innocent souls never got to meet their fathers — when the project was completed, so were the relationships. The men went back to their Australian wives and families while these vulnerable young girls were left to tidy up the mess.

Ken hadn't professed his love for me, but I felt it. And if he truly loved me, I knew he would wait and respect my wishes and values. We shared meals and laughter with the occasional kiss, and it was enough to keep us content.

We spent a lot of time with Lenny and Anni. We came home with them one Saturday night about midnight, and heard the sound of a couple arguing. Lenny and Anni were too drunk to care, so while they passed out on the floor, Ken and I went to investigate the commotion. We saw my boss, Bill, walking towards his apartment while Wendy took a left turn, heading down the steps towards the beach. It was pitch black where she was headed. We followed her into the darkness but I stopped at the top of the stairs.

'Hey! Wendy, just hold on,' Ken called out, rushing down the steps.

But Wendy was crying and on a mission. 'No, Ken. I'm going to take the dingy out and I don't care where it takes me. I'm done with this forsaken island. I've had enough.' She was obviously intoxicated.

Ken finally caught up and managed to talk some sense into her, but she was so distressed. 'Did you know that Bill is screwing the chef? The one that he assigned to look after him?'

'This is not how to deal with it. I can help you to go back to Australia,' I heard Ken say. It saddened me that one of my people was responsible for her tears tonight. I was ashamed and embarrassed. I was so proud of Ken — he was only 29 years old and yet spoke with such compassion and maturity.

If Ken takes me to Australia, how would I cope if he became unfaithful? I thought as I sat at the top of the steps. I'd be trapped in a foreign country just like Wendy. Wendy stopped crying and they started their way up from the beach. We walked her back to their apartment, as she wouldn't listen to my advice to take a vacant room for the night.

When we got back to my room for coffee, Ken could see something had upset me. 'Don't you worry, Liva. I'll make sure Wendy gets home safely if that's what she wants.'

'But she could be me one day in Australia. If you have an affair. If that happened, I would probably do what Wendy tried to do tonight. I would be as alone in your Australia as Wendy is in my Tonga.'

I couldn't stop the tears flowing freely as I felt the weight of Wendy's pain as if it was mine.

Ken got up, came around my chair and pulled me into his arms. 'Shush. That's never going to happen.'

He pushed me away from his shoulder so he could see my face. He looked tormented as he kissed me and led me to bed. 'It's very late. You need some sleep.' I felt so loved with his arms around me.

Exhaustion overtook us and sleep was welcomed until we were woken by Lenny and Anni with lunch. They had got up and snuck out to do an underground 'Umu for Sunday feast. We shared what had gone on with Bill and Wendy while they'd been asleep, laughing and gossiping about the other mixed racial affairs that were going on around us. Ken seemed troubled and distant. I sensed a bit of possessiveness in his behaviour as he kept trying to hold me even in front of Lenny and Anni.

The following Saturday I didn't see Ken all day, which was unusual. I heard he was sick, so the next day I finished my shift at noon and asked the driver to drop me off at his house. Ken shared a house with Joe, while Leo and his family lived next door.

When I got there, the door was unlocked — no one locks their doors in Tonga — so I took my shoes off, which was customary, and entered. I poked my head around the living room, but Ken wasn't there. 'Hello? Ken, are you home? It's me,' I called out.

Eventually, I heard Ken's voice. 'Oh! Hi Liva. I'm down here. I'm not feeling too good.'

A staircase to my left led down to the bedrooms. I followed it down to where his voice was trailing from.

It was the first time I'd ever been in any man's bedroom, although I'd been to his house many times. I paused at the doorway, unsure of what to do or say next. I saw him in his bed looking miserable. I entered his room and straight away, I could see that my visit had brightened him up.

My eyes darted around as I inspected my surroundings. How neat his bedroom looked! He even had a couch. He also had a bedside table with books, a clock, a jug of juice and a ziplock bag of tablets, not to mention the best view of Vava'u harbour.

I climbed onto his single bed and gave him a cuddle. I knew the risk I was taking — if he'd asked for me then, it would have been a struggle to resist, but he didn't take advantage of the situation.

I was lost in the moment until we heard a door slam. Voices drifted down from the entryway. I froze. I couldn't be seen in Ken's bedroom, regardless of how innocent my visit was.

'Quick, get in the closet,' Ken said, getting out of bed.

'What? Where are you going?' I was horrified.

'It's five o'clock so I'll go for a beer. Nobody has to know you're here.' He closed the closet door and I was in total darkness.

What a stupid culture. I hate it. Why can't I be free? If I was a boy in a girl's bedroom, no one would bat an eyelid. The more I thought about it, the angrier I got.

I heard Ken rustling about, then he checked in on me and gave me a peck on the nose.

'Oh god, Ken. I'm sorry, but my shoes are at the front door,' I whispered back.

'That's okay. I'll take care of it.'

'How?'

'Don't you worry about that. I won't stay too long. I'll see you in an hour.'

He left his bedroom door open while I was locked in his closet. He took my shoes with him, pretending I'd left them there a previous time.

Not long after Ken left, I heard Joe and his floozie in the bedroom next door. *Please Lord,* I thought, *make it quick and let them leave before Ken gets home.*

My prayer was answered and soon after, they too left. I sighed with relief but didn't dare come out in case they came back.

I grinned at where my rebellious nature had got me, thinking, *this will be a funny story to tell my grandchildren one day. What would Grandma Nane say if she found out?*

By the time Ken got back, I was fast asleep. He helped me up onto his bed and we cuddled and chatted about Joe and his floozie. I was wondering what it would be like to stay there with Ken forever when he spoke. 'Would you like to go back to the hotel or home?'

'I would like to go home please,' I answered, looking at him. *Wouldn't you like me to stay? Such a gentleman.*

He looked at me as if he could see my soul. 'Let's go before we live to regret this moment.' He jumped up, dragged me off the bed and we were on our way.

We drove home to my village and, even though Ken didn't speak my language, he thoroughly enjoyed hanging out with my family. We visited my dad, who lived a few doors away from Grandma and Grandpa. Ken always enjoyed his company. Not only did Dad speak good English, but he also loved a beer or two.

I'd been so self-conscious when I'd first brought him to my village. My grandparents' home was a Tongan hut with a coconut thatched roof and not a single piece of furniture. We sat and ate on the floor. At night, we slept on a mat on the floor, which was later upgraded to a kapok mattress. Despite that, it had always been a home full of love and laughter. Ken hadn't seemed to care about that from the start. He had no problem sitting on the floor with us, sharing a meal, eating with our fingers.

That Sunday we had dinner at Dad's house but ended up at my grandparents' place for dessert. I couldn't go past Grandpa's famous pawpaw dessert, baked underground in coconut cream. I've never had any pawpaw with coconut cream that tastes as good as my grandpa's. It was one of Ken's favourite Tongan cuisines, too.

Ken left by 11 p.m., feeling a lot better than when he'd started the day.

'My mum and dad are coming for a visit,' Ken announced one day. It was mid-1980 and we'd been courting for nearly twelve months.

'Huh? When? For how long?' The questions poured out of my mouth as I went into panic mode. Fear crept into my head at the thought of the two cultures about to collide. What would Ken's parents think of their precious oldest son falling for a black native girl? I never let Ken know the turmoil I felt because of the colour of my skin.

At least I still had a few more weeks to enjoy him all to myself before whatever verdict his parents delivered after their visit. I wondered if I should have given myself totally to Ken and hoped that would have been sufficient evidence of my love for him. But if that was all he was after, there were endless choices available. The fear of losing him was crippling.

Ken's parents, Norman and Mona, arrived in August, and Ken went to pick them up from the airport. He didn't ask me to come, nor did I wish to go.

Coming from Melbourne in the middle of winter only to be confronted by a hot, humid day upon their arrival in Vava'u was just the beginning. Ken was invited to a school opening festival that day and he thought it would be a great idea to introduce some of the cultural differences straight up.

Different, all right — his parents had no idea what had hit them. The school football oval was lined with tables (I call them 'tables' but they were on the ground). Then it got tricky because Ken couldn't sit with his parents. In my culture, it's an honour to have a guest, especially a palangi, dine at your table. Therefore, they were taken to separate tables, surrounded by island people who couldn't speak English. His parents had no idea what the food placed in front of them was. We all sat on the ground and ate with our hands. I could see them screwing up their noses at some of the food; they'd never seen or tasted anything like this before. They bobbed their heads in time with the Tongan music and seemed to enjoy the local girls dancing, their skin dripping with coconut oil.

I could see the two of them getting tired as the night wore on — this kind of function could go on for over five hours. When they tried to get up, both of them struggled, but some of the townspeople tugged on their hands to help them. One of the Tongan men who could speak broken English then slapped Norm on the back. 'Norman, you're lucky we've given up eating white men since corned beef arrived.'

I worried that Ken's dad would take offence, but he couldn't stop laughing.

Ken understandably didn't come by the hotel that night. I wondered whether he was telling his parents about me, about *us*.

The next day, I was so excited when he dropped in at the hotel. I was desperate to know what he'd told them but was too scared to ask. Instead, I said politely, 'Did your mum and dad enjoy themselves last night? What do they think of Vava'u?'

'I think they had a good time but freaked out at being separated from me and not knowing what to eat or say. Dad complained about sitting on the ground for so long, but he got over it.'

I got the impression he had enjoyed exposing his mum and dad to my culture on the first day they'd arrived. But it made me worry. What would they think of my way of life? 'It must have been a big shock for them,' I said.

'Can I pick you up after work to go to the house and meet them?' he asked with a grin.

'Of course. That would be lovely,' I said, pretending I was excited. *Oh dear,* I thought, *that means you told them about me.*

When he left, I felt so nervous it made me sick. I thought all parents, no matter what colour or race, would have a say in the choice of their children's partners. That's what happened with Tongans. Of course, my grandparents had no say in my choice, but only because I made a promise to myself long ago.

I was frantic, trying to work out what to wear. I tried on four dresses and was hot and bothered so decided to wear the last one I'd tried on. A green dress.

Ken picked me up around 6 p.m. 'You look nice,' he said.

'Thanks, I didn't know what to wear. I'm so nervous I feel sick.'

'They don't bite,' he said, helping me into the ute.

I was quiet on the drive until he broke the silence. 'I asked my parents what they would think if I brought home a Tongan girl.'

This home or Australia? 'Oh, dear! How did that go for you?'

'They were okay with that. By the way, I wasn't asking for their permission, only their thoughts. At the end of the day, it's my choice and I'll do what I want to do.'

'Yeah, right. Whatever,' I said with a nervous little laugh.

After his parents left, he told me that his dad had staggered backwards onto a chair when he'd told them. His mum, however, had been cool about it and happy for him. 'About bloody time, son,' she said. Once his dad had recovered enough and gathered himself up, he found the right words. 'Well son, we don't care what colour, race or shape as long as you know she'll be happy away from her family.'

But during this visit, Ken was trying to calm my nerves. 'Mum asked if you could stay for tea. She's cooking.' *Oh! It's going to be a long night after all. What happened to meet and greet? I hope I will keep up with the English conversation.*

When we arrived at the house, Ken was beaming like the cat who caught the mouse as he introduced me to his parents. His mum was normal and relaxed as she stepped forward and gave me a hug. But his dad was as awkward as I was.

After some small talk, I went to the kitchen to help Mona before sitting down to eat. That was the first time I'd had mock fish — grated potatoes mixed with eggs, seasoned, then fried. Potato wasn't my favourite vegetable but the way Ken's mum cooked it, it was delicious.

The conversation around the table was fluid and pleasant but I lost my tongue — I was scared that anything I said would sound backward or stupid. So I kept my mouth shut, only opening it to answer a question directed at me.

After helping Mona with the dishes, Ken took me back and I heard him telling his parents not to wait up for him. This pleased me. I needed his reassurance.

It was late when we got back to the hotel. No one was at the bar so we opted for coffee on my balcony.

While I was making the coffee, Ken said, 'You were very quiet tonight. How did you find my parents?' He didn't wait for my answer as he continued. 'My parents are very easy and simple people, Liva, you'll see. Just give it time. I know you'll love them.'

'Yes, I know. They're lovely people, Ken. I like them but I'm worried about my poor English. I didn't know what to talk about. I felt very inadequate.'

'I wish you could drop this nonsense about your English. It's fine. You speak quite good English.' *Talk about backing your own horse!*

'Yes. They were very nice, but way above my level. But it was a very successful day and thank you,' I said.

Norman and Mona stayed for six weeks and, true to Ken's word, I grew fond of them. I hoped they were fond of me too. We shared many meals and lots of outings on yachts, snorkelling and boat trips to outer islands. They taught me how to play cards and we spent many fun nights playing until late.

Mona cooked every night we got together. I watched in awe. Ken proudly told me, 'Mum's a good cook.' Maybe he was pre-empting that I should become a good cook one day. *Dig me a hole in the ground and I'll show you good cooking,* I thought.

Everything went well with his parents, but where did that leave us? I wasn't sure what the next step was. Had he meant what he said about taking me to Australia?

3

The proposals

Unbeknown to me, when Ken's parents left Tonga he had given his dad a few tasks to do upon his return to Australia. Lots of paperwork was required by the Tongan government if he was to marry a Tongan girl. He needed an original copy of his birth certificate and proof that he hadn't been previously married.

Funnily enough, he did all this without proposing. Norman sent all the required paperwork within a week of returning.

After their beer o'clock one day, he leaned over and whispered, 'Can I come back and see you after your shift tonight? I want to talk to you about something important.'

'Hmm! that's sound serious. The answer will be … a no,' I teased.

He gave me a wink then he left.

'I won't finish until nine,' I yelled after him.

He came back about 7 p.m. and waited at the bar. By the time I'd finished my shift and joined him, he said, 'I think I may have had too much to drink. I won't ask you now or you'll think I'm not serious. Can I see you tomorrow?'

'Hmm, whatever.'

He left me worried all night. Was he going to end our relationship?

The next day after their few beers, he leaned over and in a low voice, 'I'll see you tonight.' He came back at the same time as the night before and waited at the bar, drinking a can of Coke. When I finished my shift, we went to my room. If it was bad news, I knew I would cry and I preferred to do that in the privacy of my room.

While having coffee, he said, 'I guess we can get married now, so will you marry me?'

I nearly choked on my coffee as I cracked up laughing. I thought it was the biggest joke of the year. 'I read in a magazine somewhere that in the white man's culture you get down on your knees.'

'Oh my god, you've read too much rubbish,' he said gruffly.

I'd always imagined that when Ken proposed, he would have a ring and be on his knees with a red rose between his teeth. That's what the magazine had led me to believe. Instead, he started to laugh.

Ken was not the romantic type, but this was perfect for me, as my culture forbade any public physical shows of affection. But hell, we were alone and normally he was more relaxed and very attentive and loving, but he was popping the biggest question of his life and I thought he was joking. He must've been gutted that I thought it was funny.

A week later while having a coffee on my balcony, Ken asked, 'Have you thought about what I said last week? Will you marry me? I think we should.' He still wasn't on his knees and I still didn't see a ring.

I looked at him. Maybe we were playing games now and he was digging his heels in with the kneeling thing. I would've forgotten about that too but this time it was a bit more serious, like a command.

I was scared by the intensity of the question. This was my last chance to emphasize to Ken how important my race, my family and my culture were to me. My insides were dancing with happiness and excitement at the prospect of being this white man's wife. What would it be like to be called Mrs Mac? I loved the sound of that.

But what blurted from my mouth was completely different from what I felt inside. 'Are you serious?'

'For the second time. I was serious the first time too, in case you didn't notice.'

'If I were you, Ken, I would consider that long and hard, because marrying me is like marrying the mafia — you'll have to marry my mum, dad, aunty, uncle, grandma, grandpa and my whole village. It's a big ask. You know there's a Tongan proverb. "It takes a whole village to raise a girl" and I hope you've been here in Vava'u long enough to understand what that means.'

Ken stared at his coffee without saying another word. It was my turn to be serious as I spelled out the cons of marrying a native girl.

'My grandparents are ageing and I have to look after them. As much as I love you, I could never abandon my duty to my grandparents, who gave up everything for me. I'll have to help out with my sister's education. As your wife, would you allow me to help them?'

The look of disappointment he gave me broke my heart. I was in overdrive trying to sugar coat my stupidity. I thought I'd lost my chance, but it was better to be all out — at least we'd both know what we were getting ourselves into.

When Ken left that night, I doubted our relationship would survive our cultural differences, duties and responsibilities.

It only took a couple more days before Ken took me out to dinner and he didn't have a drink. He was unusually quiet and very serious. Afterwards, we went to my room for our usual coffee and chat. I turned the kettle on, went to turn around and nearly tripped over him.

'Will you marry me? And the rest of your family.' Ken was on one knee, asking for the third time.

Heaven knows, he didn't have to go down on his knee, as I was aching to be his wife and thought I'd busted my chance the previous times. Looking down at him, tears blurred my vision. I put my hands on his face to urge him up. He apologized that there was no ring as he couldn't buy one in Vava'u. I couldn't have cared less, as a ring is only symbolic. Tongans don't have wedding rings, anyway. What was important to me was the declaration of our commitment to each other.

I couldn't believe my ears when he said, 'I'd like to ask your dad but I want you to come with me.'

'If you're going to ask my dad then you better ask my grandpa too,' I told him. 'My grandfather has more fatherly rights to me but I understand, my dad will always be my dad.'

He had no problem with that.

The next night we went to see my dad. He was so proud, but I wished he'd stop calling Ken 'son' all night. *Not yet!* I thought. Afterwards, we went to my grandfather's. The language barrier was always going to be a challenge. Somehow, the spirit of asking for my hand was lost when I had to be the interpreter. How I wished that Grandpa could comprehend the words from Ken's mouth.

Nonetheless, my grandpa understood perfectly the significance of what Ken was asking. He was touched and couldn't hold back tears of happiness as he tried to find the right words. 'Ken, grandson, you made me a very happy and proud father and grandfather. I know you will love and take care of our Liva. I wish you both a wonderful, happy future together. I pray that god will shine the way and bless your new family.'

He turned to me and reached out for my hand. 'Liva, you have always been a good girl, and this is the prize — a very good man. Look after him.'

'I love you lots, Grandpa.' I hugged him when we left for the hotel, very happy.

'We've got both your dad's and grandpa's blessings but you haven't given me your answer,' Ken said afterwards while cuddling me.

'I thought my reaction was sufficient. Didn't I say yes? There! I just said it. Yes. And not only am I delighted to be your wife but I can't wait to be Mrs Mac.'

Ken tilted my head up and he had love and happiness in his eyes, which didn't take much to start me off again.

'On one condition,' he said.

That made me nervous. 'Bloody hell, I thought you loved me unconditionally but now you added a condition?'

'Please don't make me wear those stupid mats.'

'Sure,' I said, laughing. It was not the place or time to be arguing over stupid mats.

Fine woven mats from pandanus are an important part of my heritage costume for special events. Ken had been in Tonga long enough to see that special mats were worn for different occasions. A traditional wedding costume consisted of multiple layers of fine woven mats. It wasn't the most comfortable and would be a shock for a palangi. But

I knew that once the wedding day came, Ken and I would have no say over what we wore.

It was the end of September 1980 and we'd decided to marry on 16 December. Ken's contract would be finished in May the following year and he wanted to get married before we left for my new home. Australia.

I was consumed with wedding plans and was shocked when Ken told me he was going back to Australia before the wedding. Even though my heart told me everything was good, I hated the thought of him going away. What if he ran and never came back, just like the other Australians?

He left on a cargo ship MV *Sami*, via Western Samoa. I stood on the wharf and waved him off, then I waited until the ship disappeared through the narrow channel. I was sure it was the last time I'd see his face. It was only for two weeks, but it was so long as I battled with the negative thoughts in my head.

There was no phone call or communication while he was away. I waited until he returned before I continued with our wedding plans, just in case … I didn't want the embarrassment of cancelling the wedding if he didn't come back. It happened a lot with mixed relationships.

I was hunched over my desk one day when I saw a shadow across the door. When I looked up, I couldn't believe it was Ken standing in front of me.

I jumped up and launched into his arms, ignoring the eyes on us. 'I can't wait for the sixteenth of December,' I whispered.

'Me too.'

I told Ken later of my anxiety and it saddened him greatly. Our declaration of love for each other should've been enough assurance for me but I didn't know how to drive the demon of self-doubt out of my head.

Ken was busy, as both projects were close to being finished. He started the process of applying for my entry visa to Australia. Working for the Commonwealth government made things a little easier. 'I want to make sure that once my contract is finished, we're both going home together,' he said.

'Wouldn't it be easier to apply after the wedding?' I asked, fearful in case my application was denied.

'What if immigration says no?' he said.

'Oh well, easy. You can leave, then I will follow,' I said with a pang in my stomach.

'Not if I have anything to do with it. We either both leave together or we'll stay.' He tugged at my flat nose.

While I was waiting for an interview with the Australian High Commissioner, my passport arrived with my permanent resident visa granted. If I was marrying Ken just to get out of Tonga, a resident visa in my passport was gold and still in my maiden name — bonus — so I could've run. The trouble was, not only did Ken have my heart, but I envisaged my future with this white man as a very bright and happy one.

Wedding of two cultures

Leading up to our wedding day, I often wondered what was going through Ken's head. *Does he miss his family and friends? Is he lonely amongst my people? Is he worried if Australia will accept me?* Maybe he thought about all of these things.

A Tongan wedding traditionally involves both the bride and the groom's family but I was on my own with ours. That was the price I paid for falling for a white man. Ken and I decided that there was no point in sending invitations to Australia as there was no time and our wedding date was too close to Christmas. This was a decision we later regretted as we found out there were friends who would have forfeited an Australian Christmas for a Tongan one.

Ken's parents had just recently returned from Tonga and we didn't expect them to come back. Another decision we very much regretted. They wished Ken could've hinted about getting married to an islander, so they could've planned their trip to coincide with the wedding. However, it was an advantage that I got to meet them before the wedding.

I had words with my grandma as the day grew close. She was adamant we were getting married in traditional costume. 'Please, Grandma, be mindful of Ken. He doesn't fully understand our Tongan culture. I can wear your mats, but he can wear a suit. That's his culture.'

The look she cast my way was enough to burn a hole through my eyebrows. 'What did I tell you, Liva? It's happening already. Your differences will always be a problem between you two. This is what you want, against my advice, so you'd better tell your palangi man this is how it's going to be.'

I woke up alone for the final time as a single island girl. I felt a single tear rolling down onto my pillow but didn't understand why.

It was Tuesday, 16 December 1980, and a beautiful warm sunny day beamed down on us. We couldn't have asked for a better one.

We had a booking with the magistrate at the registry office at 10 a.m. Any administrative or legal requirements, weddings included, are tended to before the court case proceedings for the day. There's only one magistrate in Vava'u and it was important we were there on time.

Ken was planning on picking me up from the hotel and we were getting dressed at my great-aunty's place. She was going to wrap our ta'ovala (mats) for the day. The mats worn on the wedding day are different from the ones worn on the celebration day. There's a different one again for the first Sunday of married life. Grandma was on a short vacation to the United States but there was no word on when she would arrive.

I got up early to check on my clothes, which had been left with the dressmaker. A simple dress to be worn underneath all the mats. I walked 2 kilometres from the hotel only to find the dressmaker's shop was closed even though it was after 9 a.m. This was not unusual, as the whole of Vava'u operated on island time.

While I was standing there contemplating what to do next, knowing we had to be at the courthouse by 10 a.m., someone called out that my grandma had just arrived from the States. I headed out to where they motioned and nearly collided with Grandma Nane and Uncle Manu, who had accompanied her back from the States. They were looking for a taxi to take them to my village. I was so excited I forgot about the time, let alone that I was getting married in less than an hour.

Meanwhile, Ken had been to the hotel, then to my aunty's place, but I was nowhere to be found. With no phones or way of contacting me, he kept driving in circles, looking. Just as well Neiafu, the capital of Vava'u, is so small he could drive around it in ten minutes. He finally spotted me in a crowd. As soon as I saw him, I was so excited and called to him, oblivious to the time. 'Hey! Darl come, come.' I beckoned him to get out of the Mini Moke. 'Come and meet my Uncle Manu from the States and, of course, Grandma Nane is here too.'

Ken looked a bit flustered and signalled to his watch to remind me that we had to be at the courthouse in half an hour. He reluctantly came out to shake Manu's hand as I introduced him.

'Hi Manu, pleased to meet you.' He turned to Grandma and gave her a hug, 'Hi, Nane. So glad you make it back for our wedding, but we have to be at the courthouse in half an hour.' He rattled on even though Grandma didn't understand a word he said. Poor Ken never got used to Tongan time and he was obviously stressed.

'Relax, Ken. While in Tonga, we'll do what Tongans do. Ten a.m. means eleven,' I said.

Once I'd assured Grandma that Aunty was ready with our ta'ovala, she was happy to leave Ken and me in the capable hands of my great-aunty. She was eager to get to the village to check on the church decorations before we got back.

Ken and I went back to the hotel for a quick freshen up. On the way, he told me. 'I thought you'd bolted. That was my last lap. If I didn't see you, I was afraid the wedding would be called off.'

'Yeah right, Ken. You would have driven all day until you found me,' I teased.

'I probably would. Call me an idiot, but I love you, Liva, and I wouldn't leave Tonga without you.'

Gosh, how lucky am I? Thank you, Lord.

When we got to Aunty 'Ana's house, we found ladies from my village had already gathered there. They fussed around us, singing and chatting happily while wrapping our ta'ovala. Phew! To my relief, there were only two mats each. We made our way to the courthouse feeling fat and hot.

'Can you breathe, Ken?' I asked mockingly.

'I hope I won't need to go to the toilet. By the way, how can I go to the toilet?'

'You just don't. Ha ha!' I laughed. 'Brace yourself, this is only day one.'

We rode in the Mini Moke with three of my cousins piled in the back seat. They giggled, as every time Ken hit a pothole one of them was nearly thrown out. 'Slow down, Ken. You'll get married today, so why the rush?' one of my cousins yelled.

We arrived at the courthouse a little after 10 a.m., family and friends already awaiting our arrival. The small white building looked more like a church than a courthouse. We were called forth shortly afterwards. It was show time and there was no turning back. Even if Ken or I had wanted to run, it was impossible with the mats around us.

It was my first time inside a courthouse and it was very intimidating. We entered through a side door, to the right. The judge sat behind what looked like an altar. To the left were rows of long benches, just like a church. The judge peered above his glasses as we walked in. Undoubtedly, he would've seen the name 'Ken' and guessed he was a palangi. If he thought it was odd, he didn't show it.

I couldn't remember or understand what was said, but it got serious when we were handed a Bible and Ken and I had to swear an oath. We had to sign legal documents with my aunty as my witness and Lenny as Ken's. The judge then rolled the paperwork up, handed it to Ken and said, 'Take these to the minister next door to complete the marriage sacrament. I wish you both the very best.' He shook Ken's hand.

On my aunty's advice, we took the paperwork to my local minister in my village instead. I welcomed the idea as there had never been a mixed marriage in my little village. The normal practice was that a couple went to the magistrate and registered the marriage, then proceeded next door to the minister or, if you were Catholic, a few doors away to the priest.

My little village was buzzing by the time we got there. Ken handed the paperwork to the minister. He opened it and scratched his head with a worried look. 'Where's the rest of the paperwork?' he asked, looking up at us.

Ken and I looked at each other, bemused. 'What paperwork? That's all the judge gave us,' Ken said.

One of the elders intervened. 'Next door to the courthouse has the rest of the paperwork. Normally, that's where newlyweds go. Lopeti will go back with you to get it.'

'Oops! It would've been good if someone had bothered to inform us. There's nothing easy in this place,' Ken said, looking frustrated and hot. I felt sorry for him being in a foreign place wrapped in mats on a hot day, having to drive back to town to get the correct paperwork.

An hour later, Ken and Lopeti returned to find everyone fast asleep under the breadfruit tree. 'It was weird to go back to town with one of your relatives dressed in these stupid mats while you were left behind. I must look like an idiot,' Ken whined.

'For better or for worse, in hot or cold and, by the way, you look beautiful in those mats. They suit you,' I laughed.

'I'll be glad when the day is over.'

It didn't take long to raise everybody with the church bell. The villagers of all different denominations started to pour into the tiny Methodist church. The little building stood on coconut logs. A cyclone had smashed it up 20 years earlier and the congregation had salvaged what they could.

There were more people outside the church than in. Most onlookers were just sticky beaks, curious to witness the odd couple's union. Some of them were my critics and I was proud to prove them wrong.

When I linked arms with my grandpa as we walked the first few steps, I blinked away tears and hoped I made him proud. *For all the care and love you and Grandma bestowed on me, today your duty is complete. This is it. I'm going to miss you. Thank you, Grandpa.*

As we walked, my grandpa stopped when he reached his older brother, Tonata. Out of respect, he let Tonata walk me the rest of the way and hand me over to Ken. Respecting your elders and knowing your rank in the family is the oxygen of our culture. I kissed Grandpa as I whispered through tears, 'Love you lots.' He just patted my hand without another word. He turned but not before I noticed a single tear escape his eyes.

I watched Ken through a haze of tears, standing there all alone, and thought my heart would burst. He had no groomsmen and I had no bridesmaids, but we had each other and that was all we needed. My grand-uncle shook Ken's hand as they locked eyes. I saw the dark look of unspoken words: 'You'd better bloody look after her.'

Ken took my hands as we looked deep into each other's eyes. For better or for worse, 'til death do us part.

When we exchanged our vows, the minister started off in his native tongue, knowing full well that Ken didn't speak Tongan. However, Ken was doing so well repeating after him until the minister increased the length of the sentences and Ken was lost. He looked at me, seeking help, but I was already in hysterics.

It got worse with the blessing of the ring. I didn't have a ring for Ken. That was something I would have to source later in Australia. When he handed the ring to the minister, I wasn't sure he knew what to do with it. The minister had the shakes and kept dropping it. Finally, Ken got hold of it and started to put it on my finger. We both had no idea whether it was the right sequence, but Ken wasn't going to give it back in case the minister lost it for good.

Ken gathered me in his arms and gave me a kiss. That wasn't appropriate either, but no one was going to tell him otherwise.

After the ceremony, my family had prepared a small feast. All were invited back for lunch. This was a low-key affair because the celebration day was Saturday.

In my culture, the bride and the groom still had to live separately until the first Sunday after their wedding, where the celebration commences with a church service or mass, followed by the wedding feast. Only then could the bride and groom finally be united as a couple and consummate their marriage.

We'd spoken about it before but either Ken refused to listen to another cultural thing or thought I was teasing as usual. After lunch, I whispered to him about it, but he looked at me in disbelief. This time he dug his heels in and found an ally in my uncle from the United States. 'I've done everything according to the culture and respecting Liva's family, but now that we're married, I'm done with waiting. This is beyond ridiculous. We're starting our married life today, not a week later.'

We left my uncle with the hard chore of smoothing things out with my grandma and her cronies.

Ken moved in with me at the hotel. My boss was happy to accommodate us and I intended to continue my role there.

Bill had organized a dinner party that night to celebrate our big day with all our expat friends. It was nice to see Ken celebrating our special day with his people, dining at tables instead of sitting on the ground. This was only the beginning of our wedding celebration. There would be a long week of celebration as everyone continued the tradition until Sunday.

No more pressure from culture and family. We were free to explore without fear as we embarked on our life journey as husband and wife, white and black, Tongan and Australian.

Oh shit! Sex! What do I do now?

A new wave of fear came over me. Remembering that someone had told me it hurts the first time, I was scared, but with Ken's love and understanding, we got there.

Very early the morning after, Ken got up to open the curtains of our hotel room, stark naked. I couldn't believe how easy it was for him to stride around in the nude, something I wasn't ready to do after day one. I was still lying in bed, covered up to my neck, marvelling at this white body in front of me. It was like watching a movie in slow motion. *That white body is mine.*

He started to draw the curtains open and, as quick as a flash, he yanked them closed again. He spun around and strode back towards me, waving his fingers furiously. I could tell he was trying to keep his voice down. 'Get rid of them.' He pointed towards our balcony, where I could hear singing. 'What more do they want from me?' He disappeared into the bathroom.

'The morning after consummation, the bride's female relatives come and collect the bloody sheet as proof of virginity and purity. It's something to be celebrated,' I attempted to explain.

Ken couldn't believe what I was saying. 'That's disgusting. This is ridiculous!'

I went out and dragged Grandma in for a private chat. 'Grandma, Ken is very uncomfortable with this particular part of my culture but out of respect for you and our tradition, you can damn well have the bloody sheet but it's not for every Tom, Dick and Harry to see, no ifs, no buts.'

Grandma wasn't happy, and I didn't care. Ken was my priority. She begrudgingly gathered her followers and disappeared without taking the sheet. There was no joy if she couldn't brag about it to her gossiping friends and relatives.

The wedding vibes were still in the air, so too the feasts every night, waiting for bloody Sunday. Any excuse for the villagers to gather around playing their banjos, singing and dancing, whether we were there or not.

It wouldn't be a party without a bowl of kava, the local alcoholic drink. The root of a kava plant is dried and pounded into powder form then mixed with water. I'd never tried it, but Ken said it tasted like muddy water and it numbed his tongue.

'Why would people drink that shit?' he said.

We were looking forward to the end of the week when we could have a bit of privacy and people would leave us alone. Hopefully, they'd stop staring and kids would stop following us around. Ken found it amusing and didn't mind but I wished I could tell them to piss off.

Saturday was our celebration day. We arrived at my grandparents' house and the atmosphere was buzzing. People were singing, dancing and cooking, dogs howling, pigs squealing and there was smoke everywhere. Before Ken turned the ignition off women raced towards us, laughing and making weird noises as they scooped Ken and me up and carried us off separately. Ken had no idea what was going on. I didn't know what was going on either so couldn't offer any explanation. All I said was, 'Just try to enjoy the moment.'

I was planted in one corner of the hut and Ken in another. There was a beautiful tapa cloth for us to stand on during the mat-wrapping ceremony. Tapa cloth is made from the bark of the mulberry tree and is an important element of our cultural collection.

Surrounded by my village elders, I started to well up. I couldn't be any prouder to be an island girl bringing a white man, my husband, to be dressed by my respected village ladies. There was no escaping as we became prisoners of these elderly women with no teeth, according to Ken. He looked at me without uttering another word. I'd never told him about the earlier discussion with Grandma when I'd tried to excuse him from wearing a mat.

Silently, he understood and, for the first time, I felt sorry for him. It would have been a disaster if he'd refused, and an embarrassment for me and my family. But once the layers of mats started to pile on, I heard Ken calling in a panicked voice. 'Liva ... Liva ...' The old ladies were smacking his legs to spread them apart, and with the language barrier Ken had no idea why he had to open his legs. 'Well, if you still want to get married, you'd better spread your legs,' I said.

'We're already married,' he said, trying not to sound too annoyed.

I was killing myself laughing, watching how distressed he was over such a simple request. His face was red and confused. Only then did I release him from agony. 'You need to spread your legs while they're wrapping you up, darl. If you don't, not only would you look like a cigar, but you won't be able to walk.'

He gave me a wink with a smirk on his face as he relaxed again.

It took over an hour to complete the mat-wrapping ceremony. By that stage, it was approaching 1 p.m. and the lunch feast was laid out. We had approximately 20 expat guests and 200 locals. A wedding feast was not only family but a whole village affair.

I couldn't fathom the abundance of food in front of us. There were lines of spit-roasted succulent pigs, endless rows of lobsters and other varieties of local delicacies. This is my Tonga, and I will always treasure that wherever I go. Everything is effortless and, certainly, my people know how to put on a feast.

Ken and I took up our position at the head of the table, sitting on the ground. During the feasting, we were entertained by the local girls, who performed our cultural dancing, their skins dripping with perfume-infused coconut oil. Being the oldest of seventeen siblings — six from Mum's new family and nine from Dad's, as well as my sister Selai — we were honoured by three of my younger sisters leading the dancing celebration.

Ken delivered his speech first and I translated it to Tongan. He was a bit emotional when he announced, 'My wife and I'. The noise was deafening with people whistling and clapping when Ken made his first public declaration. I was emotional, too, hearing Ken refer to me as his wife for the first time since our wedding. It was a bit tricky to translate that phrase myself. I was overwhelmed with pride. Then I delivered my speech in English first, followed by my native tongue.

There were a lot of speeches but when my grandpa made his speech, it was a heart-wrenching one. My Uncle Manu translated for him.

'Keni, today I have lost a black sheep but gained a white one,' he said, and everyone roared with laughter. 'Thank you for loving our Liva and for that, Nane and I love you too and are proud to have a palangi grandson. Wishing you both a happy and fruitful long life. When you continue on your journey to your home in Australia, don't forget you have a home here in Vava'u too.'

Afterwards, our getaway vehicle was a motor scooter. With both of us on it, I felt every loose stone and pothole we went over, but it was convenient for us to have a quick getaway without hitchhikers.

Alone at last after a long, hot day trapped in those mats, we chatted about our day over a beer for Ken and a much-needed cup of tea for me. We laughed and cried but they were happy tears. The mat-layering saga was all but forgotten as we became entwined.

The next day we went back to my village for the Sunday service. Because we'd already lived together as a married couple since Tuesday, the service was more symbolic than anything.

The mats were only two layers this time. Ken was relieved about that. Thank god we weren't made to sit in the front pew, which we were both very happy about. We got to enjoy the singing as only Tongans know how.

We came home to yet another feast, but not as lavish as the celebration day. By this stage, we'd eaten enough to last us a lifetime. This was a low-key Sunday lunch with just the family. We also made it our farewell lunch with Uncle Manu, as he was leaving for the States the next day.

After lunch, we bade farewell to everyone as we knew the next day Ken and I would both be going back to work.

Back at the hotel, fatigue overtook us and we both succumbed to mental and physical exhaustion as the angel of dreams took possession of us.

'Thank you, Ken, for the happiest day, week of my life,' I whispered, but I wasn't sure whether he heard me as I knew he was already asleep.

I cannot begin to think how Ken survived all that ordeal. Not once had he whined or complained about anything. Apart from the ladies outside our balcony the morning after the wedding, he'd grinned and borne everything I'd put him through.

It was worth the sacrifices as I overheard Ken telling friends years later about our wedding day. 'As painful as it was at the time, I am very happy and proud that I did it. It was memorable. Our wedding with a difference.'

5

Wife, a different life

Our first Christmas holiday as husband and wife was also the season for the inter-village netball competition. This was something I'd participated in every year and I'd been team captain for the last few years. I'd been single and free then.

Tongan husbands didn't usually let their wives play sports. It was the controlling and possessiveness of Tongan men in taking ownership of a woman once they were married that I deeply resented. But now I had to tell Ken that I was playing. I mulled over this for a few days as I had no idea how an Australian wife should behave. Maybe the Australian men did the same, but I didn't know yet.

Instead of asking Ken, like a Tongan wife, my rebelliousness reared its ugly head as I blurted out in a defensive mode. 'I'm going to play netball with my old team, Ken.'

Ready for my first fight, I was shocked when he said, 'Okay, when and where?'

Wow, this is good. It was easier than I thought. 'Oh, I don't know yet. I haven't told the team I'm available. I didn't think you were going to let me.'

'Huh! Let you? Can I stop you? I didn't know you're a comedian, too.'

I did my best to ignore his little dig.

Next, I had to see whether the team would allow me, a married woman, to play. If I was allowed, how would other people judge me? A married woman in Tonga must be dressed conservatively. Nothing too revealing and skirts not above the knees. *Ah well, stiff shit.* The team was delighted and I resumed my usual position of goal attack.

Ken came to watch me play the first game. He didn't like it that much; he said, 'It's too rough and you could get hurt.'

My friends laughed, telling me every time I'd fallen over, they could hear Ken crying out, 'Ooh!' louder than I did.

I played three games and I started to feel nausea all the time. I had to stop playing, which delighted Ken. But it quickly turned to concern as I continued to feel sick and I thought I had a virus. Doctors were consulted and I was given antibiotics and anti-nausea tablets, to no avail. I also had a blood test.

Finally, the blood test result came and Ken's worries turned to elation as the doctor announced, 'Congratulations, there's a baby Mac on the way.'

'What? No way! That can't be right. We've only just got married,' I said in disbelief.

Ken was beaming as he shook the doctor's hand. 'Thank you, doc, that's the best news. I was worried that I might have to take home a sick wife, but now, only a pregnant wife.'

The doctor laughed, congratulated us again then left.

I sat down at the end of our bed in our hotel room and buried my face in my hands. Ken shut the door and turned around, saw me and the smile left his face. He came over and just hugged me while I cried.

I was scared and overwhelmed, then I heard his voice. 'Liva, my closest friends, even my younger sister, they've all had kids, now it's my turn, our turn. We're going to be parents and have our own little family. Why aren't you happy?'

I was shitting myself. *What will I do with a baby? Gosh, I'm still a baby at twenty.* 'Darl, this isn't what I envisaged the beginning of our marriage to be. I need time to explore my new husband, get to know his family, his country, before embarking on a new career as a mum. What was I thinking, having unprotected sex?'

My fear turned to anger and accusation. 'I don't want to start a family yet. You planned this all along. What am I going to do with a baby without my family?'

'Shh, everything will be okay, you'll see. Please be happy with me. I'm not getting any younger and I'm your family now. I'll be there all the way. I love you,' he said, tilting my face up as he often did.

Ken was ten years older than me and, of course, he would be excited at 30 to be a dad, but we hadn't discussed this.

Oh, dear lord, he's just like a Tongan husband, I thought. *Get married then I'm suddenly the incubator, popping a kid out every year. No thank you. I have things to do, places to go, dreams to catch, but it looks like I'm just an ordinary girl. That's what's expected of me. Get married, have kids, cook, clean. There's no escaping being a woman, no matter what colour.*

It reminded me of when I'd been in Year 12 and we'd had to write an essay about our ambition. I couldn't write about my fantasy of being a pilot. I knew I'd be laughed at. So I thought I'd write about being a mum — the unrecognized, unappreciated and thankless career. For my effort, I got 100 per cent and excellent remarks on the context and depth of my essay, but I was also summoned to the principal's office.

My principal was a big Irish priest, a very clever man at that. He also happened to be my English teacher and the one who'd given me the excellent marks. I entered his office and I saw my essay on his desk while he was tapping his white fat fingers on it with a sarcastic smirk.

Without warning he roared. 'Face 'Utulei.'

'Utulei was an island across the bay. I was shaking like a leaf but I did as commanded.

'Touch your toes,' came the second roar as I shuddered.

I was not sure why I didn't wet myself. I knew very well what came next. It had taken until my final year for me to receive the infamous belt. The ferocity and intensity of twelve straps on my back was like nothing I'd ever experienced before, but I never flinched or made a sound. My defiance was stronger than the pain his strap was making.

The unspoken message the principal taught me was loud and clear. *You're better than that and being a smart arse will get you nowhere.* I left his office feeling like shit. It took weeks for the lumps and the bruises to subside. I never told my grandparents about it.

So here I was now with a bun in the oven and the essay I'd written all those years ago about being a good mum was nowhere to help me. I never discussed my feelings with Ken. I had no time. Netball was the first casualty of my pregnancy, then my job.

I was sick all day every day and hated being pregnant. I hated Ken's aftershave. Years later, when I was at the shopping centre, if I got a waft of that aftershave smell I'd start to feel sick. I couldn't stand the sound of his alarm in the morning. I hated his toothpaste. These were just a few of the most annoying things about being pregnant.

I craved weird stuff. One of them was sea urchins. Ken had never had to collect them before, but there was a first time for everything. After giving Ken a crash course on how to fish them out of the water, we went down to the beach and he'd snorkel out and spear them one at a time and bring them over to where I was waiting. The first time he brought one, I knew he was sitting in the water, watching me. I tenderly chopped off the long black spikes with a knife, being careful not to spike myself, as the barb would break under the skin and it could be very painful. Once they were all cut short, I cracked it open. Stuck to the shell was the much-anticipated, delicate yellow eggs I was after. I scooped up the eggs and slurped them in. I could hear Ken bobbing under, saying, 'Gross! Yeek! Brrrrr!' but he continued to bring them again and again. I had a good feed, vomited them up, then we went home.

I was losing weight and I could see Ken's early excitement at becoming a dad was being dulled with concern. He was worried that I might lose the baby and medical help in Tonga wasn't to his satisfaction. He just wanted to take me home to Australia.

6

The end of the project

The hospital and the fuel depot projects were approaching the finishing line. The King of Tonga, Taufaʻahau Tupou IV, came from Nukuʻalofa for the opening ceremony. It was March 1981 and the weather was hot and humid as we were just coming out of what was normally the cyclone season. I was struggling with morning sickness and we were running late but managed to get there as the Tongan national anthem was being played as the King arrived.

Ken was dressed in my Tongan costume of a taʻovala. He looked handsome and hot but he was proud to show off to the King his Tongan side. Thanks to Ken, I was privileged to be seated with him in the front row together with Leo and Joe. I was honoured to be standing next to my white husband feeling very important.

The Australian team got the accolades they deserved from the King. ʻI thank you, Leo, Ken, Joe and the Australian government for the much-needed help for our people. The hospital looks beautiful and the people of Vavaʻu will be forever grateful to you in years to come. I'm delighted to see we managed to convert one of the Australian team members.' He looked towards us, smiling, and the crowd laughed. We bowed in acknowledgment.

After the hospital-opening ceremony, the three Australians were summoned for a private meeting with the King before proceeding to the fuel depot. It was the first time I'd shaken my King's hand. I was nervous; being a commoner, I'd never thought I'd come close, let alone touch his hand. Our culture would have required me to drop to my knee and crawl up and kiss his toes. However, the King looked genuinely pleased as he shook Ken's hand first. 'Congratulation Ken, I'm glad you've got yourself a black pearl,' he laughed. 'And by the way, you look good with the taʻovala. Thank you for this beautiful hospital. I wish you all the very best.'

'Thank you, Your Majesty,' Ken said.

The King didn't say anything to me. He shook my hand with a smile as I curtsied.

The opening of both the hospital and the fuel depot spelled an end to Ken's contract. There were still some final fittings to do but he was told his job was done and it was time to go back to Australia.

A few weeks later, we were both staring at our one-way tickets for Australia. *Oh dear, it's real. I have to follow my beau and leave my Vavaʻu.* I was mesmerized by this ticket in front of my nose. I'd never seen an aeroplane ticket before, let alone an international one. While it was scary to be going to live in another country, I was excited about my first plane ride.

Ken looked sad as he stared at the tickets. But after the initial shock, there was excitement on his face. 'I can't wait for you to see Australia and our home. You'll love it.'

Before we knew it, there was a mad rush of tying up loose ends as we prepared for the trip of my life. My subconscious reared its ugly head again as the unknown loomed ahead. *How will Australia receive this black girl? What will Ken's family and friends think of me?* These were paralysing thoughts. Fortunately, those thoughts never stayed on the surface for too long.

'I did tell you I've got a house?' Ken said one day.

'Yes Ken, you did. And a car too. That's why I married you,' I teased. 'I can't wait to see.'

He ignored what I said. 'I came home one day and told my father I'd bought a house. He looked at me and didn't say congratulations, he lectured me instead. "Why did you do that? You're a bloody idiot, son, you'll never be able to pay it off."'

'Well, Liva, I was determined to prove him wrong, and you and our baby gave me the extra determination. I bought it two years before I came to Tonga. It's your own house and you don't have to answer to anyone but me. If you want to sleep all day, you sleep all day. Not every Australian bachelor has a house, but I worked hard knowing that one day I would have a wife and my own family.' He looked smug.

I was so proud of him. *Oh my god, I've got a house in Australia,* I thought. *I don't have to live with Ken's parents. And I have a car as well. Could somebody wake me up, please?*

He'd come to Tonga as a bachelor and was now going back with a native wife who couldn't drive, couldn't cook, spoke broken English and was pregnant with his child. *A bloody gold digger! An opportunist.*

'I've never driven a car myself,' I said. 'Ken, aren't you ashamed to take me to your family and friends knowing I'm so backwards in every way?'

'How many times do I have to tell you that I don't care what they think? I'll teach you to drive and you will drive, Liva, I know you will. It would be a shame to have a car waiting if you can't drive it.'

The day before our departure, we went to my village to say goodbye. We received a lot of gifts of local artefacts from my people. My grandparents gave me a tapa cloth. Tapa cloth is made from the bark of a mulberry tree. The bark is stripped, dried and beaten in a way that doesn't rip it but expands it. The pieces are joined with special natural glue — tapioca. Once the desired length is achieved, it's painted with special ink extracted from the bark of a Koka tree (red gum), boiled to get a rich dark colour. It's a long, slow process and requires the help of the whole community.

'Take this, Liva,' Grandma said through her tears, 'and hang it where you can see it as a constant reminder of where you come from, and your heritage. Don't ever forget.' It was later hung in our home and covered a whole wall in my dining room.

'Thank you, Grandma, you don't have to worry about that. You and Grandpa have etched it deep in my heart, never to be forgotten. I don't need a tapa cloth to remind me but I'll treasure it.'

Grandpa gave me a 'ukulele he'd made from a coconut shell, even though I didn't know how to play. There were mats, baskets and table mats. Unfortunately, we couldn't take everything, but we took enough souvenirs.

6 THE END OF THE PROJECT

There were lots of tears as the minister who'd conducted our wedding ceremony came and said a farewell prayer for us. I was broken to say goodbye to my family, my beloved village, my life as an island girl.

Ken took me in his arms and hugged me, whispering love and promises of a happy future in Australia. 'We'll come back as often as you want.' This was a promise he kept.

I looked around one last time as we drove away from my village. I wanted to engrave everything into my mind, never to be forgotten.

As we crossed the little causeway that connected my little island of Pangaimotu to the main island of Vavaʻu, a sound of pain involuntarily escaped my lips. I closed my eyes and inhaled the sea air as if it was my last breath. Ken's gigantic hand took mine without a word and kissed it. I was lost in my own sadness for the rest of the drive.

I was sad about the separation but had no regrets. I wanted to be with Ken more than anything in this world. No island, no family and no friends would keep me away.

7

Bon voyage

When we got to the airport, we boarded a small aircraft. Fifteen passengers squeezed in, with some of the big Tongans taking up nearly two seats each. Ken let me sit at the window, then he took the aisle seat.

The aircraft engine started squealing. Within seconds, we accelerated down the runway. I squeezed Ken's hand harder as the aircraft became airborne. As we took off it started to lightly rain, but I could make out my village as we flew over it. I was glued to the window, in awe of the aquamarine colour of the ocean below, beauty I'd never experienced from a bird's-eye view. Once the dotted islands of Vavaʻu disappeared, the Haʻapai — the middle group of the archipelago — appeared, with more beautiful white sandy beaches below. The rain got heavier after that and I couldn't see below any more.

The flight got bumpy and the little aircraft tossed all over the place. Suddenly it dropped and I reached for the sick bag and spewed. Ken just held my head. So much for the excitement of being on a plane.

'Ladies and gentlemen, we're on descent to Fua'amotu airport and the latest weather forecast reported heavy rain in the vicinity of the field. It shouldn't be an issue for our arrival, please ensure your seatbelt is securely fastened,' the pilot announced on the PA.

'Yeah, right. If it's not an issue, then why is everybody sick? Surely they're not all pregnant,' I whispered to Ken.

It was raining so hard the poor old plane was leaking, with the water coming inside. I spotted a local passenger pulling out a Bible. She started to pray. Things look a bit grim when you see people praying.

We seemed to have been descending a long time when suddenly we hit the runway. *Hmm I'm not sure about this pilot dream of mine,* I started to think.

'Whoa! Did we land or get shot down?' I said, half-crying and half-laughing.

'Glad the pilot saw it because I didn't,' Ken muttered.

We stayed at a hotel in Nuku'alofa overnight. The next morning, my mum, who lived on the mainland with her family, met us at the airport and drove us to the family's home for yet more feasting.

'Argh! More feasting,' Ken said in exasperation.

Food was laid out under the 'Ovava tree. My stepfather said grace, which went on for too long for my liking, but you could never eat without blessing the food, no matter where you were. With morning sickness, I couldn't stomach any more. Ken, on the other hand, was polite. 'I'll miss the fruit,' he said. 'You'll never get bananas that taste like this in Australia.'

Then it was time for more teary goodbyes as we boarded the biggest plane I'd ever seen. We were headed for Melbourne, via Auckland. We taxied down the runway, coconut palms rushing past us as we accelerated. Shortly after, I felt the floating sensation as we became airborne. I was speechless. The aircraft turned away from the runway and soon the coconut palms were replaced by endless blue ocean below.

Then it hit me. *Oh no! Tonga is behind me now.* As I looked toward the horizon, I whispered, 'Goodbye, my Tonga.' I wondered if my god would keep his promise to bring me back for a visit one day. I closed my eyes and sent a silent prayer. My thoughts were interrupted by the ding-dong of the 'fasten seatbelts' sign as it flicked off. The hostess was busy handing out hot face washers. No sooner had they come around to collect the used towels then there were drinks and nuts, followed by a tray of unidentifiable food for breakfast.

The three-hour flight to Auckland seemed like an hour as I watched with curiosity while my god ordered more food and drinks. He showed me how to use the headphones so I could hear the movie that was playing on the big screen. I couldn't understand the movie because they talked too fast and I had trouble keeping up.

The flight was so smooth as we floated across the Pacific; such a difference from our flight from Vava'u to Nuku'alofa. I watched in awe as my god filled all our arrival documents.

When we arrived at Auckland airport, we didn't have to use stairs like in Tonga. There was a bridge that came out from the building and connected to the aircraft door and we walked straight out into a lounge. Ken took me out to the airport's observation deck to look at the city. I couldn't believe my eyes. There were millions of cars darting around on the road below. I turned to Ken and asked in bewilderment, 'Are these all the cars in the world?'

He smiled. 'Wait until you see the cars in Melbourne.'

I was glad that my god knew where we were and where to go. I had no idea. I had no sense of direction. I felt as if I was in a web, trapped by fear. This one building was ten times bigger than my whole village.

Before long, we were queuing up again to board another plane. This one was even bigger. It dawned on me as I examined my surroundings that I was the only non-white passenger. I kept my head down and followed my god closely, but I could feel everyone's stares boring holes in my skin. I didn't like it when Ken pushed me ahead, as I didn't know where to go or what to do. He must have realized that we were no longer in Tonga and he could now hold my hand in public, so he grabbed it with possessiveness and dragged me wherever he went. This simple action drew a lot of attention, as if people had to look again to be sure that their eyes weren't playing tricks, but my god didn't see them. I couldn't get to our seats quick enough.

I took the window seat. Not only did I like to see out, but I could hide behind Ken and didn't have to talk to the hostess. I spoke enough English to save myself, but if the conversation moved too fast, I was gone.

I just wanted to sleep. We'd been in the air for about three hours and it was pitch black outside, when I was jolted by Ken's excited voice. 'Look, darl. Can you see the lights? That's the coast of Australia.' It didn't take long for my eyes to adjust to the blackness outside. 'Oh my god! It's beautiful.' If there was a heaven, in my eyes, this was what it would look like. I stared down at the promised land with my love beside me. I forgot all about my sadness at leaving my Tonga, family and friends as the excitement of my new country became real.

I was deep in thought as the aircraft kissed the runway and taxied for a long time before we pulled up at the terminal.

If I'd thought Auckland was big then Melbourne was gigantic. I'd never seen so many people as I did in the airport terminal in my entire life. I could make out different races but not many black people as other flights came in. I didn't see one other mixed couple.

We seemed to walk a lot then queue up for miles. Finally, the big automatic sliding doors opened out into the arrival hall and I was hit by the lights and noises.

8

The promised land

Ken's mum and dad were among the waiting crowd, and there were others with them, too.

'Welcome, Liva. How was the flight?' Norman and Mona said in unison as we embraced.

'Thank you, good to see you again. The flight was really good and smooth. Gosh, Australia is so big.' I had so much to tell them but there were others to greet.

Ken's brother Bruce and his wife were there, too. Ken shook his brother's hand then introduced me.

But what bowled me over was a frail little white-haired lady who had come out in the cold of the night to meet Ken's new black bride. She was Ken's 80-year-old grandmother, Nanna McLeod. I watched Ken hug this little lady with so much love. It warmed me as I thought of my own grandma.

When Ken introduced me, she had tears in her eyes. *She doesn't see me as black*, I thought as I hugged her as if she were my grandma. I felt welcomed, and with his loving family around me I was excited about my new adopted country.

Our first stop was Nanna's house in Northcote. We had tea with yummy treats that filled what looked like a trolley. Two tiers full of cakes and biscuits that I'd never seen before. Tea and biscuits, not yam and pigs like Tonga. I suppressed a smile.

We left Nanna's house and proceeded to Ken's parents' place. Bruce and his wife came back to the house, too. There were more cups of tea and everyone seemed happy that we were home, and we chatted until late into the night. I was exhausted. Morning sickness didn't help, but I'd never been in a car for so long before. We had stopped multiple times while driving, for me to chuck on the side of the road.

Ken must have sensed my weariness and whispered, 'Is it okay if I tell them about our little bun in the oven?'

I looked at him, horrified of the reaction I'd receive. But before I could answer him, he blurted it out.

'We're going to have a baby,' he said. 'Liva is pregnant.'

'What? Congratulations! When?' everyone asked at the same time.

I could understand the look of surprise and disbelief in their eyes, but I wasn't sure whether it was because I'd got myself pregnant so quickly or because I didn't have a belly. I wanted the earth to open and swallow me up right there and then. I felt cheap and stupid.

Well, it wasn't my fault I got pregnant. I'm only twenty, but my god should've known better.

There were kisses and handshakes of congratulations and a call for celebration, and there was a new understanding of my fatigue and vomiting.

We were staying at Ken's parent's house for the night. Unbeknown to me, we took his parents' bedroom, which is a big taboo in my culture. How ironic that my first night spent in Australia was in my parents-in-law's bed. I could see my grandma admonishing me. 'Where's the respect Liva? That's not how you were brought up. On the floor, girl.' *Ah, Grandma, I'm here and it's beautiful, like the Promised Land.*

Sleep was welcomed as my head was spinning. It was a freezing night, — the beginning of winter. Although it was cold, I was mesmerized by the warmth of the bed that apparently came from an electric blanket. I felt spoilt. *Am I still on the same planet?* I wondered.

The next day I was awoken by the smell of something delicious. Unfortunately for me, that was my cue for a chuck.

Knock, knock. *Oh god,* I thought, *I can't let anyone see me like this.* I jumped up, trying to control my afro, but Ken was onto it.

'Good morning! How did you sleep, Liva?' said Mona.

'I slept well, thanks,' I said, uncomfortable that my mother-in-law was in my bedroom.

Ken met his mum halfway and took the tray from her. He brought it back and set it on the bedside table.

'I made you tea because it's better for you first thing in the morning,' Mona explained over Ken's shoulder, oblivious to my discomfort. 'It's a cold day. I've put a warm dressing gown here for you.' She pointed to a sheeplike pile at the end of the bed. 'Enjoy your brekky.'

'Thank you M—' With that, she walked out of the room. Ken shut the door and returned to bed and started to fuss with the tray of breakfast. I'd never seen anyone get so excited about food as Ken.

As he handed me a cup of tea, he noticed the tears on my face.

'Oh gosh! What is the matter now?' he asked, returning the tea to the tray and sitting down to cuddle me, rocking me back and forth.

'I nearly called your mum "Mum". She's doing the things my mum should be doing. In my culture, I should be doing that for your mum. Unacceptable.' I sobbed.

'You can call her Mum if you like. She wouldn't care. She would like that. So stop these tears. We can't let this yummy breakfast get cold.'

My first breakfast in bed — eggs and bacon, cooked and served by my mother-in-law. Another cultural collision.

'She's my mum and we can have breakfast in bed. It's a treat for special occasions and our first breakfast in Australia is special, let alone that you're with child. Stop tormenting yourself. You're not in Tonga now, so enjoy,' Ken said, hoeing into his scrambled eggs.

Breakfast was so good but not for long — what goes down must come up, as my morning sickness didn't take a break.

After that, we went out for some fresh air. It was cold but was good for morning sickness. I was excited to see my Australia in the daytime.

Ken's mum and dad had a modest weatherboard home. There was a half-acre backyard with fruit trees and a swimming pool. I looked at Ken accusingly. 'Wow! you never told me that your mum and dad are so rich.'

'They're not rich. They're comfortable.'

'You never told me that you had a swimming pool in your backyard,' I said as I peeked over the fence.

'What are you doing?'

'Checking to see whether the neighbours have swimming pools too.'

'You're being stupid now. Of course not everyone has a swimming pool but Mum and Dad aren't rich. We have a very big swimming pool at our house.'

'Really? You never told me that either.'

'Yeah, it's called Port Phillip Bay.'

'Huh?'

'The ocean.' He laughed.

Oh, dear! I thought. *This is where Ken comes from and he's had to endure a primitive kind of living when he came to visit me in my village. How can I ever measure up?*

There were apple, pear, blood plum, apricot and lemon trees in the backyard. It took me back to Tonga — apples were reserved for only the rich and famous and here I was, walking around among apple trees with abundant fruit as if I was in the garden of Eden. Which apple should I have, red or Golden Delicious? I wished my little sister was with me so she could have as much as she wanted.

'I miss you, Selai,' I said, looking towards the horizon as if she could hear me.

Ken was too busy to notice the sadness that came over my face. 'I used to mow the lawns,' he said, looking up at the house. 'See that part of the house? I helped Dad build that extension so I could have my own bedroom. I bought a colour TV for my room but I finished up with everyone in there. So I moved the TV out to the lounge room. When I bought my house, Mum and Dad bought me a new colour TV and they kept my old one. You'll see when we get to our house.'

It was still foreign for me to hear Ken talk about our house.

With the help of fresh air, I felt a bit better, so we went back inside, where Mum and Dad were waiting for us. They had planned a drive for us to meet with Ken's sister, Linda, and her family, and to pick up Ken's car that Linda had babysat while Ken was in Tonga. It was another long drive to the country, although it was beautiful scenery, with the road winding through forest and tree ferns bigger than I'd ever seen.

I fell in love with my sister-in-law instantly. She lived on an acreage with a few horses, and when we arrived she had gumboots on and was feeding a horse. She would be perfect in Tonga. She stopped feeding the horse when we approached. She had a big smile on her face as she rushed up and embraced her brother. I looked on, feeling warm and fuzzy at the display of love. She didn't wait for an introduction as she let go of her brother and gave me a bear hug. 'Welcome to Australia. Sorry about the gumboots but we're in the country after all,' she laughed.

Her dark brick house looked bigger than their parents' house. This was the first time I'd seen an open fireplace inside a house, although it was a bit more controlled than the type of open fire we had in Tonga.

Linda was excited to hear that we were expecting our first baby and she gave me a lot of much-needed warm maternity clothes. Ken's four-year-old nephew, Mark, who happened to be the only grandchild at the time, came with us back to Ken's parents' place for a sleepover. We seemed to be driving a lot and my head was spinning yet again. I didn't want to complain but all I wanted to do was to see Ken's house, my house, that I'd heard so much about; but we stayed again with his parents for another night.

Ken wanted Mum's help to buy me some warm clothes, so the next day we went shopping. I had never seen shops like these before — so many under one roof, it was insane. We bought a lot of clothes, shoes and ugg boots. I stared at all these new clothes and shoes that had been bought in one day. They were more than I'd ever acquired in my whole life. Before this, I would have been lucky to get one new dress for Christmas. It was as if all my birthdays and Christmases had come at once. I was embarrassed and felt greedy at the amount spent on me. 'Ken, can you afford all these clothes?' I asked. 'Do I need all these?'

'Of course I can and believe me, you'll need these, as winter is yet to come. You've never experienced being cold before and you'll be thanking Mum and me when the time comes.'

'Well, we've only just arrived and I have no job or money to buy all these,' I whispered so his mum couldn't hear.

'That's my problem, not yours. Don't worry your pretty little head over it. Your job is to tell me whether you like them or not,' he said, tugging my nose lovingly.

'Thank you and yes, I love them all. I love anything Australian,' I grinned back.

We returned to Mum and Dad's house where Bruce and his wife joined us for a roast dinner. As if I hadn't bought enough clothes, Bruce's wife gave me a white woollen cardigan she'd knitted. It was beautiful but instead of being grateful, I felt inadequate; I couldn't knit. Was I required to knit? Tongan wives are expected to weave. I made a mental note that I would learn to knit in due time.

The next day we finally set out on the last sector of my long journey to my new home — my home with Ken. Mum, Dad and Mark, Ken's nephew, followed us. Only then did I understand why Ken had wanted us to rest for a couple of days at his parents' to break up the drive. My excitement was tarnished by the endless driving, with my usual stop on the side of the road to chuck.

I'd given up being awed by houses, street lights and the vast distances we'd driven in the two days since we arrived. I was exhausted from so much information to retain. But when I saw the ocean and beaches, I found some reserved energy. Ken had told me that he lived by the sea, but seeing it with my own eyes gave it a different beauty. It was clean with a white, sandy beach and we drove alongside it for the next 30 minutes.

'There's your swimming pool,' Ken said smiling. 'And it's free.'

'Yes, just like what I used to have, but I bet this one is cold,' I said.

'Oh, yeah. Brrrr.'

We turned inland, away from the beach, for another ten minutes with a series of turns, then transitioned from bitumen to an unsurfaced road. I sensed we must be close to our home. We then turned into a narrow street full of potholes and it almost felt like I was back in Tonga. The houses that lined the small street were small compared to what I'd seen. It felt very country-like. 'I spy with my little eye, which house is ours?' Ken said excitedly.

'Oh, are we playing that stupid game again? This one?' I said.

'Nope.'

'I give up. I can only see trees, no houses.'

He slowed down along a high timber fence and stopped in front of a brown gate.

'This one,' I screamed.

The grin on his face said it all. He jumped out and opened the gate to reveal a long, crushed rock driveway with a reddish brick L-shaped house at the end with lots of tall windows. It looked the best out of all the houses we'd passed.

I unsuccessfully tried to blink away hot tears then allowed my emotion to take over. 'Wow, this is my house. My home,' I mumbled, unashamed of my excitement. 'Darl, you were telling the truth. You really did have a house and it's mine too. It's beautiful.'

I got out of the car, my legs wobbly with excitement. I couldn't wait to see inside. Ken unlocked the door and before I knew what was going on, with one swift motion he scooped me up and carried me into the house. I protested, as his mum and dad were right behind us.

'Since we were married, it's been always about your culture. This is my culture. I have to carry my bride over the threshold for the first time.' He beamed mischievously.

'Huh! How come I've never heard that one before? You never told me of such a thing.' I blushed but didn't want it to end as I continued to tease. 'It took you three times before you got down on your knees, but here you are remembering to carry me over the threshold. If you'd done this in Tonga, you would only have had to carry me over the broom; short and sweet.'

We both laughed as he put me down — in the kitchen. *How appropriate*, I thought, but we kept our arms linked while he took me through his, but now our, house. To our left was the lounge room. Then it was back to the kitchen and dining area. Through a door off the hallway, we turned right to our bedroom. I looked at this huge bed and wanted to curl up right there and then, but we had Mum and Dad and our nephew in tow.

'Ken, this is unbelievable. Kitchen, bathroom, toilet, all indoors, and there's hot water coming out of the tap. It's absolutely magical and it's all mine!'

'All yours and our baby's. Do you like it?' he said. Huh! If only he could have seen my heart dancing, my thoughts full of gratefulness and appreciation for all he'd given me. Security, comfort, but most importantly, love.

I began helping Mona prepare lunch in my new kitchen when Norman walked in, shaking his head laughing.

'What's so funny, Norman?' Mona asked.

'Ken just can't help himself. He's out in the laundry polishing the washing machine and the dryer with his hankie,' he chuckled.

That was my introduction to Ken's world of fastidiousness, so far removed from mine. What was I thinking? From a thatched-roof hut and my primitive and humble kind of life, to this. I had failed to envision that Ken's world might be totally different. In my eyes, his house looked like a palace and I hoped I could look after it like a white wife would. There was so much new machinery I had to learn to operate.

Those thoughts were amplified by Ken's nephew asking the funniest question of his nanna and pa. 'Uncle Ken is going to sleep here but where is she going to sleep?' He pointed at me. Such an innocent query but I was probably the first black woman this little fella had ever seen. *Does he really see me as an outsider?* I wondered. *He obviously sees it as odd that I'm so different and maybe don't belong to Ken. Not suitable enough to stay in his Uncle Ken's house.*

It took a bit of explanation, but he still looked confused. *One day you will understand, Mark,* I thought. At the time, I felt sorry I'd been born the way I was.

Ken took some time off work to help familiarize me with my new surroundings. My world was spinning out of control; there was so much to take in.

Our first week was spent at home, mostly in bed, exhausted. We felt at last as if we were having the honeymoon we'd never had, with no families, no work and no noise. But the quiet was deafening and foreign to me, as all my life in Tonga had been lived in a very open house. If it wasn't people who made noise, it was the pigs or the dogs or the chooks mixed in with the church bell. Always noisy.

Here, I was surrounded by unoccupied homes. 'Ken,' I said one day, 'there's no noise or life coming from those homes.'

'They're holiday houses.'

'Holiday houses? What do you mean? They're not hotels, people can't go there for holidays. They're not big enough.'

'Not that kind of holiday, silly.' He started to laugh. 'Some people have two houses — one to live in the city for work, and one by the beach for their holidays.'

'That's insane. The people on my island couldn't even get half a house, let alone two. Do you have a holiday house hidden away somewhere, too, Ken?' I teased.

'Nope, this is it. Why do we need a holiday house when we have Tonga for a holiday?'

The thought of holidaying back in Tonga hijacked my thoughts for a moment as I hung on to those words of hope. 'Yes. I can't wait.'

'We will, sooner than you think.'

9

Finding my niche
in his world

I feared what would life be like when Ken returned to work.

'Ken,' I said one day, 'I love this world where it is just the two of us. I am so content, so happy. Your love is all I ever needed to breathe, to function and to live, but understandably, that is not the reality.'

'Unlike Tonga, we have to work here,' he replied. 'You can't just go to the bush and climb a coconut tree or ask the neighbour for some food. This is a working country. No money, no funny!' he said, mimicking what Lenny used to say.

We went to the bank to add my name to Ken's account. I'd never had a bank account. What I used to earn, I spent and shared with my family. Bank accounts in Tonga were held by husbands only, the head of the family.

Ken took me to the supermarket to buy groceries. The size of one shop to buy food was intimidating. I didn't understand why there was a need for so many different brands of the same thing. The lights and colours were enough to make me dizzy. 'Do we need a trolley? Are we going to buy the whole shop? It's only the two of us.'

'I only shop once a week,' Ken explained. 'I don't have time to be running back and forth to the shop every day. So I stock up.'

We shopped on demand in Tonga. We didn't have money to buy for the following day, let alone the week.

Nearly all of what he put in the trolley was a mystery to me. It was embarrassing to ask what things were or how they were used. I would have to wait until we got home. I didn't want to draw any more attention to my presence than I already had. There was no other black person in the whole area, let alone in the supermarket. The occasional stares from customers were discreet but they were there. Fear, apprehension and a lack of confidence made me keep my head down so I didn't have to make eye contact with anyone, and I stayed close to Ken.

I thought of my family, especially my little sister with Grandma and Grandpa. *What are they having for tea?* I wondered. If only they were nearby so I could share my trolley full of goodies.

I was daydreaming as usual when Ken jolted me out of it by asking, 'What ice cream flavour do you want?'

'Ice cream? In different flavours?' I'd only ever known soft white ice cream that came out of a tap. I later learned that was called 'soft serve'. 'Oh, I don't know. You pick.'

'Okay, let's have Neapolitan so you can have three flavours in one tub — vanilla, strawberry and chocolate.'

'Whatever, darl. I'll be happy with any ice cream.'

The more I had, the more I felt guilty and sad for what I couldn't share with my family.

'Are you okay, darl?' I heard Ken ask. 'Is there anything else you want?'

'Yes, I'm okay and no, I don't need anything else. I'm sorry.'

What astounded me was that Ken paid so much for the loaded trolley, maybe the equivalent of two months' salary in Tonga. I thought that was disgusting.

When we got home, he unloaded the shopping and explained every package before putting it into the pantry, where each had its own spot. I tried to absorb as much as I could; however, I paid special attention to the boxes of food that had pictures and were pleasing to my eyes. I made a mental note that I would check those mystery boxes first. 'Pantry' was a new word to add to my vocabulary. When I'd been growing up, we'd had a cupboard with flyscreen doors and the legs had stood in empty corned beef tins filled with water so the ants couldn't get in. Not that we'd had much food to store.

The best part of the shopping was the ice cream. So when Ken suggested lunch, I laughed. 'Forget lunch, I will just have ice cream.'

'No, you can have as much ice cream as you like but only after you have something substantial first. You have a baby to feed, or have you forgotten?'

'Oh! Such a bubble burster. I am going to teach this baby to love ice cream too.' I scoffed down a sandwich as quickly as I could.

In the evening, Ken busied himself making tea while I watched. I couldn't boil an egg, let alone turn on a stove. I was scared of burning down the house or something worse. The Tongan men do the underground 'umu while the women prepare the food to be cooked, but I couldn't find that kind of food here, and there was no hole in the ground to be found. I learned later that Ken was bad at cooking but at that time I didn't know any better; whatever he cooked tasted delicious. The first meal he taught me to cook was spaghetti bolognese. It was amazing.

I was having the time of my life having Ken all to myself. He loved taking me everywhere, showing me his Australia, but I think what he enjoyed the most was watching my excitement at the simplest things. I loved watching TV, as I'd never had that in Tonga. Sometimes he had to drag me out of the house. I would've been happy to stay at home watching *Sesame Street* and *Humphrey B Bear*, followed by *Play School*. Much to Ken's amusement, I had my breakfast watching kids' shows. Not only did I enjoy the kids' programs, but it was invaluable in helping improve my English.

I was scared to be left on my own when Ken returned to work. I was very pregnant, couldn't drive, couldn't cook and the small town of Rye where we lived was quite remote.

It was the middle of winter and I'd never been so cold. It intensified my loneliness the first morning Ken went back to work. It was dark when he left. I wanted to wave him off, but he insisted I stay in bed with a cup of tea because it was so cold.

'Please Lord,' I prayed, 'look after him and bring him safely back to me. I don't want to be left on my own in this white foreign world. What would I do?'

He left at 6.30 a.m. and got home at 5.30 at night. It was a long, lonely day for me. I missed my little island with its warmth and outdoors, where there was always someone around. I peeped out at the sound of every vehicle from 5 p.m. onward.

With Ken at work, a different anxiety entered my being. *What will I cook? A coloured wife with no job, no talent, I'd better pick up my game.* So I mirrored the spaghetti bolognese that Ken had shown me before. We had that for five days in a row before Ken said, 'Darl, do you know that there are other things we can eat? We don't have to eat the same thing every day. We're not in Tonga anymore.' This was the first criticism of my housewife qualifications and I burst into tears.

'Now, now, there's no need for tears. You will have to watch my mum because she's a good cook.'

What the fuck? Is he saying I'll never measure up? If he thought he was being helpful, he was mistaken. 'I'm sorry, but if you want me to be your mother then perhaps you should've married a palangi. You knew I couldn't cook.'

'Okay, I'm sorry. Forget I even said that.'

Ken never liked seeing me in tears. We put the cooking episode behind us but yes, I watched his mum and learned to cook a lot better. I became adept in the kitchen and enjoyed cooking and entertaining. After all, food is in my DNA.

Ken always said that once I got my driver's licence, life would be easier.

I had a driving lesson each week with a driving school. Then on weekends Ken took me for extra driving. Somehow, those drives always finished up with me in tears. I wasn't sure whether Ken was an impatient driving instructor or if he feared I would kill us both in the process. I had no idea of road rules even though I'd studied them for my Learner's. On the island, it's fast one first go; there were no such things as stop or give-way signs.

During my first driving lesson with an instructor, I confessed my inadequacy. 'I'd never been in a proper motor car until I came to Australia a couple of months ago.'

She looked at me as if I was from another planet.

'Seriously, I don't know the difference between a clutch, brake and accelerator,' I said again.

'Okay, hop in,' she said, motioning for me to get into the driver's seat.

Is she kidding me? Hell! She's going to let me control this car? Once I realized she had another set of pedals on her side, I relaxed a bit.

We spent my first driving lesson on my driveway and in our street. Could you believe it? A whole hour! I had to familiarize myself with the new language associated with driving, blinkers, clutch, brakes and first, second and third gears.

She found out the hard way that I was going to be a challenge for her when I went through the T-intersection without stopping. She had to override with the brake on her side. *Phew!*

The world of automatic appliances that Ken provided meant that, as a housewife, I had so much time on my hands. I would go for a walk and try to remember how to get home. I didn't know how to read a street map so I tried to memorize how many left or right turns I made, then reverse it on the way home.

'What did you do today?' Ken would ask when he got home, eager to hear about my day.

'You would be proud of me,' I replied one particular day. 'I walked to the shop and I took my spoon with me for when I bought my ice cream. On the way home, I sat on the side of the road to eat, but there were cars tooting. Not sure whether I did anything wrong. But I ate my ice cream then found my way home again.'

It must've sounded so stupid, but Ken never made me feel that way. He was proud that I was brave enough to venture out. He never stopped me or suggested that it wasn't normal to sit on the side of the road eating ice cream. He was always excited to hear about my day of exploring.

Ken's mum drove me to my doctor's appointments. The gynaecologist was a bit concerned as I'd gained so much weight. No surprises there, as I started my day with tea and toast before Ken went to work, followed by cornflakes, then porridge. I ate all this before lunch. I was like a kid in a candy store with so much variety of food at my fingertips and there was nothing else to do but entertain my tastebuds with these delicious, readily available foods. And Ken had told me that he only shopped once a week so I thought I had to eat everything before the next shopping day.

The gynaecologist learned of my relationship with food and advised against having three breakfasts. Only then did Ken tell me that I didn't have to eat everything in one week and assured me I would never run out of food.

Ken continued to work hard inside and out so the house would be baby-ready. I struggled to understand all the fuss. Ken's house was a three-bedroom brick house with a big yard, both front and back.

That was big enough for a family and yet Ken was already planning to extend. I compared it with Grandma's hut, with one common room where ten people slept on the floor at any given time. And Ken thought it necessary to build a second storey on top of the house. I didn't see the rationale behind it but I remembered something that he'd said before we got married which bothered me. 'I would like four kids, maybe four girls, one day.'

'Well, would you now? Have you factored in four weddings? Hope you have a good stash for that.'

We already had three bedrooms and I knew I was only carrying one baby.

We bought a lot of baby equipment. Ken was busy cleaning, painting and decorating the room close to our bedroom and turned it into a nursery.

'Hang on a minute, Ken. Are you saying that the baby is going to sleep in a room by him or herself?' I asked, baffled.

'Yes, the baby has to learn to sleep in his or her bed,' he said.

'Oh, really? That's weird. That's not going to happen in my house. My baby is going to sleep with me, just like in Tonga.'

'Well, we're not in Tonga and this is how we do it in Australia. We need our rest here,' Ken said in a 'discussion closed' manner.

'Hmm, the Australian mum is very precious then. We'll see about that,' I said sarcastically. *What on earth?* I thought. *There hasn't been any accident with mothers rolling over on their babies in Tonga.*

No sooner had we cleaned the bedroom than we filled it with baby things. Ken's mum bought us a wooden cot. His sister Linda gave us her cane bassinet and we got a hand-me-down English pram. I found myself wandering around in the baby's room touching and playing with all the baby stuff I'd never seen before, feeling very grateful. *How amazingly lucky is my baby to have a room to him or herself,* I thought. I sat on the floor of our baby's room feeling very pregnant and missing my grandma. Surrounded by baby stuff my mind's eye drifted away, thinking of a Tongan mum lying on the floor cradling a newborn baby as it suckled from her nipples, full of warmth and love. She never had all these things. I turned out okay.

But this is a different world.

'I am very lucky. Thank you, God,' I whispered, but there was no one there.

10

A friend in need is
a friend indeed

Without any medical history, Ken's family doctor referred me to an obstetrician at Mornington Bush Nursing Hospital. I didn't understand the health system. Ken had to pay a lot of money for me to go to this hospital as I wasn't covered by a private health fund.

I was unaware of the extra financial burden of my pregnancy. If only I'd known, I would have demanded to go to a different obstetrician who operated from a public hospital. 'The women in my village have their babies with an ancient midwife in the village,' I explained. 'Neither an expensive doctor nor a fancy hospital is required.'

'You're no longer in the village,' Ken said.

When we visited the gynaecologist, he suggested it would be a good idea to attend a prenatal exercise class with a physiotherapist. The nearest class was a 20-minute drive from our house. That was a problem. Despite having started driving lessons I still had no driver's licence. To attend my prenatal classes, Ken pre-booked a taxi to get me there and when I finished, I had to ask the physio to order my returning taxi. When I requested my taxi one day, she looked surprised. 'Do you come by taxi every time?'

'Yes.'

'Why? Don't you have a car?'

'Yes we have a car but I can't drive. I don't have a driver's licence yet. I'm still learning,' I said, lowering my voice so no one could hear.

'Does anyone live near Pardoner Road to help pick up and drop off Silva?' she announced before I could protest.

I was the only non-white girl in the whole class and now everybody knew I couldn't drive either. I looked down, feeling embarrassed and inadequate. I wished the physio had asked for my permission before enquiring about a charity run on my behalf. I braced myself, waiting for no one to offer. That would have been more degrading.

'Yes, I can, Helen.' I turned to see where the voice came from and to my surprise, the attractive petite lady with short brunette hair who always sat behind me in class raised her hand. I was glad it was her. I liked her but we'd never spoken at length other than to just say hi.

Wow! I thought. *That stranger is going to take me home and pick me up.* But then another wave of fear and insecurity crept in. *What will I talk to her about?*

She smiled back at me. 'Hi, I'm Lynette.'

'Hi, I'm Silva. Thank you, but I don't mind catching a taxi.'

'I don't mind, I pass your place anyway.'

I found out later that Lynette didn't live near me at all.

I was excited at the thought of making my first friend in Australia but nervous about how to make conversation. Ken was the only one who understood my broken English. I followed Lynette out to the car park where she stopped and opened the door of a big blue van. *She's way too small to be driving that big truck*, I thought. I watched her haul herself up and I had to follow suit. Soon both of us, with our big fat bellies, were sitting high and off we went.

'I saved you money today, Ken,' I said when he got home.

'How so?'

'I've made a friend and she brought me home, so I didn't use a taxi.'

He looked pleased. 'Does the friend have a name?'

'Her name is Lynette and she's going to pick me up every week.'

'Oh, that's nice. What did you two talk about?'

'Babies,' I laughed.

Ken could see I was very happy and he hugged me. From that day forward, Lynette picked me up and dropped me off every week for the rest of my pre-natal classes. She dropped me off one day and I invited her to stay for lunch. I was so excited to show off my cooking skills. Ken's mum had taught me how to make steak and kidney pie. Needless to say, that was what I prepared for lunch. Lynette was very complimentary and ate her portion. Later I found out that she didn't do kidney. Oops! I couldn't imagine what she would've been like on her drive home. Probably dry retching all the way.

Asking people whether they would like something to eat or drink is rude in my culture. We dish up for our guests and if they don't like the food, they can leave it on the plate. When Lynette came over, I hadn't given her the opportunity to decline my steak and kidney pie that I was so proud to show off. I dished it up like a Tongan. That was the polite way in my culture.

Bit by bit, Lynette educated me on many Australian ways. We continued our weekly ritual until she had her baby girl, Amber, one month before my baby was due.

One day, Ken took me to the bank to show me one more time how to make a withdrawal. While queueing up, a man with receding red hair came out from behind a desk and called us to a different counter. 'Can I help you?' he smiled and directed his question at Ken but looked at me inquisitively. We moved over to his counter and Ken started to engage in conversation with him. The conversation was way too fast and foreign for me to keep up. He looked at me then said, 'Are you Silva?'

'Yes. Are you Brian?'

He nodded. 'I'm Brian, Lynette's husband.' Lynette had told me that her husband worked at one of the local banks, but I hadn't expected to meet my new friend's husband this way. It felt too formal and I froze up.

Brian recalled later that what he saw was a cold, terrified young girl. That was an understatement — I panicked that I wouldn't understand any question that came my way.

I continued with my driving lessons and the instructor picked me up one day early in September. She looked at my bulging stomach but didn't say anything.

We were only fifteen minutes into our one-hour session when she asked. 'When are you due?'

'Today,' I replied.

'Left blinkers. Left again and let's call it a day,' she instructed.

That's early. What have I done?

'I'll book your licence test after you've had the baby.' She appeared quite calm, but I knew she didn't fancy my waters breaking in her car.

11

'Elisapesi: Gift of God

The day after my last driving lesson, I felt pain in my lower back. *Could this be labour pain?* I wondered, as fear and loneliness crept in. I didn't want to be a high-maintenance black wife and alarm Ken at work. So I soldiered on until loneliness got the better of me and I had to call the only lifeline I had.

'Hello?' Ken answered on the second ring.

'Hi darl, it's me.' I started to cry. 'Can you please come home? I'm scared.'

'Are you okay? I'll call the doctor and I'm coming home right away.'

I hung up and waited. It was the loneliest I'd felt since my arrival in Australia. When Ken got home, I threw myself into his arms and cried more. 'I'm scared, I wish my mum or grandma were here,' I sobbed. Ken just held me without a word.

When I looked into his face, I saw my mum, grandma and my sister, as he was the only family I had. When we left Tonga he'd promised me that he was my family and he would always be there for me, a promise he kept. I knew that Ken was by my side and that had to be enough.

He loaded my hospital bag, which was already packed and ready, into the car. It was just the two of us on the half-hour drive to hospital. On arrival, it struck me how clean and white the hospital was. The foreign smell of antiseptic reached my nostrils as I called for a bowl.

Our baby decided to be a high-maintenance one. Ken was by my side for three days and nights of continuing hell. Then, after what appeared to be never-ending pain, my waters finally broke. As I was wheeled into the labour ward, I heard a scream from next door: 'Mamma mia!'

I started to laugh but I was only masking the terror I felt as I squeezed Ken's hand harder and never wanted to let go.

How lucky am I? I realized. Tongan husbands aren't allowed to be present at the birth. They could usually be seen gathered outside or in the bush awaiting the news. I was so grateful that Ken was with me as I didn't think I could face it alone without my mum or grandma.

Then the thought of Ken in the room brought me back to the present. *Oh god, he's going to see me in a not-so-pretty way. This can't be happening.* But I couldn't bring myself to send him out. He was the bridge between me and these medical strangers.

Another contraction came and I pushed, then I heard a voice saying, 'The baby's head is showing. Pant now.' The midwife brought a mirror over so I could watch the birth just as I had another contraction. As I exhaled, I let out a scream. 'Take the bloody mirror away.' I was baffled at the concept of how anyone could watch their rear end while in pain, giving birth with blood everywhere. *Sorry, I don't find anything beautiful about that. It would put me off sex for life. Weird Australians.*

My thoughts were interrupted by another contraction, and as I screamed one more time, the baby entered the world with the loudest cry I've ever heard from a tiny little thing.

'It's a girl,' the gynaecologist said.

I looked up, exhausted, to see Ken tearing up as he kissed me, but I hated him for the pain I'd endured.

'Oh, darl, you did so great. She's beautiful. Well done,' he whispered.

I had held his hand so tightly during labour that his wedding ring had dug into his finger. All I remembered was my legs strapped to some poles and the baby on my tummy as I drifted off through the clanging of instruments.

By the time I woke up, Ken was sitting beside me, holding our new baby girl. Yes! He was smitten.

I took the baby for the first time and she was beautiful. Long black hair, a button nose like me, but she was very white.

'A little palangi loi (pretend white baby). Where's me in this baby?' I asked, but I was proud that she was all Ken except for the nose. 'I hope you won't mind having a black mummy in this white world of yours,' I whispered while kissing my baby's ear.

'Don't be stupid. God, you can be so clever and so dumb sometimes,' Ken said, annoyed. 'Of course she'll be proud, she'll never see you as being different. I wish you'd stop calling yourself black, by the way. You'll always be her mummy. The end,' he added, rubbing the baby's chubby cheeks.

At the hospital, the babies were kept at the nursery and mothers could only access them for feeding. They were like monkeys in the zoo, where they were on display along the windows for visitors.

I saw people pointing, 'Look at that baby with so much hair.' As I approached, they looked at me and I could see the silent understanding on their faces.

I was so proud that my baby had white skin and lots of black hair while the rest of the babies had none or very little hair. I didn't want my baby to be burdened with brown skin and always be second class to the superior white race. I didn't want any obstacles that might disadvantage her.

I would have preferred my baby to stay with me in my room, just as I had beside my mummy on the floor of our Tongan hut, snuggled into her bosom, smelling her milk. That was how mums and bubs bonded island style, but in Australia, they preferred the precious mums to have complete rest before taking the baby home. Just as well Grandma wasn't here; she would have had none of this separation.

When it came to naming our baby, I found it hard to accept that we as parents decided on the name for our baby. In my culture, the firstborn is named by the father's family, out of respect.

'Here in Australia, she's our baby and we're free without prejudice to call her any name we like,' Ken told me.

'She has to be connected to her ancestors,' I argued back.

After going through some of Ken's female ancestors' names, I declared. 'I like Elizabeth. "Gift of God". This can be translated to 'Elisapesi, the Tongan version. What do you think, Ken?'

'Yes, I like Elizabeth too.'

I knew that my family would approve of a biblical name for my firstborn, so we agreed on Elizabeth, after Ken's paternal great-grandmother, and we both liked the name. Ken's mum's name was Mona Joyce so we decided on Joyce — 'cheerful' — for her middle name.

Elizabeth Joyce McLeod entered the world on 9 September 1981, the first fruit of our love. A cheerful gift of God. How appropriate. Like most new parents, we were the proudest ever.

Ken took time off work to bond with our little gift of God. I had no idea how to raise a baby; I was merely a baby myself — a mum at twenty-one and knowing nothing. *Where are you, Mum, Grandma? I need you*, I thought. However, I felt blessed as Ken was very hands-on. We were at his mum and dad's one day when he showed off how to fold a cloth nappy and change the baby. I didn't think his father approved but Ken was proud to show off his newfound skills in front of his family. I was proud, too.

At home, I was very spoilt as Ken was the one who got up through the night. He paced the hallway with Elizabeth, trying to burp her or pat her to sleep. He introduced Elizabeth to a honey-dipped dummy. She loved it, but mums of today would cringe at that.

Years later, I heard Ken telling friends, 'Liva would sleep through a bomb. If I hadn't got up, god knows what would have happened to Elizabeth.'

'Why should I get up, Ken, when you beat me to it every time?' I smirked, poking my tongue out at him. 'Someone at least gets some sleep. I'm not as stupid as I look.'

'Yeah, right. Whatever!' Ken said, rolling his eyes.

We settled into parenthood but my inner self kept nudging me. *Liva, you promised Grandpa never to forget where you come from. Where do you take your baby for her first outing?*

'Yes, I know, Elizabeth. I will have to approach the subject cautiously with your dad,' I mumbled tickling her tummy. It didn't help that my grandma kept asking when Elizabeth would be baptized.

I finally built up the courage. 'Can we baptize Lizzie?' I asked Ken. 'What for?'

'Because that's what we do. I can't take Lizzie out until I take her to church first to be baptized. I was baptized, so I want her to be, too.'

Ken went quiet so I took it as a maybe. The next day I rang the local Catholic priest and he wanted to make an appointment to come to our house for a chat with both of us. I knew that would be a big ask for Ken so I thanked the priest but declined the offer. But I wasn't going to give up, so I dialled another minister from a different church. We booked the christening for Sunday and I didn't care what denomination as long as my baby was christened.

It was hard work to get Ken to church in the first place but he succumbed to my nagging. I cringe when I recall that event. I can still hear the minister's words: 'Let little children come unto me. For the kingdom of God belongs to such as these. Take care of her, as she's God's child.'

When we sat down Ken whispered, 'That was a lot of BS waffling.'

'Oh Ken, shush.'

'Hope to see you again soon, Ken,' the minister said when the service was over.

'Take a good look because you won't see me here again,' he mumbled when the minister was out of earshot. I pinched him so hard he nearly yelped.

After the christening, I was happy that another part of my heritage was fulfilled. I was free to go out and Ken suggested I go back and get my driver's licence. My instructor took me for another refresher.

On my driving test day, I felt confident until a police officer, who would conduct the test, hopped in. The pedals on the instructor's side were covered so she couldn't interfere with them while I was in control. I freaked out but once the police officer told me where to go and what to do I was like a robot, business as usual.

After an hour of driving, I pulled up in front of the local police station where we'd started. 'Congratulations!' the officer said from the back seat.

'Oh my god, thank you.' I beamed. I was so happy. Then we went inside to finalize the paperwork and pay.

'You've got your licence, but you will need reassurance to build your confidence up.'

'Oh yes, I've got insurance,' I blurted out. My instructor and the testing officer looked at each other and burst out laughing. They tried to explain to me the difference between insurance and reassurance.

Thank god that with my colour, they couldn't see how red I was. Nevertheless, it was exciting to come home with my P plates.

Ken was right — life was definitely a lot easier with me driving. I took Elizabeth to the community health centre for her health checks, and met lots of new mums there. I always felt uneasy at these gatherings, where I felt inferior to other mums. Once Elizabeth was checked, I was out of there in a hurry unless Lynette and Amber were there.

Neither Lynette nor I joined the mother's group, as we had each other. We got together every week so our little bundles of joy could play as we compared notes and shared our minimal baby knowledge. We hung out all day and had lunch, but one thing was for sure: steak and kidney pie was no longer on the menu.

Watching my baby grow and reach little milestones only intensified my yearning for my mum or grandma to share in my joy. I lived in the hope that maybe Ken would take us back to Tonga soon.

12

New identity

'I think you should consider becoming an Australian.'

Since our arrival in Australia, Ken had wanted me to become an Australian citizen. I wasn't sure whether I wanted to lose my Tongan identity but at the same time, I wanted to belong to Ken and his world wholeheartedly.

'I might get another job overseas,' he explained, 'and it would be easier if we all travelled on Australian passports.'

'Okay, I get it, but I don't want to lose my identity. I never want to forget who I am and where I come from.' I remembered my grandpa's last words before I'd left Tonga.

'That's something you have on the inside.' Ken pointed at my chest. 'And no one will ever force you to give that up, and no piece of paper can ever take away who you are.'

I knew he was right. However, I suspected that Ken was fearful that one day I might get up and leave, taking Lizzie to Tonga with me, and he would be powerless to do anything about it. If only he knew that my whole being belonged to him, especially now, with our precious little girl. Leaving him would never be an option.

In the end, I reluctantly chose to forfeit my Tongan citizenship. I knew in my heart that Ken was right — Australian citizenship would never take away the Tongan in me.

In November 1981, I attended the shire office at Rosebud for the naturalization ceremony. I was among a few others who were naturalized at the same time. I was called to the stage and I felt humbled to become an Australian and yet, at the same time, felt like a traitor to my Tonga. *Please forgive me,* I thought. *I am only simplifying things for my family but I'm still true to my culture and my heritage. I am Tongan through and through.* I apologized to my ancestors in spirit as I pledged, 'I solemnly and sincerely promise and declare that I will be faithful and bear true allegiance to Her Majesty Elizabeth II, Queen of Australia, her heirs and successors according to law and that I will faithfully observe the laws of Australia and fulfil my duties as an Australian.'

Less than twelve months after pledging to be faithful to Ken, I also pledged to be faithful to his queen and country. That was an enormous commitment I carried with me. Following the receipt of my citizenship, Ken moved to apply for an Australian passport for me and Elizabeth. He had to apply for a new one of his own, too, as he had to return the diplomatic passport he'd previously travelled with. It was a privilege he could only retain if travelling for the Commonwealth. It didn't take long for us all to get our passports, which ignited new hopes of going back to Tonga so we could introduce our Elizabeth to my family.

It was mid-December and I knew it would be a hopeless dream to go to Tonga before the year ended.

Ken was at work and I was busy with baby chores at home one day when there was a knock at the door. I went to open it only to find a stranger with a basket of yellow roses. It was beautifully arranged. I stood there with my mouth open, confused, as the stranger enjoyed my stunned reaction.

'Happy anniversary,' she said.

'Oh! You must be at a wrong address,' I said. What I wanted to say was, 'My name is Silva.' I didn't understand the word 'anniversary' and I thought she was looking for a person called Anniversary.

'Are you Mrs McLeod?' the woman asked.

'Yes.'

'Well, happy anniversary.' She shoved the basket of yellow roses into my hands and left. *I've heard of happy birthday but never heard happy anniversary.*

I was oblivious to the fact that we'd been married twelve months. I looked at the flowers and spotted a card. I opened it and it was from Ken. It simply read, 'Happy anniversary, darling. All my love. Ken xxx'. Tears gently rolled down my face and I felt special even though I didn't know the meaning of 'anniversary'. I was loving this new world that Ken had created for me.

Nine days after the excitement of our first anniversary, Christmas arrived. It was my first in Australia and my first away from Tonga.

My whole being was occupied with thoughts of my childhood Christmases. On Christmas Eve, we'd always go to church and watch the nativity play. Outside the church stood a big Christmas tree decorated with balloons. I would always take a wrapped gift from home to put under the tree for me to open later. Grandma usually wrapped a manioke tama (grated tapioca mixed with coconut cream wrapped in banana leaves) baked in the 'umu, as we didn't have anything else. After the service, we'd sit around the Christmas tree to open the gift we'd brought. I'd always been so embarrassed to open mine in front of other kids who unwrapped their gifts of toys or something special. I watched these lucky kids and wished that one day I would be able to give my kids a Christmas present not a grated tapioca. Afterwards, we'd sing carols from house to house until dawn, which was a lot of fun. Every time we finished singing at a house, we'd be rewarded with candies or keke (doughnuts) for our good cheer.

Then on Christmas Day, we'd have the best feast ever. There was always roast succulent pigs, crayfish, sea urchin, oysters and all sorts of seafood. Lots of my family would come from abroad for it. It had been loud and happy.

Now I was in a different world, far removed from my Vava'u. I soon realized what was missing — sharing. So I continued my Tongan tradition on Christmas morning in Australia. I baked shortbread and made little Christmas treats and shared them with my neighbours, friends and extended family. This small action warmed my heart and kept me closer to my heritage.

I found it odd that we celebrated Christmas but didn't go to church to commemorate what Christmas was all about. Instead, we had a special breakfast then watched how spoilt our little girl was with so many presents. Afterwards, we made the marathon drive to Ken's parents, where we joined the rest of the family for the Christmas feast. I thought Tonga was quite lavish but on my first Christmas in Australia there was turkey, pork, chicken, Christmas pudding, pavlova and other treats. *Where's the seafood and the suckling pig?* I thought. *I wonder what Selai is having. Do they have enough food? Are they fending off a cyclone?* As tears threatened to intrude once again, familiar loving arms came around my shoulder. Ken understood without me saying a word.

After a long lunch and more presents, we came home exhausted, but I wanted to call my family. I knew they'd be as eager to hear about our first Christmas in Australia as I was to tell them, and I wanted to hear about theirs without me.

Calling home was never easy. I called the telephone exchange first and requested a message to be passed on to my family to come to town. Then I'd hope not to fall asleep during the two hours that passed or my family would have to wait in town all night. Once I heard my grandma's voice, I went into meltdown mode. Then I spoke to my grandpa. My pa, my saviour, so wise, was the one who always pierced my heart. I loved my grandma, but I loved and missed Grandpa more. Shh!

'Hello, love! How are you and Ken? How is 'Elisapesi?'

I loved it when he tried to pronounce Elizabeth's name in Tongan. I smiled through tears as I heard his gentle, loving voice. 'Pa, we're all fine, I miss you. I miss our humble home. I miss our village. How was your Christmas without me?' I broke down uncontrollably, grateful for the crackling line.

'We missed your loud laugh — Christmas is not the same without you. 'Ofa atu Liva and 'Elisapesi. Here's your sister. Don't talk for too long. It must cost Ken a lot.' I smiled at the thought of Grandpa, who always considered the expense.

'Merry Christmas, sis,' I heard Selai's voice.

'Merry Christmas, Lai. How was your Christmas? What did Grandma wrap for the Christmas tree gift? What did you have for lunch?'

'Gosh, I got the infamous manioke tama as a gift, so embarrassing.' She told me about what they'd had for lunch and she was full of gossip from my little island. She always managed to make me laugh with all her animated news. God, it was nice to hear her voice.

I couldn't tell Selai of all my gifts and how spoilt I was, knowing that she'd had none. She loves anything sweet and when she heard about the Christmas pudding, trifle and pavlova, I knew she would be drooling.

'I wish I was there,' she said. 'You wouldn't have to clean up because I would lick everything clean.'

'One day Ken will bring you over to Australia for Christmas, I promise. I'll send some photos as soon as I'm able,' I said before hanging up.

After speaking with my family back in Tonga, I felt a bit depressed, missing my village, and yet I knew my heart belonged to Ken and Lizzie. *It will pass,* I told myself.

With no TV or newspaper, my family relied on photos to put together the puzzle of my new world. The postal system wasn't always reliable. When we sent some money for Christmas, I had to send it in early December via registered letter to ensure it got there in time.

Tonga had no pension for the elderly. Instead, they had to rely on family. Ken was supportive of this concept and never begrudged me sending money to my family as long as our bills were paid and there was food on the table.

Ken promised we would save up and go to Vava'u in the coming year. However, when Lizzie turned one, I started to feel unwell, a feeling I knew too well. Lo and behold, I was pregnant with child number two.

That certainly messed up my plan. 'There goes Tonga for another year. How can this happen?'

'Well, I don't know,' he said sarcastically, poking at my belly.

Ken was elated that we were having another baby. Maybe he saw it as a cheaper alternative than going to Vava'u.

As I had been with Elizabeth, I was sick as a dog and not happy. Having morning sickness with a one-year-old in tow was no fun. *This 'married with children' sucks,* I thought. It was amazing how quickly it changed my reality. No Tonga, no life, no fun.

There was no denying that Ken worked hard as the sole earner and the pressure of providing must have been overwhelming, but I was in tunnel vision within my own turmoil.

I had been sick all day one day when Ken came home in a funny (not) mood. Everything I did was wrong. He complained that dinner was tough and I was sick all the time. He was tired and he still had to do the dishes. I watched him when he walked into the lounge room and ran his finger on the top of the TV then said, 'How long since you've dusted this?' He was looking for a fight. Being pregnant and emotional, the only defence I had was running off in tears. He followed me to the bedroom.

'Liva, why don't you stand there and fight me instead of running off? How will I know what you're thinking?' A constant collision of the two cultures.

'You know what, Ken? You keep your shiny house and your fancy stuff. I'm going back to Tonga where there's no TV to dust, floor to mop or plates to wash. I was kidding myself to think that I would be enough, but obviously I'll never measure up and I'll never bridge the gap. And I'm taking Elizabeth, the only thing that I brought with me into this marriage,' I hissed.

I have failed, I thought. I heard all the negative voices from long ago; the village people who'd doubted our union came back to haunt me. I wanted to go home, back to my village, back to my island life, where I belonged. I needed my family around to help me, but they were nowhere to be found.

Ken held my face in his gigantic hands and tilted it as he looked into my eyes. 'You listen to me and listen well. That will never happen. I won't allow it. Are you listening? Never.' He pulled me into his arms and held me so tight as I convulsed. 'I'm sorry you felt that way and I'm sorry to upset you like this. I love you and I can't function without you and Lizzie and the new baby in there.' He rubbed my belly.

I'd never seen Ken upset like this before. It was our first serious argument. I wondered: if my family was with me now, would I be threatening to leave? I missed that family network.

Ken might have lived to regret giving me permission to fight back because I never lost an argument after that. He'd given me permission to stand up and let my voice be heard. That was a foreign concept in my culture.

13

Temaleti: Goddess of the sea

From past experience, I knew it could only be labour pain. By mid-afternoon on 30 April 1983, my contractions had become more frequent. It was time for the now-familiar hospital run.

Ken's mum and dad came to look after Elizabeth. Ken did his best to drive and breath-coach me on the way. Arriving at the hospital, the administrator asked him to fill in the pre-admission forms at reception just as another contraction came.

'Stuff the forms, Ken. I'm going to push,' I screamed.

'Do you feel the urge to push, Mrs McLeod?' the admission clerk asked.

'Yes.' As another contraction crippled me.

I'd never seen people move so quickly. They put me in a wheelchair and rushed me to the labour ward. I was sure they didn't want me to make a mess in the reception area.

Morning sickness didn't happen in the morning only; sometimes it was an all-day event. I was still vomiting while I was in labour, but

I had a strong urge to push. The midwife was there but I scanned the room for my obstetrician, who was still not present.

'Where's my doctor?' I said.

'He's on his way. He'll be here soon but I'm here if you need to push,' the midwife reassured me.

No sooner had the doctor entered the room than the contractions and the urge to push came more frequently. He pinched the membrane and a rush of warm liquid poured out, together with the screech of a baby crying.

'A baby girl,' the doctor said.

Ken was still holding my hand with a face washer on my forehead and a bowl by my side where I had another chuck. Ken beamed from ear to ear as yet another healthy baby girl entered our world. He gave me a kiss and whispered, 'Two down, two to go.'

'That's not funny at all,' I said through sweat and tears but what I really meant to say was, 'That would be with someone else, Ken.'

We didn't have a name picked, as I'd thought I was having a boy. If it had been, he would be an heir and would be named after Ken's family also, according to my culture. 'Can we call the baby after my mum?' I asked Ken. 'Temaleti. We can still shorten it to Tema and it may not sound too foreign.' I would've liked to call her after my grandma Nane but there had been already too many kids named after her.

With my name 'Vaisiliva' being so long and difficult to wrap your tongue around, I thought Ken wouldn't want any of his kids to have a Tongan name. But he was in euphoria — I could have asked for the world and he would have said yes, so we called our new little bundle of joy Temaleti (goddess of the sea) Ann.

'If she grows up hating her name, then Ann will be the fallback,' I said.

'She'll love it and I hope she can be half the woman your mum is,' Ken said.

I got the name I wanted but worried about how Ken's family would feel. Would his people accept my baby with a foreign name? I could imagine Ken's father saying, 'How can people pronounce that?'

'Well too bad, they'll get used to it,' Ken said firmly and left the hospital.

I wondered whether he was truly happy with another girl. Did he want a son? In my culture, I'd be considered a failure for not producing a son — an heir — for him. I hoped he wasn't disappointed.

The next day, Ken brought Elizabeth to meet her little sister. She was delighted, as she thought Tema was a doll to play with. I watched her with so much pride. It was picture perfect — Ken holding Elizabeth over the crib asking her, 'What do you think of your little sister, Tema? She looks just like you when you were a baby.' He was happy with his girls.

Ken's mum and dad came to meet Temaleti, and I couldn't have been any more wrong about their reaction to the name. They loved it and had obviously been practising it since Ken had told them. They pronounced it perfectly. Mum and Dad took Elizabeth home and Ken stayed for the rest of the day.

'I can't wait to tell my mum,' I said.

'Hope Grandma won't get her nose out of joint,' he said.

'She'll be happy. There've been a lot of grandkids named after her but not my mum.'

When I rang my mum, she was overjoyed. 'Never in my wildest dreams did I expect you to name your daughter after me, especially since it was Grandma's sweat and tears that raised you, but I'm so honoured.

Thank you, and Ken. I can't wait to meet my only grandchildren. I love you, Liva.' She hung up, but not before I heard the tremble in her voice.

Ken's father had retired when Elizabeth turned one, so it was easy for them to stay for as long as I needed. I could only be grateful for the love and support his parents gave me and they treated me like a daughter, taking care of Ken and Elizabeth and doing the washing and cooking.

We settled into our new routine with two babies at home. Ken went back to work and, of course, I was very domesticated by this stage. It felt like a lifetime since I'd left Tonga. I didn't walk to the shop any more for ice cream. The roads were unsealed and full of potholes, which made walking with the pram difficult. With two babies, it was impossible.

Ken continued getting up at night to help with baby Tema, as he had with Elizabeth, something my grandma would have frowned upon. 'That's not how you were brought up. Shame on you, Liva,' I could hear her saying, waving her little finger frantically.

'Oh well, sorry Grandma, but I don't have anyone else to help, so Ken will have to make do.' *I wish you were here, though.*

14

Token of my love

Once the excitement of creating such perfect little people subsided, being just a mum was not enough for me. It was far from what I'd imagined my life with Ken would be. I dreamed of going back to school to be somebody or finding a dream job and capitalizing on what this country of opportunity had to offer. Now that I was stuck at home with so many responsibilities, it didn't look so rosy after all. I needed a job.

Every day after Ken had gone to work and the kids were asleep, I combed through the newspaper looking for job vacancies. The ideal job for me was something that I could do from home, like bookkeeping. Ken's mum had taught me how to knit after Elizabeth had been born. I can proudly say that I'm an above-average knitter. I accomplished an earlier wish to be able to knit like my sister-in-law.

I came across an advertisement in the local paper: knitter required to work from home. I applied without Ken's knowledge. The job was for a handicraft shop that sold handmade goods. The more garments

I could knit, the more money I would make. I had to knit the jumpers from graph patterns. It wasn't easy but doable, and I would get $100 for each completed garment. I was happy with that.

I had never knitted from a graph before but there's a first time for everything. There were nights I knitted until 2 a.m., trying to get as many garments done as fast as I could. It didn't go down very well with Ken. 'Bloody hell, Liva, the money you're going to make won't cover the electricity bill. Get to bed before that needle pokes out your eyes.' I ignored him and kept knitting. I was on a mission. I dropped off my final item and was happy with my $300 reward. That was my first earnings in Australia with my own hands, and it was very rewarding.

When Ken and I had got married, I hadn't been able to afford to buy him a wedding ring. I'd always had in mind that one day when I earned my own money, I would buy him one. I was excited when I took Ken to a local jeweller and bought a nine-carat gold wedding band at last. It was simple, but I'd earned it.

Ken didn't care and hadn't wanted a ring before because of his job. 'Electricity and metal don't mix,' he said. But I was pleased from the day I put the ring on his finger as a token of my love, for better or for worse, in sickness and in health, till death do us part.

He wore it proudly.

15

Homecoming

After Tema was born, I feared that a visit to Tonga might never happen. It was a big ask financially. I was sad but understood that Ken's income wouldn't stretch as far as to buy four plane tickets.

Nevertheless, Ken promised we would go to Tonga for Tema's first birthday. And in mid-April 1984, we got ready for our trip. It was strange that, given I'd been in Australia for three years, I still regarded the trip as going home. I was excited beyond belief and had been shopping for months. I bought clothes for my little sister and my grandparents. There was a case full of food — the kind we didn't have in Tonga.

When Ken saw the suitcases lined up, he frowned. 'Bloody hell! Liva, we're going for four weeks, not four months. What are you taking now? We're going by plane, not by boat, don't forget.'

'I'm taking a bit of my Australia for my family. Some clothes for Selai, and …'

This is the only surviving photo of my mum, Temaleti, as a young girl. I believe she was only seventeen years old in this photo taken by a tourist.

Ken and I in Tonga, 1979.

My humble cooking hut when I was growing up on my island of Pangaimotu, Vava'u. 1980.

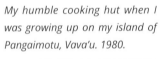

Ken with his Tongan electricians. It shocked him that they wore no shoes while working on powerlines. Ken single-handedly built this water-tank tower.

On our wedding day, my grand-uncle handed me over to Ken. But I couldn't stop laughing as Ken tried to repeat after the minister in the Tongan language. My little Methodist church in my village of Pangaimotu, Vava'u. 1980.

Our wedding celebration at the Port of Refuge hotel with Ken's expat friends.

Our getaway scooter after our wedding celebration day. 1980.

My Grandfather Tai, Grandma Nane and my Uncle Manu on my wedding day.

Receiving my Australian citizenship, which was captured in the local newspaper. 1981.

My first time arriving in Australia, my new home. Walking through Melbourne airport was mind boggling. 1981.

The tapa cloth that my grandma gave me as a reminder of where I came from was hung on the wall of our dining room for years. 1981.

Lynette and I with my new afro at the back beach of Rye. I think this was taken in 1983.

Our little family was complete with the arrival of Temaleti in 1983.

Temaleti's first birthday and christening. This was the last time I recall Ken wearing a ta'ovala and Tupenu (mat and skirt). I think, secretly, he was proud to wear my traditional costume. 1984.

I love this photo. It keeps me grounded. My humble home where we sat on the floor sharing a meal with laughter. My grandparents with Uncle Lopeti and Aunty Kava with Ken junior. 1984.

A Tongan feast was prepared
for Temaleti's first birthday
at my grandparents' home.
1984.

Ken sailing with Lizzie and Tema in Vava'u. 1988.

Elizabeth and Tema with their
father at the end of every day. Just
before his diagnosis of cancer.
1989.

My mum preparing traditional
food for 'Umu. Meat with Lu (taro
leaves) and fresh coconut cream
wrapped with banana leaves. Yum.

This is the cockpit photo of the Boeing 777 that hung on my wall since 1994. It was the motivator in my pursuit of my dream but I never envisaged that I would be flying it. In 2010, some sixteen years later, I finally sat in the cockpit of the B777 instead of looking at it.

A very proud moment when I graduated from the flying school with my wings. 1993.

Each set of wings represents airlines I've worked for spanning 28 years. 1992–2020.

My brother Saia helping me with refuelling before I took him for a scenic flight over Melbourne. I think this was 1994 or 1995.

My first day at work with Royal Tongan airlines. I couldn't get the smile off my face. 1998.

Ken came with me on my flight to Niua Fo'ou, one of the very remote islands in Tonga. 1999.

This photo was taken after Ken lost his hair the second time with his chemotherapy treatment. 2003.

Ken and I in 2005 as proud parents and grandparents.

My time with the Royal Flying Doctor Service, flying Beechcraft Super King Air 200 will always be the most special time of my flying career. 2006.

One year after Ken had the stem cells transplant, with his hair grown back, he walked with Elizabeth on her wedding day. 2005.

'This is going to cost a fortune. I can see that.' But he never mentioned it again and I kept packing.

Eventually, the day of departure neared. I was too excited to sleep the night before. I checked and rechecked our passports, tickets and baby food. There was not an inch available in our station wagon by the time Ken finished loading our luggage. When we arrived at Melbourne airport it was buzzing with people. I had no idea what to do or how to help, so I just hung on to the kids and watched my white beau in action. He juggled all our suitcases one by one onto the weighing belt, sorted out the excess baggage, tickets and passports. No other passengers had so much luggage. If Ken felt embarrassed about it, he didn't show it. We boarded our flight and before long we were airborne. Only then did my muscles relax.

Getting to Tonga wasn't easy. There were only two direct flights from Melbourne to Nadi a week and a weekly service from Nadi to Tonga. To align the flights meant we had to stay three nights in Fiji before the connecting flight to Tonga.

We finally arrived at Fuaʻamotu International Airport, but I hadn't told my mum we were coming. It was going to be a big surprise. Ken wheeled our luggage out while I tried to figure out whether there was a taxi. Because the international flight only came in once a week, it looked as if all of Tonga was at the airport and I didn't know Nukuʻalofa at all.

'Taxi! Taxi!'

I turned to see a taxi driver beckoning to me. Phew!

'Can you please take us to Haʻalalo?' I asked.

'That's a long way away,' he replied with a doubtful look on his face. It was unusual for a Tongan to arrive from overseas with no family to meet the flight.

'Yeah, Mum lives there but she doesn't know we're here. I'm a Vavaʻu girl.'

'Oh dear, you'll be in deep trouble then, young lady.' He rushed around and helped Ken put the luggage into another taxi then we all climbed into his car.

About mid-morning, we pulled up outside my mum's house and while Ken was sorting out the fare with the drivers, our luggage was already headed for the door. One of my half-sisters appeared; she had only been three when I'd left.

'Oh my god, it's Vaisiliva,' she announced with a shocked look on her face.

My mum was at peito, the outdoor cooking house. She heard the commotion and ran around to investigate. 'Why didn't you let me know that you were coming so I could come and meet my grandchildren at the airport? You arrived like a homeless. That's unacceptable, Liva,' she wailed.

While crying and chastising me, she was unaware that the buttons of her blouse had come apart while she'd been running and she didn't have a bra on. Her breasts were clapping together happily.

'Er, Mum,' I said, pointing.

'What?' she looked down, then at Ken, who was giggling. She frowned but did her blouse back up. 'What does that matter when I get to meet my beautiful grandchildren for the first time?' She gathered them in her arms. 'And to have one of them named after me, that's pretty special.'

'Okay, okay, Ma, how about a hug for me?' To hug my mum after three years was the best feeling ever. I saw her embrace Ken with tears of gratitude. 'Thank you,' she said. She couldn't speak English, but she managed those words.

It was good to see my mum, but I was eager to get to Vavaʻu. To my village, to Grandma and Grandpa. The next day we boarded the small aircraft for the one-hour flight. Not long after we became airborne, the familiar dotted islands of the Haʻapai group came into view and I knew that the archipelago of Vavaʻu would be next. I watched in awe at the beautiful colour of the pristine water beneath us. *I'm home.*

As we approached the field, I could almost reach out and touch the coconut trees as they swept past. The De-Havilland Twin Otter aircraft touched down, screeched to a halt and the inside was filled with the smell of kerosene that poured in from the reverse thrust. We then taxied slowly back to the little tin shed terminal. It was three years since I'd left but time had stood still on Vavaʻu. Everything was the same, even the terminal.

Tears dripped down and wet my top. Ken was obviously excited as he gave me a squeeze. 'Are you happy? Welcome home.'

'Yes. Very. Thank you. I'm very happy, thank you. I can't believe I'm finally here. Three years felt like a lifetime away.' I whispered blinking the tears away.

Unlike our unannounced arrival in Nukuʻalofa, my grandparents were already at Vavaʻu airport. Mum had made sure of that — she'd broadcast our arrival on the Tongan radio. The show-off in her wanted the whole island to know of our arrival. Some of the people who worked at the airport had also worked on the hospital project and they recognized Ken straight away, and were genuinely happy to see him back. This was like a homecoming for Ken, too.

Through the crowd I spotted Grandpa and Grandma. I wanted to run and throw myself onto them as I had as a child, but I noticed they'd both aged since I'd left. When we hugged, as I inhaled the coconut scent mixed with smoke, I knew I was home. How could it be that I'd left as a young girl and returned as a mum of two?

We all bundled into the back of a 3-tonne truck for the ride to my village of Pangaimotu. The 40-minute ride brought back memories as we bounced over potholes on the dusty unsealed road. We passed the hospital, the hotel and the fuel depot, then crossed the single-lane causeway to my island village.

We slowed down as we descended the steep hill leading into the village, to give way to kids, dogs and pigs, and to wave to villagers who were raking leaves or hanging out washing. When they realized it was me they dropped whatever they were doing and hurried towards Grandma and Grandpa's house to greet us.

It was heart-warming to see that my village people still held Ken in high regard. The village elders invited him into their circle under the mango tree with their kava bowl, which was customary for receiving important guests. I could see the big mound of dirt — the telltale of an 'umu soon to be opened up for a yummy feast. The local boys played their 'ukulele and banjo while the kids danced happily to the music. Elizabeth and Tema were snatched up and taken for a walkabout.

I smiled and watched Ken, so relaxed and at ease, smiling the whole time. 'Don't get a big head, Ken; it's not for you, it's for me and the kids,' I said proudly. I knew they wouldn't have gathered like this if it was only me.

As I approached my grandparents' place, I noticed that beside the old hut stood a new weatherboard house. I went in to inspect and was pleasantly surprised that it had three bedrooms and a common room but no kitchen or bathroom. But it was a big upgrade from the thatched roof and mud floor I'd known.

Ken has never stayed under my grandparents' thatched roof before. Thank god it's a tin roof now. How will he cope with the lavatory — a hole in the ground — cold showers, minus all the comfort he's accustomed to? This was a far cry from the Vava'u he'd known with his nice house on top of the hill and its sweeping ocean view. But staying at the hotel would insult my grandma and my people and Ken was aware of that. He would never offend them that way.

In the early hours of our first morning, Ken nudged me to get up from the blow-up mattress that had been our bed. I'd brought it with us from Australia. 'Someone's calling,' he said.

'It's only the roosters, go to sleep.'

Then I heard the familiar voice that used to wake me up for church many moons ago. 'Liva, Liva, get up. What do I need to do for Ken's breakfast?' It was Grandma.

'For Christ's sake, Grandma, it's bloody 5 a.m. Ken can fetch for himself when it's breakfast time. Go back to sleep,' I yelled.

But Ken got up and helped Grandma light the fire to boil the water for coffee. I could hear Grandma yakking away in Tongan and Ken answering with something random. They didn't understand each other but were enjoying their time together. When I got up, I could see that Ken had made a fork from a coat hanger so we could have toast on the open fire for breakfast. The kids stared at it with wide eyes and took their slices quickly, gobbling them up.

'Here you go,' Ken said, handing me coffee and toast. I thanked him and dug in but noticed my grandmother's eye on me.

She scowled. 'Ken shouldn't be making coffee and toast for you. That's your job, or have you forgotten? Is that what Australia's done to you?'

'Whatever, Grandma,' I said, trying not to look at her.

'You're embarrassing me. That's not how you were brought up.'

'I must be one big disappointment to you then.' I pulled faces at her behind her back.

Thank goodness Ken didn't understand any of what Grandma was saying or else there would have been no more coffee for me.

After breakfast, Ken wanted a shower, so I took him to the outdoor washhouse, cringing at the reaction that could bring. 'You know there's no shower,' I said. 'You have to use a small basin of water.'

He raised his eyebrows as I led him inside the makeshift wall made from woven coconut leaves. Being 6'1", he towered above it. 'Great. I'll be able to talk to the neighbours while I'm washing.' I worried that he was upset, but he seemed amused.

Sure enough, as he washed, he chatted to our neighbours, watched the dogs chasing the chooks and everyone else walking past. Some kids tried to peer through the holes in the woven coconut leaves. Ken pretended he didn't see them, then splashed water into the holes and the kids ran off, squealing. I heard them chattering to each other as they ran past. 'How did the palangi see us? Did you see his white bum? Let's go back.' They ran back, peering through the holes again until Ken splashed them and they ran off.

Eventually, he came out of the washhouse and glanced around, frowning. 'Where are the girls? I can't see them anywhere.'

'Relax, Ken. They're fine. My sister's taken them around to show them the village. Someone will bring them home.'

But as the hours ticked on and the girls didn't come back, Ken's frown grew darker. He wore out the linoleum at Grandma's house with his pacing up and down.

'The palangi is not happy, Liva,' Grandma whispered with a smirk.

'He'll get over it.'

By the end of the day, the girls were back, bathed, fed and fast asleep. It took Ken a few days before he stopped worrying. Then he relaxed enough for us to rediscover Vava'u.

We caught up with Lenny and Anni — Ken and Lenny went spearfishing while Anni and I waited at the beach, and we had some more night picnics. We also invited them to join us for Tema's first birthday celebration. We decided to celebrate her birthday on Sunday, 29 April, one day before her actual birthday. However, there had been something bothering me for the last twelve months. Tema hadn't been christened. I knew I had to capture this opportunity — the Tongan in me was calling. *But how am I going to persuade Ken?* He probably thought I'd forgotten about it.

It was now or never.

'Ken, I have been thinking, how would you feel if we baptize Tema on Sunday together with her birthday service? If we're going to church, we might as well make it worthwhile.'

'Seriously? You're not making me wear a dress again.' We both laughed, remembering our wedding day with the mat-wrapping saga.

'We have to go to church anyway for Tema's birthday and yes, you'll have to wear a mat again. I'm sorry about that, but Tema hasn't been baptized and I haven't forgotten. We can't baptize one and not the other.'

He grimaced. 'I knew it. More bloody mats.'

'Just think about it — one mat for two events, otherwise, you'll have to do two separate ones. I promise it's going to be the last time and it's a simple one-mat event.'

'I've been there done that and I'm not doing it again. No,' he said firmly.

'Thank you, thank you, I will tell Grandma to get the ta'ovala ready and advise the minister,' I said, ignoring his protest. 'If you hadn't made it difficult to baptize the kids in Australia, we wouldn't be having this conversation. So stop it, the mats didn't kill you.'

A loud sigh of acceptance escaped his lips.

On Sunday, the church bells started ringing at 5 a.m. 'That's one thing I haven't missed,' Ken said, rolling over.

'The bell will keep ringing until enough people come, so you'd better pray they hurry up.' I smiled, but he couldn't see me in the dark.

Christenings and first birthdays were significant milestones on the Tongan calendar. They were always celebrated in a big way. My family didn't fail me as they prepared a big Sunday feast, with everyone from the church and the village invited back for lunch.

Ken accepted everything thrown his way, but the palangi in him complained a lot about not having some privacy. Every time he came near me, I froze. There were always too many people around.

'Liva, can you please tell me how the Tongans have sex?' he asked one night in bed. 'There seem to be endless kids around. This is bullshit. I think a hotel stay next time would be a great idea.'

'Maybe that's why they go to the bush all the time,' I said, teasing. 'Have you noticed how they go in pairs?' I kept laughing but Ken didn't

126

think it was funny. 'I don't know when and how, Ken. Shall we go into the bush too?'

He smiled. 'You're an idiot, Liva, but I love that idiot in you. Don't ever change, even for me.'

He reached for me, but I pushed him away. 'My grandparents are sleeping in the next room with only a paper-thin wall made of Masonite between us. You know Grandma sleeps with one eye open.'

He laughed at me.

We spent three weeks in Vava'u and I surrendered to a week at the hotel in Nuku'alofa — a break away from family and the heaviness of my culture. It saddened me that we couldn't stay with my mum, but I couldn't have it my way all the time. Secretly, I was looking forward to a hot shower, comfortable bed and some alone time for the last week of our holiday. The kids were bitten by mosquitoes badly in Vava'u and Tema's skin had started to form little blisters, which provided the excuse we needed to justify the hotel stay. My mum was understanding and didn't mind. We spent the days at her house and the nights at the hotel.

We arrived at the hotel and the kids were so excited; they stayed in the shower for an hour, enjoying the running hot water again. I was torn between the comfort of my new life and love and respect for my humble beginnings.

When we got back from Mum's house one night, Ken suggested we go to the bar for a drink. After putting the girls to bed and getting a babysitter to watch them, we were excited to go out on our own. It was about 9 p.m. when we entered the half-lit bar. There was a live band playing and it was very noisy. The patrons were all Tongans, and a lot of them were drunk. Ken was the only white person there but he didn't seem to notice it. It was too crowded for my liking, but Ken hung on to my hand and propelled me towards the bar. 'Can I have a Foster's and a Fanta, please,' he yelled. 'Charge it to room 206.'

We had a great time, Ken maybe a little too much. He was a little unsteady when we left. Fortunately, I remembered to ask the barman for the account.

'Sure. Here,' he said, handing it to Ken.

Sure, why not? Just give it to the white man, you piece of shit. I'm the sober one here. Ken scribbled his signature without checking. I didn't trust the barman. From my experience, it was common for unexplained charges to appear on guests' accounts. After Ken signed the bill, I pulled the account over so I could check. I didn't even get a chance to see the total when the angry barman snatched the bill off me. *What the fuck?* But I didn't challenge him. When we turned to walk away, hand in hand, he yelled, loud enough for everyone to hear, 'Fokisi!' He was calling me a prostitute.

I stopped, frozen on the spot at the ferocity of the word. I didn't know whether to cry or wish the floor would open and swallow me up. Everybody turned and looked my way. I'd never felt so cheap in my entire life. Unfortunately for the poor uneducated barman, Ken understood exactly what he'd said. He had the shock of his life when Ken turned around, grabbed him by the scruff of his neck and half-dragged him over the bar.

'Listen here, and you better listen well, you arsehole. For your information, she's my wife and you'd better apologize fast before I knock your block off.'

The barman cowered away from Ken's fury. 'Sorry, man. I didn't mean it, so sorry.'

'Come on, darl. He's an idiot. He's not worth it,' I said, trying to pull him away. But I wanted to get out of there. I feared there might be a brawl, and clearly Ken would be outnumbered — this was not Vava'u. But he was blind with alcohol-fuelled rage at this imbecile of a man.

We left the bar, but Ken wasn't satisfied. He sought out the manager to report the matter.

At 1 a.m. the manager and the barman came knocking on our door.

'Mr and Mrs McLeod,' said the barman, and I noted the deliberate inclusion of 'Mrs'. 'I am so sorry to use such offensive words towards you. It was said unknowingly and for that, I'm deeply sorry. Please, I beg your forgiveness. I don't want to lose my job. I have three kids to feed.' He was crying.

'I'm not angry but very sad that my husband of a different race and culture witnessed such unkindness from my people. As you can see, we have two kids, and certainly, I don't want you to lose your job,' I said.

But Ken was still angry. 'I won't have my wife talked to in that way. I've a good mind to check out tomorrow. You just see if we don't.'

When we woke the next day the barman came back with a basket of fruit and gifts for the kids. I advised the manager that what he needed was to educate his staff that not all Tongans who hang out with white men are fokisi. Obviously, in the eyes of the barman, I wasn't good enough to marry a palangi.

The incident at the bar tarnished our trip. It left me thinking, *where do I belong?* It was a question I frequently asked myself when I sometimes felt judged by both countries. *Is that the price I must pay for loving a white man? Please Lord, help me clear the confusion I'm in.*

16

The checkout chick

Our trip to Tonga deeply dented our financial pocket. 'I'm going to look for a proper job, Ken, and you can't stop me,' I told him when we got back to Australia. 'I can't do the stay-at-home mum thing forever. The girls will be going to school and kinder soon. I want to be productive, I want to help you. Motherhood is a tough unpaid gig and I feel guilty all the time for not contributing financially.'

'That's the dumbest thing you've ever said. Who's going to look after the kids?'

Ignoring Ken's protest, I started doorknocking at banks, motels and shops with no luck. My confidence was squashed every time I was denied. *Just let me in and I'll show you. I'm not afraid of hard work. I'll wash floors, I'll make tea, whatever. Just give me a chance.*

'Do you think, Ken, it would be this hard looking for a job if I was white? After all, I don't want to be a brain surgeon; they're all shit jobs I'm asking for and I can't even get that,' I complained after an exhausting day of job hunting.

'It's all in your head. You're smart and beautiful. You'll get a job soon. I'm still struggling to understand why you want to work while the kids need you,' Ken said.

I knew he didn't understand my struggle to be accepted, let alone helping my family without asking him all the time, but he was still trying to comfort me.

I'd been to the local supermarket numerous times in the past and had been turned down. But one day Ken came home and handed me a piece of paper. It simply said 'Georgina'. 'Go and see her at the supermarket.'

'Who is she?'

'She's the supervisor and the wife of Dave, the gardener at work.'

'What could she do for me? I've been in there numerous times. I'm sure I would've met her in one of my past enquiries.'

'Just go and see her and tell her who you are and say that her husband sent you. She knows.'

Apparently, Georgina had heard of my pursuit of a job from her husband and invited me to come in and see her. Well, she got me my first proper job in Australia. I was happy but wished I'd obtained it through merit. However, I swallowed my pride and accepted the job graciously.

Like my first job in Vava'u, it wasn't my dream job but I was happy and excited to be productive. Rye is a small seaside town and it was buzzing with holidaymakers settling in for the summer. The supermarket was busy during this time. I only worked weekends while Ken was home to look after the girls. It was an arrangement he didn't like but he knew how important it was to me so he supported it. But once the novelty of my first job subsided, Ken changed his tune and started to begrudge me going to work. 'Isn't the money I'm making enough, Liva? I don't want you to go to work.'

I needed him to be on board if I was going to make this work. It was an argument he wasn't going to win. 'Ken, you know I'm a simple girl. I grew up with nothing and I don't need much. Of course you provide abundantly, but I'd like to be able to help my family in Tonga without asking you all the time and without guilt.'

'Don't forget that I don't want you to go to work, as I can provide for you, for us, sufficiently.' He looked sad but maybe more annoyed as he continued, 'This is your family now, our family.'

What happened? You promised me when we got married that you would take care of my family too.

I could sense his male ego oozing out and I had to play along. 'Of course I know that, darl, but it's important to me to be accepted into the workforce here in Australia.'

I was so proud to be a checkout chick, proud to be working in Australia. Being the only coloured worker at the time made me even more proud of my achievement.

However, at teatime, the lunchroom was always full of people and I was very conscious of being different. It didn't take long for my apprehensions to be proven true. I went to the tearoom one day and just as my head popped up at the top of the stairs, I heard someone call out, 'G'day, Grace.'

I looked over and saw Andy laughing, as were those sitting with him. Andy had been introduced to me as one of the butchers. When I realized his greeting was directed at me as there was no one else behind me, I just smiled back, but I had no idea who Grace was. Even though it didn't feel right, I brushed it off and kept walking towards the urn. I made a coffee then sat on my own, pretending I was reading the magazine on the table. I could still hear them giggling.

A week or so passed and I'd almost forgotten when Andy found a new audience another day when I arrived at the tearoom. 'Hello Gracie, or is it Jonesy today?' Again, everyone laughed but I was none the wiser. When I returned from my tea break, I asked Vanessa at the next checkout. She'd been in the tearoom and I was sure she'd heard Andy's comment. 'Vanessa, who is Gracie or Jonesy that Andy was calling me?'

'You know, Grace Jones?'

'No, I don't. Who is she?'

'Aw, Silva, where have you been? She's a famous black model and singer. You should be proud. It's a compliment.'

'Well, it didn't feel like one, and if so, why did everyone laugh as if it was the joke of the century?' I wanted to say more but the tears were threatening to pour, so I shut up and tried to busy myself at my checkout.

I couldn't wait to go home and look up this Grace Jones. I was hurt when I saw her picture. As beautiful as she was, I didn't like it at all — it only amplified how black I felt with my afro. *Yes, I'm the intruder and I should find a way to cope with it,* was all I could think. I never told Ken.

After that I took flight and avoided the tearoom, always going home to have lunch with Ken and the girls. That was my defence. *My home, my haven, where I find Ken, who never sees me as coloured.*

I was called to the office one day and feared the worst. I knocked gently and Ethan, the store manager, opened the door and motioned for me to sit opposite his desk. His office was not very big and consisted of a huge desk in the middle with filing cabinets lining one wall. But what astounded me was the big glass window with a full view of the store below.

'Silva, you've done well at the checkout and we've watched you and are very happy with your performance. There's a vacancy at the cash office for a part-time position.' He watched me for my reaction. 'Would you like to be trained on a month's probation? If it works out the job is yours, and if not, you'll return to the checkout.'

Phew! I let out a small sigh of relief. 'Yes please, I would love to.'

So I started working in the office. One of the office responsibilities was the calculation of wages for sometimes 200 staff. It was often complicated by different awards, and mistakes occasionally slipped through the cracks. Of all the employees whose pay I could have messed up, it had to be the very butcher that I'd tried to avoid — Andy.

He nearly knocked down the small hatch where employees collected their pay, as he banged on it for my attention. When I saw him, I didn't give him the satisfaction of showing how uncomfortable he made me.

'Hello, Andy. What's up?'

'Do you think I work here for peanuts? I'm a butcher, not a baker. What have you done? This is wrong.'

I looked at his payslip, which he shoved roughly through the hatch, and realized my error. 'I'm so sorry, that's my fault. I'll correct it in the next pay run.'

'No, you won't, you'll correct it now.'

'Okay, sorry. Can you wait in the tearoom? I'll call you when it's ready.' He rattled me so much I just agreed, even if it meant I had to pay him from my own pocket.

As he turned to walk away, he said, 'Bloody useless wog.'

That's a new word. I didn't know what it meant but it was said in a nasty manner, so I knew it couldn't be good. *I'm not going to cry. I'm stronger than that.*

I corrected the error and borrowed from the petty cash tin in the safe then called him. He collected his pay and I was so relieved to see his back.

I was preoccupied with the confrontation with Andy when I was cooking dinner at home that night.

'How was your day at work, darl?' Ken said as he came in, leaning over to see what was for dinner.

'What's a wog?' I asked.

He spun me around and stared at me as if he was searching for something. 'What did you say?'

'What's a wog?'

'Why? Where did you hear that? Did someone call you that?'

'Matter of fact, yes. It was my fault. I made an error in someone's pay and he called me a bloody useless wog.'

Ken's face went red. 'That's not an excuse to be an arsehole. Who is he? I'll go there and knock his block off.'

'Ken, calm down. No one's going to knock anyone's block off. I asked you a question, just answer it. What's a wog?'

'It's not very nice,' he grumbled, but he explained anyway. 'A foreigner especially from Eastern Europe.'

'Oh! is that all? That's okay. It's true I'm a foreigner but I'm a Polynesian.'

Ken looked at me in disbelief then started to laugh.

That night after the kids had gone to bed, he said, 'I'm sorry you have to face some idiots out there, but it's only a minority.'

'I know that. There have to be more of you out there who see me the way you see me. The good will always outweigh the bad. I can handle it. I'm a big girl now.'

'God, Liva, I love you, I knew you were special, but I was worried about taking you away from your family and your people ... Now you have to endure this kind of behaviour that I didn't see coming.'

'It's character building,' I said as he took me in his arms and kissed me passionately first then hungrily as we got lost in our own world, one that wasn't racist.

My shifts on weekends were long ten-hour days and I always came home and cooked, but more often I started bringing home fish and chips.

It was late when I came home one Sunday, tired and grumpy with no fish and chips. I walked into the kitchen. Ken was watching TV in the lounge, the kids were playing and already in their pyjamas.

'Hi, Mama.' Lizzie ran up and gave me a hug.

I looked over toward the kitchen; it was clean with no sign of any cooking going on.

Ken got up and came over to kiss me. 'You didn't bring dinner?'

I was barely inside the house and I hadn't put my bag down!

'I think you should try to cook, Ken. When you go to work, you come home to a cooked meal. It's only fair that I expect the same when I come home. From now on, I won't cook anymore on days I work, or queue up at the fish and chips shop.' Exhausted, I stormed out of the kitchen.

As soon as those words escaped my mouth I regretted them, but it was too late to retract. *Dear god, it hadn't taken long for me to become Australianized.*

'Don't forget I didn't want you to go to work,' he hissed back, following me to the bedroom.

'Whatever. I'm tired, I'm going to bed.' The argument went nowhere but I was adamant I wasn't cooking. I left him to fend for himself and the girls.

The following weekend I felt guilty about our argument. He was right — it was my choice, so I'd better not complain any more.

When I arrived home, I was armed with fish and chips. I opened the door and couldn't believe it when I saw Ken at the stove cooking. I put the white paper parcel of fish and chips on the bench and walked around to where he was. He smiled and I smiled back. As we hugged, tears freely rolled down my face.

'I'm sorry,' I said.

'I'm sorry, too. I'll try, but I'm no good at cooking. You know that.'

'I know.' I let go of him and looked at what he was attempting to cook. There were two chops under the griller and two potatoes swimming in a huge pot of water. I started to giggle.

'I tried.' He smiled, pulling me back into his arms. 'I hate it when you look sad. It doesn't suit you. I love it when I see you happy and hear you laugh.'

'Well, by the look of your cooking skills Ken, I'm happy to cook or queue up for fish and chips. Forget about my little outburst. It must've been that time of the month.'

I lay in bed that night, knowing that I'd been heard. *There's no way a Tongan husband would do that. How lucky am I?*

17

Powerless without you

Ken came home from work one day looking distracted. He gave me a quick kiss hello and walked over to make a coffee. He stood there watching the kettle.

'Did you have a good day today? Is everything okay?' I said, massaging the back of his neck.

The kettle boiled and he continued making his coffee while the girls hung around his feet.

'They've asked me to go to New Guinea.' He turned to face me.

I was confused. 'Wow! This is exciting. Why are you looking sad? You've been waiting for an opportunity like this since we came back from Tonga.'

'I know, but I can't take you and the kids. I was hoping for somewhere that I could take all of us as a family, as Leo did with his family in Tonga.'

'Well, we'll be fine. I can drive now, Lynette is here and your mum and dad aren't far. You must go. How long is the job?'

'Six months, extendable; it could finish up like Tonga where it went for two years.'

'You must go and try. At least for the first six months, then reassess afterwards.'

He hugged me without another word. He was torn.

'I don't want to be the reason you miss out on yet another adventure, darl,' I said, returning his hug. I didn't let on that I was petrified to be left in his country on my own. I thought of taking Lizzie and Tema to Tonga, but I knew Ken wouldn't like it so I kept my mouth shut.

The day Ken was due to sign the contract, I was filled with dread. *Will he really leave me with the kids in his country, alone?* I didn't want to hear the answer, therefore, when he came home, I didn't dare to ask. I busied myself with dinner, cleaning up and putting the kids to bed.

'Can you please sit down? You're making me nervous,' he finally said.

I sat down, bracing myself for the inevitable.

He sat down and roughly pulled me into his embrace. 'I didn't take the job. They told me there's a rape cage in the house and I would be trained in how to use a firearm. I thought about it, but if I can't take you and the girls then I won't go. I've declined the contract.'

Tears of selfish joy threatened to tumble while my heart sang. At that moment I felt ridiculously in love with him all over again.

Sadly, he never got another offer after he turned down the New Guinea job. I carried an enormous sense of guilt over this.

In 1986, we decided to spend our annual holiday in Australia instead of going to Tonga. We spent six weeks on a driving holiday to Queensland, then visited Sydney Harbour Bridge, the Opera House and the war memorial museum in Canberra on our way home. I couldn't comprehend that we'd been driving for days and were still in the same country.

We'd only been back from our holiday about a week or two when the phone rang and I went to pick it up. 'Hello?' I heard a little pip and I knew it was an international connection. It could only be Tonga.

'Hello, it's a call from 'Ana. Will you accept the charge?' 'Ana was one of my half-sisters on my mum's side. She was about fifteen years old.

'Yes, that's okay.'

''Liva? Hello! How are Tema and Lizzie? How's Ken?' I loved it (not) when they always asked about the kids and Ken but never me.

'They're fine. What's up 'Ana? Is everything okay?'

'Mum's not well. She asked for you to come home, so you'd better come now.'

'What do you mean? That sounds serious.' I knew my mum wouldn't ask for me unless she'd reached the point of no return. She wouldn't want me to leave Ken and the girls unnecessarily.

'She keeps vomiting and she's very weak.'

'Can I speak to her?'

'No, she hasn't uttered a word since she asked for you this morning.'

'What do you mean she can't talk?' I yelled; my heartbeat was racing. I couldn't hold my fear at bay any longer.

Then I heard my stepfather's voice and Ken was by my side, taking the phone from my hand.

'Oh, god. Ken, she can't talk to me.' I started to cry.

'Shh, shh,' he said. 'We'll get you on the first flight to Tonga.'

Our finances were stretched to the limit after our holiday, but Ken found a way for me to go.

It was Saturday, 19 April 1986, when I arrived at Fua'amotu airport. I scanned the arrival area and spotted my stepfather. He was with a stranger who he introduced but I didn't get her name. She was the driver. On our way, I realized we'd passed the turn to my mum's village. 'Where are we going? Shouldn't we have turned back there?'

'Mum's at a faith healer's place in Nuku'alofa,' my stepfather said.

'Whoa! What? Not in hospital?' That was news to me. They could've told me that on the phone.

I watched him trying to make sense of the senseless. 'We've been to the hospital and we've exhausted all medical help, so your mum wanted to go to the most prestigious doctor of all.' He pointed skyward.

Oh my god, I can't believe I'm hearing this. I was cold with fear at the finality of those words. 'Doctor of all? Please, please take her to hospital. The doctors there are blessed by the doctor of all.'

'I can assure you, once you see your mum, you'll agree that the best for her right now is your prayers and your unwavering faith. Don't forget, you were a strong Christian and a true believer when you were growing up.'

We arrived at a house. I'd never been there before. 'Does the faith healer live here?' I asked.

'No, she only comes here for her healing sessions, morning and night.'

It was like a communal centre or a healing centre. I was stunned at the crowd that had gathered there with their sick and disabled family members, seeking help from this so-called 'faith healer'. I was ushered through a back room only to be held back — Mum wasn't ready, they told me. I felt sick.

'What's this? She's my mum. Try to stop me, I'm going in.'

I moved towards the closed door. The door opened up and I saw a figure lying on the floor. I screamed at the top of my lungs. 'Oh, god! No! No! This is not my mum. How long has she been like this? You all lied to me.' I dropped to the floor and cradled her head, kissing her face, but got nothing in return. I rocked back and forth as if I were cradling a child. 'Oh, God, please, please can we take her to the hospital?' I begged.

'Pray and ask God to strengthen your belief,' my stepfather said.

I couldn't believe that I allowed myself to be influenced into agreeing. To keep Mum at this pagan voodoo house was insane.

I forgot to ring Ken until the next day. 'How are things with your mum?' he asked.

I told him everything I'd faced the day before.

'Liva, you take your mum to hospital right now,' he demanded.

'You don't understand. If I take Mum to hospital and she dies, I'll never forgive myself and the rest of the family will never forgive me. Oh, Ken, I wish you were here. No one would argue with you. They don't think shit of what I say. I'm too late, she doesn't know I'm here,' I sobbed. 'What I need most is your arms around me to empower me, to take charge. I feel powerless without you right now.'

Ken allowed me to pour my heart out, then he said, 'I'm thousands of miles away. You're an intelligent girl. You take your mother to hospital if you want her to live. Give my love to Tema, and I love you. Take care and call me again tomorrow.'

I was sure if he'd been there, his influence as a white man would have been valued and the outcome could have been different.

There were so many people staying in that centre, it was unbelievable. At night-time there wasn't a vacant space on the floor. We were lucky to be given a room at the back of the house. Five of my half-sisters and a brother all slept on the floor with Mum. People camped outside the house, singing all night. It made it hard to get any sleep.

The faith healer came the following morning, as we were all sitting around Mum. She placed her hands on Mum's breast and prayed. I watched her instead of closing my eyes. I tried so hard to believe because that's what I was meant to do, but it didn't work. When she finished praying, she said, 'I've received a message.' She raised her head toward the sky. 'Tema will wake up on Tuesday at 7 p.m. precisely.'

I was astounded. *I believe, I believe. NOT!*

The following Tuesday, Mum was still unresponsive. I bathed her that morning, wishing that she would say, 'Ah, that's nice.' But it never came.

'Mum, it's me.' She turned her face and looked blankly at me. *Does she hear me?* I believed so, so I pushed on. 'Lizzie and Tema send their love, and Ken too.'

She blinked and kept staring at me. 'Mum, don't you want to see Tema junior again and Lizzie?' They were still her only grandchildren.

I watched a single stream of tears roll down her face. I bent over and kissed her. 'I love you, Ma,' I said. 'I know you can hear me. I'm sorry I can't take you to hospital. Please forgive me for my weakness and thank you for everything.'

The 'faith healer' also came that morning and told me and my stupid family, 'I have received another divine message from above. Temaleti will regain consciousness today. It is the seventh day since you came to me. Tonight at 7 p.m. Temaleti will wake up and she'll speak again.'

Who the fuck do you really think you are? Are you playing God now? But even with those thoughts, I hung onto every word she said.

By the evening, there was still no change. My stepfather called the family to pray at about 6 p.m. Everyone came except my sister Selai, who was still in Vava'u with Grandma and Grandpa. I stroked Mum's face, wishing with all my might that she would say something. I moved to hold her hand in case she returned my squeeze. Nothing. I moved to feel her pulse on her wrist. None. My heart thumped faster. I bent over and placed my ear on her chest, looking for any sign of life. I was panic stricken when I couldn't find any.

I turned to my stepfather. 'Can you please feel Mum's wrist? I can't find her pulse.' But I knew the truth. *She's dead. You're the biggest idiot of the year, Liva!*

'She's fine. Give her some water,' he said.

I tried to spoon in some water but it ran out of her mouth. I started to panic, my voice rising. 'Please feel for her pulse. I can't find it.'

'Tema, Tema,' my stepdad called. Of course, there was no response. 'Go and fetch the faith healer,' he commanded to no one in particular. I was happy to get out of there, so 'Ana and I went, as I didn't know where to go and it was already dark.

The faith healer's house was crazily eerie. She was having tea when we walked in. 'Mum's gone,' I said without any pleasantries.

She shook her head. 'No, your mum is pretending. I've received a message that she's in the process of a heart replacement. Go home. I'll be there shortly. Hold steadfast to your faith and be strong.'

Is she kidding me? A heart replacement? What the …?

We got back to where Mum was and, by this stage, more people had arrived for the faith healer's evening session. They were singing, oblivious to the fact that my mum was lying dead in the back bedroom. These vulnerable people believed whatever BS brought them comfort and hope.

The faith healer arrived not long after we got back. She knelt down, placed her hands on Mum's breast as she had before, and prayed. It was the longest prayer I've ever endured. In the end, she ran out of praying magic — her god continued to ignore her.

'I'm sorry, but I was mistaken with the interpretation of the divine message.'

Imposter.

'Now I realize that the seventh day meant for Temaleti to be given eternal life, not mortal.'

Bogus.

'There are seven days of the week and there were seven commandments of Jesus Christ.'

I looked at her in disbelief. I wanted to drag her out of the room and shut her up. She was a fake!

Mum was declared dead at 7 p.m. on Tuesday, 22 April 1986.

A couple of weeks after Mum passed, I heard that the so-called faith healer had been admitted to the psychiatric ward of the hospital with mental health issues. I was glad she couldn't put any other families through the hell she put us through. I couldn't bring back my mum, but a small justice had been served.

I took Grandma back with me to Vava'u after Mum's funeral to see Grandpa. I was excited to go back to the island I'd once called my home. It was where I felt free and loved. I only wished that my Ken was with me.

It had been two years since I'd last seen my grandpa and sadly, his most recent stroke had taken its toll. When he saw me he cried. 'I thought you're your mother when you came through,' he said.

'Aw, Grandpa. I'm sorry. I wish I was as pretty and fair-skinned as she.'

That broke his sadness and he started to laugh. 'How are Ken, 'Elisapesi and Tema?'

'They're all fine and wished that they could've been here too.'

'How long are you staying?'

'Only two days. Just enough to hug you.'

'Good, go back to Ken and the girls. Bring them back for Christmas.' He welled up again.

'I'd like that, but money talks, Grandpa.'

My two days went too fast and it was time to bid farewell once again. I hugged him as if I knew I would never see him again. 'Please stay strong until I can afford to bring Pesi and Tema to see you.'

'Give them a kiss for me and always tell them of my love.'

Saying goodbye previously, when I'd been with Ken and the girls, had been one thing. This time it was different — I felt as if I was abandoning my grandparents.

My world hadn't stopped since my return — it was spinning as if it was out of control. I'd achieved so much in very little time but I was still hungry for more. I wished I could go back to school but that was a farfetched dream in my current situation.

Ken always hinted about having another baby but the thought of morning sickness for another nine months didn't appeal to me at all. He became resigned to the fact that we had two beautiful healthy daughters and eventually let the subject slide. However, gnawing questions lingered in my head. *Does he want a son? An heir to carry the family name? Have I failed him? I would have to keep trying for a son if I'd married a Tongan.*

But I never stopped wanting to be something more than just an island girl with lots of kids. I was done. Our little family was complete.

18

Post tenebras lux:
Light after darkness

On Monday, 29 February 1988, I went to answer the phone.

'Liva, is Ken there? It's Uncle Manu. I'm ringing from America.'

'Yes, Ken's here. What's going on? Is everything okay?' My gut feeling told me this was not an ordinary phone call. I looked at Ken, my heart picking up the pace.

'Liva, Grandpa Tai passed away,' Manu said in a broken voice.

That was all I managed to hear as the phone slipped out of my hand.

Ken spoke with my uncle briefly then hung up. Then he was beside me, wrapping me up with his gigantic arms, allowing me to cry it out. 'Shh, Shh. I've got you,' was all I heard as I buried my face deeper into his chest.

Ken hadn't been at my side when I'd lost my mum. I'd yearned for his hugs and support on that painful day. Now I was confused at what hurt the most — not being able to say goodbye or knowing my grandfather wouldn't be there to greet me next time.

'This is the price I have to pay for love. I've been punished for my selfishness.'

'Shh, shh. I'm sorry.'

'Ken, I'm sorry, but I must go.'

'Yes, of course you must. Stop your crying until you get to Tonga. I have to find out the quickest way to get there.'

Ken took care of the travel arrangements. I had to make a coffin cover for my grandfather — it was a duty expected of daughters and granddaughters. *How do I do that?* I wondered. I wished I'd paid attention all those years ago. I reached out to Lynette for help. My Australian sister. Somehow, between the two of us, we managed to create a beautiful lace cover with tiny red ribbons. The red symbolized Christ's death on the cross and the white purity and safety. *Not bad for someone who's never done something like this before.* I knew my grandma would be proud to display it on my grandfather's coffin.

Because the mourning period for a Tongan funeral could go on for ages, I decided to take the girls with me this time. I was the first to arrive from overseas.

Our house in the village was like a sea of people wearing black. It was hard to make out which was my grandma. I wanted her to myself, but all the village ladies surrounded her. When she finally saw me, she said, 'Oh Liva, Grandpa's favourite.'

I bent down to hug her.

'He's gone, Liva, he's gone. Never to return.'

'Shh, shh. I know.' I couldn't help her with her grief. I could only cry with her.

At Grandpa's funeral service, I stood there with our girls, who were too young to comprehend what their mama was going through as I squeezed their tiny hands.

Afterwards, everyone started to disperse. I didn't want to leave my grandma alone, though. I wanted to grieve with her, relive memories with her, for however long she needed.

'Can I please place a collect call to Australia?' I asked the operator.

Soon I heard the familiar voice I loved. 'Hi, darl. How are you and the girls? How was Grandpa's send-off?'

'Hi, darl. I miss you and wish you were here. It was sad but all went well. It rained the whole day with only a break in time for the burial.'

'Hope you managed to get some sleep and weren't sitting up all night.'

'Yeah, the girls gave me the excuse to go to sleep with them.'

'When are you thinking of coming home?'

'I think this is a great opportunity to introduce our girls to my heritage, culture and the life I've had. I'm thinking of extending my stay for three months. What do you think?'

I could hear the frown in his voice. 'I don't think that's a good idea. What about their schooling? Liva, that's irresponsible.'

'Ken, they might be absent from their school but their little lives will be enriched by learning how to live the island way, my way, or have you forgotten they're part Tongan?'

'Let's talk about it next week. How's Grandma?'

'She's good, thanks. There are always people around her, which is a good distraction. Are you okay?'

'It's very quiet without you and the kids, but I'm good, thanks. I miss you. Please think about not extending your stay. Three months is a long time.'

'Love you, darl, but this call will cost you a fortune. I'll call again in a couple of days.' I was glad to sign off before arguing.

Eventually, I got him to agree to extend our stay. The girls were enrolled at the little village primary school I'd attended as a child. They wore the red and white uniform with no shoes, just the way I had long ago. They thought it funny that, when the school bell went, they all had to line up to brush their teeth, followed by a groom check before class.

I slipped into my island life as if I'd never left it behind — the life with manual labour and no electricity or running water. Even though electricity had moved closer to my village, it was still 5 kilometres away. *Could I live to see electricity in my village?* I wondered. *Ken could change that for me?* But with the expense of our trip and Grandpa's funeral, I couldn't bring myself to ask.

After two months, my endurance was running low. I missed Ken and all the comforts he'd provided me with. I wasn't so sure whether I could last three months but I was determined to see it through after I'd given Ken grief over it. The girls had picked up the Tongan language and they were having the time of their lives — mission accomplished. It was worth the heartache of separation.

However, I admitted defeat and called Ken, my lifeline. 'Can you please book our return flight? I'm done with cold showers, and I miss you. I want to come home.'

'Okay, great. I'll do it tomorrow and let you know.'

A few days later, I still hadn't heard from Ken. My calls went unanswered. I started to worry. *What if he doesn't want us back any more? I made it difficult for him, serves me right.* The girls went off to school and I was onto the next task of cooking lunch under the mango tree. The firewood was still wet from the rain the day before. The fire didn't start well and it smoked so much. *Who in their right mind would live on this forsaken island?* Then a car pulled up at Grandma's house. I looked up through thick smoke and made out the silhouette of a man on the other side. *What the …? I know that figure. Ken?*

He had a smile like a split watermelon. I stood up, my heart pounding so hard I worried it might jump out. I lunged into his outstretched arms. *Ooh! He smells so good. I must smell like shit.* But I didn't let him go. 'Sorry,' I said. 'I must look like shit and smell like it too.'

'That's what I love about you, darl, you're authentic,' he said, tilting my head up as he'd done a thousand times.

'Yeah right, Ken, whatev—' He didn't let me finish as he kissed my mouth long and hard without respect for my culture or care for who was watching.

'Why didn't you tell me you were coming? I was worried sick thinking you'd ditched me for being difficult.'

'I wanted to surprise you and your reaction made it all worthwhile. Where are the girls?' he asked, looking around at everyone staring at us.

'They're at school. They'll be here shortly for the lunch break. They'll have a shock. Oops, the lunch.' I remembered the cooking that Ken had interrupted, glad that Grandma had already taken over.

We heard the school bell. 'That's the lunch break,' I said. Ken had difficulty making out our girls, as they were camouflaged in the sea of red uniforms that poured out of the little school. They all walked in line, on one side of the road, until they reached their homes; only then were they allowed to break off from the line.

The girls saw their dad and screamed in delight as they raced up to him. Elizabeth couldn't shut up to let Tema talk. She told two months of stories in one breath. Tema was just content to cuddle up. My heart was warm and fuzzy, watching with pride at the loves of my life sharing a moment.

We packed up our lunch and the girls were happy to show the way to the beach like little island girls. They took their dad as if he'd never been there before.

Back at Grandma's house, Ken had two suitcases. 'What on earth did you bring? Are you staying for a month?' I said teasingly.

'Yeah, I'm staying for a month. We're staying for a month.' He looked at me for my reaction. 'Those cases are full of electrical stuff. I might as well wire Grandma's house while we're here.'

'That could be problematic — there's no power here in the village, Ken. It ends 5 kilometres away.'

'I've already taken care of that. Trust me, I've got this; I still have connections. Tomorrow, the boys from the Ministry of Works will run the powerlines and end with a pole outside Grandma's house, then I'll complete the rest,' he said smugly.

'Oh my god, Ken, Grandma will have a heart attack. I can't wait to see her face.' I'd never envisaged seeing electricity in my village, let alone Grandma living to see it. I couldn't be any prouder for Ken to be making this happen. This was the village where they'd tried to fend him off by vandalizing his Mini Moke, had thrown rocks at him, but he'd persisted and now he was stepping up to what he'd pledged in marriage — to love my family as he loved me.

Early the next day, Ken was in the roof and under the house as he worked like a dog, with Uncle Lopeti helping. It was such a tedious process with the language barrier, but comical at times. With hand signals and partial translation from me, they got there.

When darkness fell, we waited for Grandma to do the honours as we all sat around on the floor of the small living room. Grandma paraded in like a cockatoo. She stopped at the light switch and looked up at the shining fluorescent tube on the ceiling. Shifting her eyes to the switch on the wall, she smiled as she flicked the switch down for the first time — one for every room and outside, too. Let there be light and there it was. *Post tenebras lux* — light after darkness.

'Wow!' That was all I heard from Grandma's gasping mouth. Then, she started to dance without music while we all laughed. 'I'm the only one in this whole village who has lights,' she proudly announced.

'It's good to be humble, Grandma,' I said.

She came over and tapped my head but kissed Ken without saying another word.

She left the house and I found her sitting under the mango tree in the dark. 'What are you doing out here, Nane? Do you miss Grandpa? The house looks amazing. Who would have thought you'd be flicking a light switch in your lifetime?' I tried to make light of what I thought she was thinking.

I was getting ready for a tear fest, but she said, 'No, I wanted to see which neighbours came out to peek.'

'You're hilarious, Grandma. There's no one out here,' I said.

Ken heard us laughing and he came over.

'Malo 'aupito Ken ho'o 'ofa,' Grandma said.

'Thank you, Ken, for your love,' I translated.

'Peheange mai 'oku 'i heni 'a Taimani ke lave ho'o 'ofa Keni.'

'I wish that Taimani was here to share in your love and generosity, Ken.' I had to tell her to slow down as I was having a hard time keeping up with the translation.

Amid the darkness, with the love of my life beside me, I reached out for his hand and took him down memory lane.

'Did you know we had a kerosene lamp? It stank and we dodged the black smoke it spat out. Then we advanced to a benzene lamp; Grandpa had to pressurize the fuel tank before lighting it. It was a much brighter light and there was no smoke or smell, but it was a lot more dangerous. Now, with electricity, it's a switch at your fingertips. It's hard to fathom. I wish Grandpa was here to see.'

I squeezed his hand, grateful for the darkness. 'Thank you, darl,' I continued. 'My family will never be able to repay you.'

I felt his arm come around my waist possessively. 'Don't worry, you're going to pay for it later,' he said in a whisper as if Grandma could understand, but I smiled at what lay ahead.

'I used to collect and burn coconut shells and stuff the red embers into a coal iron to press my school uniform. Then it progressed to a benzene iron. Have I told you that story?'

'A thousand times, but I love hearing your stories.'

'I can't wait for Grandma to have an electric iron.'

Grandma sat quietly beside us, not understanding a word I said. I explained it to her afterwards. She loved it when I talked about my childhood, as it emphasized to her that I hadn't forgotten where I'd come from.

We all sat in silence enjoying the evening until Ken tugged at me to move inside. We left Grandma to brag to her cronies. I was delighted to share this moment with my grandma and to witness the joy she got from this simple comfort that Australians took for granted, which I took for granted also.

'This will be the last time we travel to Tonga separately. It's either we all come or we won't come at all. Promise me that, Liva,' Ken demanded once we were out of earshot.

'I promise.' But could I keep that promise?

'We are free to make love when we want and where we want; we pledged that when we got married,' he said, looking for my reaction. He thought I was going to protest but I was busy unbuttoning his shirt. For the first time, I was loving my white man under my grandparents' roof without shame or guilt.

It was time to bid farewell to Grandma. Watching her small frail body, so alone, waving to us and calling out to the girls as we left was one of the hardest things I'd witnessed.

But Ken always found the right thing to say. 'There's nothing stopping Grandma from coming over to Australia for a visit. Do you think she might like to come? Would you like that?'

'Oh! really? You would do that? For me? For her? Oh! Ken, thank you, I love you, I love you.' My tears of sadness were replaced with tears of hope.

As he'd promised, the following year, Grandma came to Australia for a visit. I'd never thought this day would come. My mum had gone, Grandpa too, so it was nice that Grandma could tick this off her bucket list.

She loved it as we and the girls took her around to see the sights of Melbourne. But eventually, the time came for her to go home — although it broke my heart, I knew that's where she was happiest.

The weekend before she left, I came home from work to find Grandma all smiles. 'Go and have a look in the garage,' she said enthusiastically, looking at Ken.

'What's all this?'

In the middle of the garage was a huge crate filled with white goods to ship to Grandma's house. There was a fibreglass moulded shower, toilet, kitchen sink, washing machine, and fridge/freezer.

'Did you rob a bank, Ken?' I asked. His generosity no longer surprised me. 'Thank you, darl. That explains the smiles.' I nudged up to him.

'That should help to make her life a bit easier,' he said.

How lucky am I to have you, Ken, so generous and loving. Would I be able to get that from another white man? He promised to marry me and my family. We didn't have much money and yet Ken was willing to share what we had and had worked overtime to fund Grandma's crate of goodies.

When the time came, Grandma was happy to go home but as always the goodbye was not something I ever got used to. 'Nane, you know I would dearly love to take you home but I couldn't ask Ken for my ticket,' I said to her at the airport. 'We've stretched our financial situation to the limit.'

'I know that, Liva. I can't thank Ken enough for bringing me here. I did the exploring for both Grandpa and me. Your world is beautiful. I'm so happy that I've witnessed it but my heart still belongs to the village. The ocean is calling, and when my time comes, I will rest with my darling heart.'

The final boarding call came and I watched Grandma walk through the security door of Melbourne airport without looking back. Out of Australia and out of my life. The hollow feeling I had was crippling. 'I was the one who always left Grandma,' I told Ken. 'This time she's walking away from me. Oh, Ken, it hurts.'

'Come on, let's go up to the observation deck and watch her flight,' Ken said, pulling his hankie out to wipe my eyes.

I gulped a big breath as we watched the aircraft below, some with their engines on, ready to taxi off.

How cool would it be to fly those machines? I pondered. 'Grandma is the lucky one,' I said, 'going on a plane ride.'

'Yeah, I thought the planes would put a smile on your dial.'

We waited until the aircraft got airborne. I watched until it became a speck in the sky, then felt his hand link with mine and beckon me to walk with him.

Bye, Grandma.

PART 2

19

Health and a new era

With Grandma gone, happy with her huge crate of electrical goodies, our household returned to normal Australian life.

But in the early hours one morning, Ken woke me up. 'Liva, can you please get me my tablets? I'm getting one of those headaches but it feels different this time.'

I jumped up as quickly as I could. My heart was thumping as I raced out to fetch his tablets. He'd been getting headaches for months but they had become more frequent lately. I was scared — he'd always been the strong, healthy one and I couldn't understand why this was happening.

After he took the tablets there was no relief. 'Can I have a bucket?'

I'd never seen headaches that brought on vomiting, but he did, again and again.

By daybreak, his eyes were bloodshot, I felt so helpless. He needed help but didn't know what to do, who to call and he was too sick to give me directions. He had emergency numbers by the phone on the wall. I was ashamed to call 000 for a headache so I dialled what I thought was an appropriate number and was eventually put through to a GP. 'Please help my husband. He's got a violent headache and I can't get him in the car.' I started to cry.

'Okay, hold the line,' said the voice on the other end. I waited for a minute, then he said, 'I've ordered an ambulance and it's on the way.' The doctor stayed on the phone until the ambulance arrived.

Ken was transferred to a trolley and wheeled out to the ambulance before he was whisked away. I cried after he'd gone. I dropped the kids off at school then called Ken's mum and dad to come and look after them afterwards.

I got to the hospital by mid-afternoon and was ushered into a small room with a desk and three chairs. 'Take a seat,' she said, taking the chair behind the desk and motioning for me to take the chair opposite. She put a folder on the desk and started to shuffle through the contents.

'There's no easy way to tell you, Mrs McLeod. Your husband is showing symptoms consistent with what we see in AIDS victims. Do you understand what AIDS is?'

My mouth froze open as I gasped for air. *I'm not an idiot. Of course I know what AIDS is. It's a death sentence.*

'I watched on TV that AIDS is a sexually transmitted disease, common with multiple partners, and there's no cure.' I shook my head. 'I don't understand.'

'We can't be sure until the result of Ken's test comes back. To help us, we need to ask you some questions. Would that be okay?'

'Yes, of course.'

'Have you had a blood transfusion in the past?'

'No.'

'Have you had multiple sexual partners in the past?'

'Hell, no.'

'Have you had unprotected sex?'

'Why would I? He's my husband.' I started to get annoyed with the questions.

'Have you had anal intercourse?'

'Oh my god. Seriously?'

'I'm sorry, but these questions have to be asked.'

I didn't hear any more, it was too much as I sobbed. I didn't understand some of the medical terms.

'As a precaution, we've isolated Ken until the results come back. You're the only person who can visit him for now. I'll get you a protective gown and then you can see him.'

A minute later, she returned with a plastic gown, a surgical mask, a hat and gloves. When I put them on, I felt like I was going to the moon. Then the nurse directed me to the ward that Ken was in.

I saw him and my heart ached. He was no longer the young, strong man I'd married. 'Oh! Ken, it can't be. Impossible,' I cried, hugging him. I tried to suppress any accusations and finger-pointing but in the end, it got the better of me.

'I am petrified, for me, for you and for our girls,' I said. 'It had to be your fault, Ken. You know you were my first. The frightening thing is, if you have it, then it's inevitable, I must have it too.'

'Can you please settle down? I don't have AIDS, so stop it,' he said, annoyed. 'The test will confirm it.'

'I'm so scared and feel dirty at the same time. They asked a lot of derogatory questions and I had to answer them.'

I bent down and kissed him and he just stroked my head. 'Shh,' was all I heard.

For two days, I visited Ken in my spacesuit in his room. Then finally, the doctor came in without a protective gown.

'Ken, the good news is you don't have AIDS. I'm sorry you had to go through all the procedures, but we had to be sure. The bad news is you have viral meningitis.'

'What the hell is that?' I asked, happy the AIDS test had come back negative.

'It's a viral infection of the linings that cover the brain. At least it's not bacterial; he'll be fine,' the doctor explained. 'You'll be moved to the general medical ward for a few days, and you can have visitors. All the best.'

'Thank you, doctor,' we both said and the doctor left.

We looked at each other with relief as we hugged in silence.

But what followed was not what I considered 'fine'. For the next twelve months, we were handballed from one specialist to another as Ken's symptoms kept recurring. One specialist eventually referred Ken to a haematologist/oncologist at Peter MacCallum Hospital, the cancer institute of Victoria. Alarm bells went off at the mention of Peter MacCallum. *Cancer? No way! That's for old people and Ken is still young and fit.*

The drive to the city took one-and-a-half hours. We arrived at the hospital early to find out where to go. We walked in and the odd smell of hospital antiseptic assaulted my nostrils, together with fear and trepidation. I started to shake like a leaf.

We were directed to the haematology/oncology department on level two. The waiting room was full of sad and old-looking people. We didn't belong there. They must have made a mistake.

Soon we were led into a simple room with a desk and three chairs. There was a thin hospital bed, a hand basin and lots of medical stuff. Soon, a skinny young person in a white coat entered. 'Hello, I'm Max,' he said, extending his hand. *Does your mother know where you are?* He looked too young to be a haematologist/oncologist.

Ken stood up and shook hands. 'Pleased to meet you. This is my wife, Silva.' He shook my hand also and we sat down.

Max, Dr Wolf, flipped through pages from the folder on his desk. We sat quietly for what seemed to be a lifetime. He looked up at us, tapping his fingers on the desk and started to ask the same questions that every other doctor had asked before.

After that first appointment, we continued this marathon drive to see this haematologist every month. After a couple of months of tests and questions, we'd still heard nothing and didn't dare ask. I was fed up with being kept in the dark, so I geared up to start asking questions on our next visit. But when we got there, Dr Wolf beat me to it.

Hmm, he looks serious, I thought, and lost all ability to talk, let alone ask any questions.

'Ken,' Dr Wolf began, 'you have a condition called multiple myeloma. In simple terms, this is a type of rare cancer of the plasma in the bone marrow. It can damage your kidneys and affect your immune system. Hence the reason you're getting infections all the time.'

I stopped listening when I heard 'cancer'. My waterworks went into a flooding rage.

'How long have we got?' I heard myself asking amid all the jargon.

'How long is a piece of string?' he said. 'With this type of cancer, normally the life expectancy is five years, but it's hard to put a span on it. You're still very young, Ken. This type of cancer is known as the old man's disease and it's common in people in their seventies but rare for a young person like yourself.'

Ken was mute, sitting there holding my hand. I could see Dr Wolf was uncomfortable with my blubbering. *Do white people cry openly like me? I'm sorry but I can't help it.*

He handed us some material about the disease. 'I'd like to discuss with my team the best way to combat this. There's a lot to digest, but I'll see you in two weeks with a plan moving forward.'

Once we were back in our car, Ken broke down. 'I'm relieved that there was a reason for my feeling like crap because I was doubting my sanity. I thought I was going crazy.'

I looked at him in disbelief. *You've been handed a life sentence and you're saying you're relieved. What planet are you on, Ken? My perfect little world has been shattered.* I'd believed I was untouchable. I'd always been a good girl and when I married Ken I thought I was being rewarded for being good. A happy life! But it was about to change.

On the way home, we made two stops. The first was at Ken's parents' house. How do you tell your parents that you've been given five years to live when you're approaching your fortieth birthday? No matter how we tried to lighten it, it was going to hurt.

'I have a disease of the bone marrow. It's called multiple myeloma. The bad news is I have cancer. The good news is I still have five years,' Ken blurted out, not making eye contact with either his mum or dad.

The looks on their faces were of utter devastation and disbelief.

'How the bloody hell is that possible? I'm so sorry to hear that son,' Dad said, while Mum still looked stunned.

'But I'll fight the bastard. I'm not going to give up,' Ken said with such defiance. *Hallelujah! At last, I can detect a bit of my feisty Ken.*

'I don't believe that,' his mum said. 'Good Lord, where could you catch that?' She was asking as if it was a cold.

When we said goodbye, I'd never seen Mum hug her son like that before. She was hurting.

Our second stop was at the home of one of Ken's childhood friends, Keith, and his wife Maria. By this stage, I didn't want to talk any more. Ken gave them the spiel and left them with leaflets as we'd never heard of that type of cancer before. 'We might as well educate ourselves together,' Ken said. We all shared a few tears then went home to our girls, who would understand nothing and be told nothing.

We picked the girls up from Lynette and Brian, who had collected them from school. We decided that they were too young and they didn't have to know, not just yet. We had a cuppa with Lynette and Brian and filled them in on Ken's diagnosis. There was disbelief on their faces too and maybe pity, as the unknown loomed ahead. I just wanted to go home where I felt safe, hold my husband and have a good bawl. It had been an exhausting day.

We got home and tried our best to be as normal as could be for the girls. *These gorgeous little faces will soon be fatherless,* I thought. I found myself trapped in what felt like a tropical cyclone as I prayed silently. 'Please God, help me. Please God, give me strength. Please God, don't take their father away.' Those words made me believe, gave me strength, at least for a few hours, until the girls went to bed. Once the kids were tucked away, I found solace in the shower. I wanted to scrub the horrible news off me. The floodgate opened as I let it all out.

I didn't hear Ken step in, fully clothed, to hold me.

'Ken, you can't bring me here and leave me on my own with two kids. It's not fair.' I dug my fists into his chest. I couldn't stop feeling sorry for myself, as if it was all about me.

We just held each other as we both wept like a pressure valve had been released. 'Whenever and wherever we want? Right?' he whispered.

'Yes, whenever, wherever.'

Tears turned to giggles as his saturated clothes fell to the floor. Ken tilted my face up. When I looked into his eyes, I saw determination and a hunger for life. 'I'm going to fight this. I'm not going anywhere. Do you hear me, Liva?'

'Yes, I believe you. I'm with you all the way.'

'Good. Let's get out before we run out of hot water.'

Ken was on a mission and he was unstoppable. He didn't sit and wait for the cancer to come and claim him. He mowed the lawns, did the garden as if the news never existed. His action was infectious and I carried on as normal, too.

That was how he dealt with it. We had two weeks of pretending all was normal until we had to see Dr Wolf again. The next visit was very businesslike as Dr Wolf laid out the plan and procedures for chemotherapy, side effects and duration. Ken was to commence immediately with a hospital stay for the first session.

We went up in the lift to level four this time. We stepped out to a foyer with another glass sliding door with a sign: 'Haematology/Oncology

Wards. To reduce the risk of infections, no flowers permitted.' We filled out paperwork and shortly after the oncology nurse came to prepare Ken for his cocktail. She put the cannula in his arm and I looked with hope at the different coloured bags of chemicals — black, orange and clear — interchanged every few hours.

Then there was the never-ending list of specialists, therapists and medical officers we had to meet. I'd never heard of a groom specialist, but she made Ken laugh. She brought in different types of wigs in case Ken required them.

'Losing my hair will be the least of my worries. People pay money to have their heads shaved. It's trendy, right?' Ken said jokingly.

'You never know, Ken, your head might get cold. You have options,' she said.

'If my head gets cold, I'll wear a beanie.'

He'd survived his first session of the feared chemotherapy.

Ken would be staying in the hospital for a while. When it was time for me to leave, he brought up an unexpected subject. As we hugged goodbye, he said, 'Do you still want to fly?'

'Whoa! Where did that come from? That's random, Ken. Yes, I do, but this is definitely not the time or place to be discussing it.' I'd mentioned to him a long time ago, when we'd been sharing our most secret desires and dreams, my dream of becoming a pilot.

'You should go and do it while you still have the chance. Life is too short. Look at me now,' he said, his voice trembling.

'You are full of drugs, darl,' I replied. 'Try to get some sleep and I'll see you in the morning.' I kissed him goodnight.

'Have a good rest and I'll see you tomorrow. Drive carefully. Love you.'

'Love you more,' I said, then left.

It was a long drive home. I looked to Heaven above for comfort as I prayed, 'Heavenly Father, look after my Ken and rid his body of this disease. Please send your angels to guard him until he returns to us. Forgive our sins. Please Lord. Amen.'

I laid in bed that night, thinking of what he'd said. The love he had for me was more powerful than any disease that riddled his body. 'Oh Ken,' I sighed as tears flowed voluntarily. But I couldn't ignore what those words evoked. Since that day long ago on the beach, we'd never spoken of it again. That fantasy to be a pilot was still burning deep inside and now there was a possibility.

But he couldn't have meant it, could he? God knows, the chemotherapy must have played havoc with his body and mind.

The next morning, I went back to pick him up from hospital. The poor darling was sick on the drive home. He spent the weekend vomiting but when Monday came, he was up and ready for work. Surprisingly, he still had his hair.

Four weeks later we rocked up at Peter Mac for more punishment. First up was the pathology department — ground floor, followed by a review with Dr Wolf — level two, then chemo — level four. A routine that became second nature to us.

'Wow! You still have your hair, Ken. I'm jealous. I don't have much myself,' Dr Wolf said, laughing.

'When did you expect he'd lose it?' I asked.

'Straight away,' Dr Wolf replied.

'At least I've done something right then,' Ken joked.

We all laughed but it was very nervous laughter.

All through this challenging time Ken never stopped living. I always admired his strength in keeping our family as normal as could be. Heaven knows what turmoil was going on in his mind and body.

He was adamant that our annual family holiday was still happening. It helped normalize our family life, but one could never take away the dark cloud hovering over our heads. Our monthly visit to the cancer institute was a constant reminder that all was not normal.

20

A love affair that defies gravity

'Happy birthday, darl,' Ken said, tugging at my nose. 'Wake up and have a coffee with me before I go to work.' It was May and it was getting cold already.

'Morning,' I said, trying to open my eyes. I'm not a very early morning person at the best of times. Reluctantly, I got up and accepted the mug of coffee and a birthday card.

While I opened my card, he asked, 'Have you made any enquiries about learning to fly?'

'Oh! Were you serious?' I nearly choked on my coffee. 'I'd thought you were so drugged up, you didn't know what you were saying. Of course, I would love to, but how are you planning to fund that? Money doesn't grow on trees.'

'I wasn't delirious when I mentioned it. Life's too short, that's all I'm saying. I haven't got you a present yet, but I'm working on it. You have a good day and I'll see you later.' He leaned over and kissed me and he was off.

I took the kids to school then played netball, as I always had comp on Tuesdays. Not long after I returned home, Ken pulled up. It didn't surprise me because he often came home for lunch. I went to turn the kettle on without waiting for him to come in. As I turned around to greet him, he was right behind me with a big smile and a bunch of flowers. 'That's lovely,' I said. 'They're beautiful.'

I leaned forward to smell the flowers but he raised them above his head. 'I'm coming back to give you my birthday present,' he said mischievously.

'Okay, you want to play games, Kenneth Neil, you can shove your flowers up your nose then.'

I turned but wasn't quick enough. He dropped the flowers on the bench and grabbed me and kissed me passionately. I didn't resist, totally under his spell.

I didn't feel the hardness or the coldness of the kitchen floor. Satiated and happy, I lay on his arm a bit longer until he broke the silence.

'So, would you like to find out your present?' he said, not looking at me.

'I thought I'd just had it,' I smiled, poking at him. 'God, I love it when you're impulsive.'

'That's a present you get all the time,' he said, trying to free his arm as he reached up for the flowers he'd discarded minutes earlier. He handed them over. Only then did I see the small white envelope deep in the bunch. I fished it out and it didn't take long for me to work out the contents when I opened it. It was a certificate for an introductory flight training session!

'Happy birthday,' he said, leaning over and kissing me.

'Wow, you're the best Ken,' I screamed, hugging him again. My heart was thumping like crazy. *My fantasy, my fantasy is going to be a reality.*

'Come on, I'm not going back to work. We're going for a drive.'

We got dressed quickly. 'Where are we going? We have to be back to pick up Lizzie and Tema from school.'

'I know. I've brought some sandwiches and my thermos of coffee. We'll have lunch where we're going.'

We drove for a while before small aircrafts buzzing overhead came into view and Ken turned in at the sign where it said Peninsula Aero Club.

'Whoa! No way,' I yelled.

'You have to go and book your flight here,' Ken said, 'and close your mouth.' I hadn't realized I had got out of the car with my mouth open. I'd never seen so many small aeroplanes up close and personal.

I went into the flying school and booked my flight for October. It was five months away but it would be spring and better conditions for flying. We sat and had our lunch and coffee, watching the small planes landing and taking off again and again.

On the morning of my flight, I was nervous and excited all at the same time.

We dropped the girls off at school, and Ken took me to the aero club and waited around while I went on my introductory flight. When we neared the airport, a small aircraft was on approach, crossing just inches above us. It looked so close I instinctively ducked my head and Ken laughed.

As we parked, I stepped out of the car and was mesmerized by the few small planes buzzing about. It mirrored what I felt in my stomach. Sure, I was excited, but a big part of me was filled with apprehension.

Ken must have seen a bit of doubt in my expression. 'Do you still want to do it?'

You can do it. Yes! you can do it. 'Of course.'

'You'll be fine,' he said encouragingly.

I took a deep breath as I built up enough courage, entered the flying school and reported in. A skinny young instructor with his one bar epaulette greeted me. He looked so young; he could've passed as my son. 'Good morning, Silva. My name is Matt. I'm your instructor for today. Are you excited?'

'Good morning, Matt. Pleased to meet you. Yes, I'm petrified,' I said with a nervous laugh.

'Nothing to be worried about, I'll be with you all the way,' he said as he pushed some paperwork forward for me to sign. 'Come with me.'

I followed him to a classroom at the back of the office. The room was lined with long desks and chairs. 'Take a seat, Silva.'

He picked up a marker and started drawing on the whiteboard. He drew an arrow upwards. 'This is the lift force.' Then he drew an arrow downwards. 'And the opposing force to lift is weight.' He proceeded to draw forward and rearward arrows. 'The forward force is thrust and opposing force to that is drag.'

He went on and on about aerodynamics and the physics of flying and I wanted him to shut up. *Please just take me up flying. I don't care about the technical part. I don't want to know the physics or Newton's*

Law of Motion for that matter, I just want to fly and feel the exhilaration of being airborne — of being a pilot.

Finally he gave me a headset and a red folder with a key. 'All aircraft registered in Australia are prefixed with VH; our aircraft rego is THF — Tango Hotel Foxtrot. The phonetic alphabet is something you'll have to learn later.'

I found the two-seater Cessna-152 with the registration 'THF'. After a thorough check of the aircraft and fuel, we finally got in the little plane. If I'd thought it looked small from outside, it was tiny on the inside. Matt started her up, ran through some checks and we taxied towards the runway. I saw Ken and waved frantically at him.

We lined up and there were some radio calls, then I heard the engine squeal as the throttle opened. The rush of the ground under me was exhilarating and soon I felt the sensation of lifting off as we became airborne.

While I was still trying to figure out what was happening, Matt said, 'Handing over. You have the controls.'

'Oh shit, what? No way.' But I obeyed and took the controls. Matt calmly showed me how to turn and keep it in a straight and level flight path without losing altitude. 'Yeeha!' I said as I manipulated the controls. Matt pointed out some landmarks. 'I'm sorry, but I'm too busy doing pilot stuff, I don't have time to be looking for landmarks.' We both laughed.

'We're heading back to the airport. See if you can find it,' he said. Now I knew why he'd been pointing out landmarks.

'Oops! That could be problematic,' I said. 'All I know is the sky above and the ground below. I have no idea of north, south, east or west.'

He laughed and directed me back to the field. 'I'm going to talk you through a landing.'

'Oh dear, don't you want to live?'

'Don't worry, I'll be with you all the way.' It was comforting to know he had another set of controls.

My first landing was a blur. 'What just happened?' I asked when we touched down.

'Silva, you just made your first landing. Congratulations.' He smiled.

He knew how to get me to do it myself. Sneaky. I'm hooked. We parked and tied down the little plane. I ran up and hugged Ken. 'Oh my god, thank you, thank you, darl. It was the best experience ever.'

'Did you like it?' Ken smiled as if he was the one that had been flying.

'Captivated.'

After a long-winded post-flight briefing, I came out of the flying school with a set of textbooks and my first pilot's headset under my arm.

My second love affair was born. Ken was not at all jealous. He encouraged it.

'Did I tell you that I'd never confided in anyone, not even my own family, that I fantasized about being a pilot one day?' I said on the way home.

'A thousand times,' Ken answered.

'Make it a thousand and one. I would've been the laughingstock of the village, if not the whole island. If only they could see me now.'

'Are you going to tell the kids?' Ken asked as we pulled up at school.

'Nope, it's going to be our little secret.'

To save money, I self-studied all my subjects. At 31 and as a wife and a mother of two, it was an enormous mountain to climb but I had the confidence that, with Ken's support, it could be conquered. *We can do it, Ken. Together.* I was looking forward to what this adventure could do for our future as we commenced the journey. My flying was the diversion we both needed to give us something to focus on instead of Ken's illness.

We could only afford one flying lesson a week. One day after I'd been learning for about three months, we'd been practising take-offs and landings when Matt said, 'Let's call it a day.'

'Roger that,' I said as I taxied the aircraft towards the apron.

'Stop here, set the brakes,' he instructed. The aircraft had come to a full stop and with the engine still running, he unplugged his headset, opened the door and said, 'You're on your own. Go for one circuit, then land and come in.' With that, he shut the door.

'Are you kidding me?' I protested, but he was gone. 'Shit! Shit! Shit! What do I do now? Holy Mary, Santa Maria, help!' I whispered. *This is your moment, Liva. Matt thinks so too. Soar like a bird.*

I meticulously ran through all my checklists as I'd done a thousand times. I taxied to the departure end of the runway and quickly checked the windsock. I took a deep breath and opened the throttle, the now-familiar squeal of the small engine loud in my ear as the Cessna accelerated down the runway. Once I gathered sufficient speed, I eased the nose up towards the sky. Without the extra weight of the instructor, I was surprised at how quickly I was airborne. I watched the earth fall away, the altimeter gaining altitude as I joined those before me who had defied gravity.

I'd been up many times but here I was, seeing the world as if I hadn't seen it before. Free as a bird, I floated and turned, no longer the little island girl. If only Grandma could see me. *Ken, I can't wait to bring you up here with me so we can share. Soon.*

'Thank you, Lord, for the white man you've given me, who took me out of poverty and helped fulfil my dream. Let him live long enough so we can share this blessing. Please guide me to land safely.' I shook myself out of my reverie and guided my aircraft around the circuit, never letting the runway out of my sight. Like a robot, I went through my checklists, talking myself through the approach.

'Keep your aiming point constant, crossing the gable mark, shift the aiming point to the runway end, shift it towards the top of trees at the far end as you arrest the sink.' Then I felt the wheels kissing the gravel runway. 'Thank you, Lord,' I said, and I finally remembered to breathe. Mission accomplished.

Flying solo empowered me to share my secret love affair with our kids, family and friends. Elizabeth and Tema were so excited and proud of my achievement, as was my biggest fan, Ken. He was chuffed, I couldn't love him any more if I tried.

But raising two kids on one income, supplemented with my two days a week of work and now embarking on a very expensive hobby made me sick every time I thought about it. Riddled with guilt, I had to offload on Ken. 'I don't know about this pilot thing. So much money in self-indulgence. It's embarrassing when my people are starving at home. I don't know where I'm going with this.'

'Are you still enjoying it?'

'Of course. I'm addicted and that's the scary part.'

'We'll find a way. Just promise me that you won't re-mortgage our house so you can fly.'

'I said I'm addicted, not stupid.'

I took advantage of fine weather one week and had two training flights, which stretched the budget beyond the limit. *That was stupid. Have I lost my mind? Ken will leave me and that would serve me right.*

I served up sausages and baked beans for the third night in a row.

'Are things that bad, darl?' Ken asked.

'I'm sorry, I shouldn't have taken a second flight this week but we'll catch up,' I said.

The following day, Ken was late coming home. It was getting dark and I was worried. When I heard his van, I couldn't get to the door quick enough.

'Is everything okay?' I asked. He gave me a peck on the nose as he walked past. He put his lunch box in the sink then turned to hug me properly.

'I had to stop and do a little job on the way. Sorry I couldn't call but I like it when you worry about me.'

He reached into his pocket and pulled out a fold of cash and handed it to me. 'That should tide us over until the next payday. We can have a nice dinner tomorrow. I told you we'll find a way.'

Those words pierced my guilt-laden heart and I promised myself that I would never double-up my flying lessons again.

I gave him a squeeze. 'Are you sure you don't want sausages and baked beans again?'

'That would be a no from me,' he replied. We both laughed.

Ken continued to do lots of little jobs outside his normal hours, which helped immensely, relaxing the tight budget so I could concentrate on my study.

'Why, Ken?' I asked him one day. 'There's no way a Tongan husband would allow me to do what I'm doing.'

'Liva, if something happened to me, I hope that by then you'll be a qualified pilot earning a good wage, which should take care of you and the girls. Tell me a better way than that? You'll be earning a living doing what you love.'

He'd said it. The uncertainty of his life expectancy was a driving force to prepare me for a life without him. His cancer was never far from his mind.

The enormous weight of a future alone without any formal qualification took my dream and fantasy to another level. I saw my flying as a way to survive.

I graduated with my commercial licence. But we were both naive to think that achieving that milestone would be my ticket to a blissful flying career. That couldn't have been further from the truth; it was only the first of many licences and hurdles.

To be employable, I needed an Instructor Rating, but that was more money. I spent days and nights feeling sick about it, but I'd come so far and spent so much, I had to go the extra length to get a job.

'Ken, I've had my commercial licence for a while and there's not much work available with just that,' I explained to him. 'I think an instructor licence will make me more employable.'

'How much is that going to cost us?'

'Ten thousand dollars.'

I could hear my heart thundering as I watched his face. The silence was deafening. He looked at me intensely, I was embarrassed and I couldn't hold his gaze. I felt sick.

I didn't expect what came out of his mouth. 'If you think that would help with getting you a job then we'll find a way. But promise me that this is it. No more money. No more courses. We have two girls to think about, Liva.' *What happened to preparing me for a solo future? He's tired. I don't want to do it anymore.*

'I'm sorry but we've come too far, invested so much, to stop now. I'll get a job and rebuild our finances and recover our cost, I promise, and you'd better hang around long enough to share that.'

I couldn't tell Ken that the ultimate pilot licence was yet to come — the ATPL (Air Transport Pilot Licence). That would qualify me for jobs with the big airlines. There was no point complicating things at that point. I knew I might never get there.

Spending that much money weighed heavily on my shoulders. That night I couldn't sleep, and I watched Ken breathe heavily beside me. *I love you, Ken. One day I'll pay you back. I promise.*

I enrolled and Ken came up with the money to pay for my Instructor Rating course. Three months later, I graduated with my instructor's licence. At last, I was employable.

21

Spreading my wings

By the end of 1995, I was working as a full-time instructor at one of the flying schools at Moorabbin airport, Melbourne. I was the only female instructor there. The job was promised to me if I did their instructor's course.

I was getting out of my car at the airport one day when one of the senior instructors greeted me with his face tilted upward, squinting. I followed his eyes.

'What colour is the sky, Silva?' he asked.

'It's still blue.' He answered his own question. I knew where he was going with his stupid joke. I'd heard it before.

'If girls were meant to fly it would be pink, don't you think?'

If he thought it was funny, I wasn't laughing. 'Go screw yourself,' I said, before dashing into the building. *Damn it, Silva, never show vulnerability*, I admonished myself.

After a few months, I found myself another flying school and didn't have to hear his insulting greetings. But once again, I was the only female instructor.

Trying to establish a career in a male-dominated industry was challenging. I had to take everything on the chin, whatever obstacles were in the way. Ken had prepared me well enough. Watching him handle his health issues, everything else was a walk in the park. Or so I thought.

At the new flying school one day, I picked up the phone on the third ring. 'Hello, Silva speaking, can I help you?'

'Can I please speak to an instructor? I'm interested in learning to fly,' said a male voice with an accent.

'I'm one of the instructors here. Can I help you, sir?'

'No, I mean, a flying instructor,' he reiterated slowly. *Here we go again!*

'Oh. You mean a male instructor?' I said trying not to sound sarcastic.

'Yes, a male instructor,' he said.

One, two, three ... breathe Liva, breathe. 'I'm sorry that you feel that way, sir. I'm one of the instructors here, female and of colour but I'm very good at my job. Please hold the line, I'll get one of the white male instructors.' *Oh god, I've lost it.* Without giving him another chance to speak, I shoved the phone to the young instructor beside me and walked off. He took the phone with a look of embarrassment and shame.

I left the instructors' room, trying not to tear up in front of others, and headed for the restroom. The advantage of being the only female was that I had the whole room to myself. I locked the door behind me and wished I could stay there forever. When I looked up at the mirror, my reflection stared back. *Toughen up, princess, this is part and parcel*

of the journey. It's just another adversity. Get out there and keep smiling.
And so I did.

The caller, whose name was Mike, turned up at the flying school with a bottle of red wine and apologized. He requested that I be his instructor. I accepted. It was a good outcome from a very awkward situation.

Ken responded well to the chemotherapy and it didn't look like he was going anywhere. He still had a life to live, places to go and a family to care for. We discussed nothing further about his life expectancy or life without him.

I continued to study for my airline licence while working full-time. There was no extra cost apart from the exam fees. Once I'd obtained my ATPL, the hunt for an airline job began. Life wasn't meant to be easy. I kept looking at the pile of applications I'd sent out and it was depressing. I was at my wits' end as to why I couldn't get a flying job.

'Ken, how would you feel if I applied for a job with the airline in Tonga? It might be easier, seeing as I'm Tongan,' I asked one day.

'Oh, that would be exciting. Do you think you'll have a chance?' he answered without giving it much thought.

'I'm continuously hitting a brick wall with finding an airline job in Australia. I don't have any airline experience. Perhaps Royal Tongan Airlines might give me that chance.'

Ken was excited at the prospect. 'You can fly and I'll wave to you from under the mango tree.' He laughed.

One of the prerequisites for employment with Royal Tongan Airlines was an aircraft-type endorsement on DHC-6 (Twin Otter). These aircraft commonly operated out of Northern Australia and were very popular with the Pacific Islands, but not in Melbourne. *Great! How can I do that? It would be easier to climb Mount Everest.* At flying school the next day, I was preoccupied with the task of getting this aircraft endorsement. The weather was not favourable for flying so I wandered over to one of the many hangars at the airport. A female pilot, Jenny, owned this one and I was awestruck at the many beautiful historical aircraft in there.

'Can I help you?'

I looked up and saw a female figure with an engineer on the balcony above.

'Hi, I'm Silva, one of the instructors at the flying school. Not good weather for students so I thought I'd come over and have a look. Hope you don't mind.'

'Not at all. I'm Jenny. Have a wander then come up when you've finished.'

Afterwards, I went up to her office. My confidence was squashed as I looked at photographs of aircraft and pioneers she had on the walls. It oozed success. But she made me feel comfortable. She offered me tea and I started to tell her of my quest for a job in Tonga. All the while she listened, nodded and scribbled on a piece of paper.

As I went to leave, she folded the piece of paper and thrust it into my hand. 'Give him a call. He owes me one and will be able to help you. I wish you all the best, Silva. Come back and visit again soon.'

'Thank you so much.' I clutched the piece of paper as if it was a precious gem and rushed back to the flying school.

At my desk I unfolded it and stared at it for a long time, wondering what to say, before I dialled the number.

'Hello, Rod speaking,' said the voice on the other end of the line.

'Hi, my name is Silva. Jenny gave me your number and I was wondering if you could help me with a Twin Otter endorsement. I'm in pursuit of a job in Tonga.'

'I have a course coming up in a month. Do you think you can make that?'

What? I hadn't expected that. I was unprepared and had so many questions to ask but none came out. Eventually, I said, 'Where and how much?'

'I owe Jenny a favour, so as long as you can get to Cairns and accommodate yourself for seven days, I'm happy for you to join my course. You can buy me a drink once you get that job in Tonga. I'll forward some paperwork but only to formalize your attendance. Bring it when you come. You have my number if you have any questions; otherwise, I'll see you in few weeks.' He hung up before I could thank him again.

The excitement quickly subsided as I thought of Ken and the girls.

As always, I had Ken's support. Lynette decided she needed a holiday and accompanied me on my course. I'd never been to Cairns before and it pleased Ken that Lynette came with me as he couldn't. We arrived in Cairns and it was hot and humid like Tonga. Luckily, the instructor picked me up every morning for the course. The mission was accomplished in five days.

With my new DHC-6 endorsement, I could only hope that would put me a step closer to that airline job. Disappointingly, the flight operation manager for Royal Tongan Airlines I'd liaised with had left the job. His replacement was a New Zealander and, strangely enough, we shared the same last name. I sent a video resume along, hoping it would work.

Just when I'd thought it was another fruitless quest, the phone rang and I heard the familiar click of an international call. I thought it was

Grandma but there was no reverse charge and before I could answer, a male voice came through.

'Hello, Silva. This is Alistair McLeod, flight operation manager of Royal Tongan Airlines. Very impressive video, but I would like to meet you in person. I'll be in Melbourne next week if that suits?'

My legs started to shake as he continued.

'How about if we meet at Melbourne airport next Sunday at midday?'

The meet and greet day came and I hired an aircraft to get there. Liz and Tema came with me and we landed at Essendon then caught a taxi for the 10-minute ride to nearby Melbourne airport.

It wasn't hard for Alistair to spot the only island girl at the airport. He looked older than he'd sounded on the phone. 'Silva?' He extended his hand. 'Pleased to meet you.'

'Captain McLeod, pleased to meet you. These are my girls, Elizabeth and Tema.'

'Please call me Alistair.'

After exchanging a few pleasantries, we ordered drinks while he had a look at my pilot logbooks.

He rubbed his bushy eyebrows before saying, 'We're not recruiting at the moment, but there's potential for someone with your credentials.'

My heart sank, but at least there was some hope.

'Having instructing experience could be useful within the airline in the future. If there's an opportunity for a job in Tonga, would you be happy with a local salary?'

'Hmm, would I be happy? Probably not, but beggars can't be choosers. I've got to be honest with you, Australia's my home and I'm hoping Royal Tongan Airlines will be the steppingstone I need to find a job back here one day.'

'Thank you for your honesty and I would be a fool to think otherwise. If, and I said, if, I offer you a job, what are you going to do with the girls' education?'

'I'll come by myself. My husband, Ken, will stay with the girls until they've finished high school.' Ken and I had spoken extensively of what we would do if I got the job in Tonga but didn't think it would come true.

Now that this seemed to be really happening, doubts and guilt crept in. *What am I thinking?* I was ashamed of my ambitiousness but I couldn't stop. *Would I be feeling like this if I was a man? It is what it is — I'm a woman, a wife, a mother and I shouldn't be having a career, especially one that takes me away from my family.* I was so used to being turned down, I'd never thought this opportunity would come.

'It was lovely to meet you and I'll be in touch,' Alistair said after a long, awkward moment.

When we got home, I filled Ken in and purposely omitted the part about him staying with the girls. I wasn't ready to engage in that painful discussion. *I'll cross that bridge when the time comes,* I figured.

'Do you think you've got a chance?' he asked.

'How long's a piece of string, Ken? I don't know. They always promise you the world but give you doughnuts. I'll wait and see. At least I still have a job here.'

As the months went by with no news, so too the hope of a job in Tonga faded. As a wife and a mother, I was happy about that. For my career, I was very disappointed. All that study and it looked like instructing would be my destiny.

That's okay, I still get to fly. I'm helping someone fulfil their dream and get paid for doing so.

22

A dream comes true

After five years as an instructor, on a day off in December 1998 I went to answer the phone.

'Hello?'

'Silva, this is Alistair McLeod from Royal Tongan Airlines. Are you sitting down? I've got some good news.' I could hear my heart thumping.

'Congratulations. I've got a position here for you …'

My break had come through — I landed my first airline job with none other than Royal Tongan Airlines at an age considered vintage in the aviation world. I was 37 years old.

After the initial elation wore off, a heavy blanket of sad reality lowered over my head as I contemplated what I was about to do. *I'm leaving my Ken and my girls in pursuit of my career. How? Why? What for?*

When I'd left Vava'u with Ken in 1981, the pilots had both been white and hadn't spoken Tongan. They'd addressed the passengers in English, oblivious to the fact that the flight was full of Tongans. None of the passengers could understand English, and therefore, they missed the most important part — the safety brief.

At the time, I'd thought, *How cool would it be if the pilot could make his or her public address in Tongan?*

This day had finally come, but there were obstacles to conquer.

I have a husband. I am a mother of two in their final years of high school. Oh, dear! What have I done? Every adversity, every challenge, every heartache carries with it the seeds of greater benefit, but at a price.

But when I told Ken, Lizzie and Tema of my news, they were overjoyed and hugged me. They'd been with me all the way through hardship, sweat and tears. They'd seen me juggle work, family life and my study, burning the midnight oil for six years.

'What's with that look? Aren't you happy?' Ken tilted my face to him.

'You and the girls.' I could control myself no longer and burst into tears.

'Oh Mum, we're fine,' said Lizzie. 'We're old enough to look after ourselves and Dad too. You've worked so hard for this. You have to go.'

Ken was still holding my face and I could feel his love burning into my eyes. 'We've worked hard together, so go and try. If it's not what you want then come home. This could open up the world for you, for us. We'll be fine.'

This was the toughest decision of my life to that point. If Australia had been my country of origin and I'd been given the opportunity to fulfil my dream, my path might have been different, but that wasn't the case.

Elizabeth would be in Year 12 when I left and Tema a year younger. But Ken, my biggest fan and supporter, never failed me. Most husbands, black or white, would have been kicking and screaming, but not my

Ken. I could never have succeeded without his 100 per cent support. We were a formidable team. *How lucky am I?*

'I don't want to be the reason you can't reach your full potential,' he said. 'It's better to see you happy than having to live with a miserable bitch.'

'Ouch! That's harsh. But you were the one who said life is too short.'

Telling Ken's parents I was going to abandon their son and granddaughters in pursuit of a career at my age was incomprehensible. Seeking the approval of parents is always at the forefront of every child's mind, regardless of age. My white parents-in-law were no exception.

I could see the disapproval in their eyes. There were no congratulations or elation. In their eyes, I could see pain and concern. Their son was going to be a single dad while I was chasing a rainbow with no end.

'Your parents don't approve of me flying,' I complained to Ken.

'It's none of their business. It's our life and if I give you my permission, that's all you need. So stop worrying about them.'

'But in my culture, a daughter-in-law will do her utmost to please her parents-in-law. I trust and hope that one day I'll make them proud as a wife, a mother and daughter-in-law who happens to be in love with aeroplanes.'

'They already are.'

But I wasn't so sure. *I'm sorry, Mum and Dad, please forgive me, but I must do this.*

I believed that Mum and Dad were worried about our marriage, but our love for each other was so strong that nothing, even my beloved aeroplanes, could come between us. I knew Ken felt the same.

'Will you trust me to be out of your sight, Ken?' I probed.

'More to the point, would you trust me?'

'Ha ha! Not funny. You'll be busy with the girls. You won't have time to scratch yourself.'

'I only have room in my heart for one person and you've occupied that. I sure hope it's the same with you,' he said with such intensity.

'It is.' I reached up and kissed his face.

Strangely enough, someone else was worried about our being apart and was never shy to voice her opinion — Grandma Nane. When I told her I'd got a job with Royal Tongan Airlines there was a pause before the wise old voice said, 'How about Ken and the girls?'

Hmm! I didn't see that coming. How about congratulations? 'Ken will stay and look after the girls,' I told her. 'We won't uproot them; they're in their final years of high school.'

'Let me tell you something, Liva. In today's age, you should always keep your man close by your side. Too many marriages don't survive a separation like that. Weigh up what's important to you.' I could imagine her little finger working overtime.

'Talk about build me up then shoot me down. Don't put me on the guilt trip. I've worked too hard, Grandma.' She didn't hear me, as she'd already hung up. *Why am I defending myself?* I was already drowning in guilt without Grandma verbalizing it.

I placed the phone back on the wall, feeling deflated. First Ken's parents and now my grandma charging me with negative thoughts. *I hear you, Grandma, but Ken is a white man and he loves me. Our love will hold our marriage together; I'll prove it to you.*

I wondered why it was so hard. *Why can't I be a man? Then I would be expected to do all this without having to fight my way through.*

My starting date with Royal Tongan Airlines was 14 December 1998. After a very distraught farewell at Melbourne airport, I boarded my flight bound for Fiji then to Tonga. Lynette, Brian and the kids came to the airport, too. I was glad they were there, not only to see me off but to support Ken and the girls.

I was based in Nukuʻalofa and not in Vavaʻu where I came from. I found rental accommodation, which I tried to settle into before starting my training. But it wasn't easy trying to stay focused while missing my family terribly.

The first pang came on 16 December. It was our eighteenth wedding anniversary and the first one Ken and I had spent apart. I came home from work feeling sad. I sat on the side of my bed, looking at the small present Ken had given me to open on our anniversary. Tears rolled down my face as I stared at the beautiful pair of ruby earrings. *I miss you, Ken.*

The phone rang, as if Ken had timed it perfectly. I reached over and picked it up.

'I wish you were here giving them to me,' I said. 'They're beautiful, I love them. Thank you. Happy anniversary,' I added with a trembling voice.

'I wish I was there, too. Happy anniversary, darl. I love you.' Ken's voice came through, then the girls took over for a while. Ken came back and we spoke at length before saying goodnight.

Christmas Day arrived and it was another tough day filled with loneliness and doubting questions. *What am I doing? Why am I here?* I started to think there was so much investment and expectation that now I was stuck with it. *Is that it? I don't know any more, except that my pain is real.* I had another emotional conversation with Ken and the girls. Later, I joined one of my brothers, Paul, who lived and worked in Nukuʻalofa, for a typical Tongan Christmas feast. I wasn't alone but I felt alone. I couldn't wait to go back to work — that was my happy place and it helped me forget about my loneliness. *If I can't have Ken then I'll have my other love — aeroplanes.*

Soon enough, the new year came around. Starting the new year without my family was weird but I was thankful for a job that kept me busy.

On Saturday, 16 January, Paul came to pick me up to go to his place for tea. While I was there, the phone rang and he went to answer, handing it to me. 'It's Ken for you.'

'How did he know I'm here?'

He gave a suspicious shrug. 'Maybe he tried your house and you're not there. I don't know.'

I took the phone. 'Hi, darl. Is everything alright?' I asked.

'Liva, there's been an aircraft accident, up north.'

I froze. *I only know of one person flying up there.*

'Liva, Charlene died in the crash, with two other passengers. Bureau of Air Safety Investigators are at the scene.'

Charlene was a young female instructor who'd been employed by the flying school after I'd started. She'd got a job with a small charter company about the same time I'd moved to Tonga.

'Oh no! Why? How? It's not fair, she's so young.'

'There hasn't been much detail out yet but the office girl from the flying school rang to let you know before it hits the media.'

'I suppose that's the risk we take every time we get into an aircraft. That's a bit too close to home, though. What a waste.'

'I'll keep you informed when I hear more. No doubt it will be on the news shortly.'

'There's no way I can come to the funeral. Can you please go on my behalf? Call me later.' I was scared. I was alone. I wanted Ken's arms around me.

'I will, but promise me you'll take care of yourself and please be careful. Love you.' Then the phone clicked before I answered ... *I love you more!*

He knew it would be a tough day for me. He rang the next day and we talked into the night and, hearing my despair, he arranged to come over in the following week.

I had been in Tonga for over two months without Ken. The night he arrived, I was waiting at the bottom of the stairs on the tarmac, a privilege I have as an airline crew member. The tarmac wasn't very well lit and I was worried I wouldn't see him among the overflowing crowd as they disembarked.

I didn't have to worry. I made out the outline of his frame and deliberately bumped into him as he stepped down. He hadn't expected me to be at the bottom of the stairs. I wrapped myself around him as tears blurred my vision, inhaling his familiar scent as I buried my face in his neck. At that moment, I felt complete.

We linked arms and walked through the small passport control area and out into the darkness to where I'd parked. Ken was happy to drive but I didn't let his hand go.

Ken's time in Tonga passed too quickly. Three weeks later, I stood alone at Fua'amotu airport, waving goodbye to him once more. *Why am I doing this?* I wondered. *To gain, I must endure pain.*

Ken sailed into some rough water at home, as Lizzie started to play up at school. I felt this was to do with me being away; the consequences of my actions didn't take long to show.

'Liva, I don't know what to do,' admitted Ken on the phone to me. 'The school called to say that Lizzie has a couple of overdue assignments and if they're not completed, she won't matriculate. I can't talk to her without yelling or getting upset.' He sounded so tired.

'Oh no, I'm sorry darl. I'm coming home, I'll call you tomorrow.' I hung up and called our airline office and organized my ticket for the next day. There was guilt, regret and sadness but I was torn as my thoughts shifted to Ken. *Does he hate me now? Will he ask me to come home? What about our girls? Elizabeth has to cope without her mum and the heavy load of Year 12.*

'Please Lord, forgive me and let everything be all right again,' I prayed.

Once back in Australia, the teacher briefed me on Elizabeth's work requirements. After he'd finished, I said, 'Lizzie won't be back to school until those assignments are completed.'

I went home to a stubborn daughter with her arms folded, her heels dug in and a scowl on her face. But I was having none of it. I locked the door behind us and took her to the dining table and sat her down.

'Elizabeth, you listen to me and listen well. In your eyes, I might be the biggest bitch who ever lived right now, but one day you will be thanking this black bitch. All I want from you is for you to complete high school. Don't throw it away. You're nearly there. If you want me to come home, I will, but please don't throw away the last twelve years of schooling.' I was crying, for her, for me. I could smell the end of my flying career. There was resentment in Lizzie's dark eyes but she didn't say anything. She had every right to hate me.

'You're going to stay in this house for however long it takes to get these assignments done, no ifs and no buts.'

'But Mum—'

'No buts. I'm not going to hear it, Lizzie. I'm sorry, you'll do it and you're not going anywhere until it's done. Hate me now — love me tomorrow.'

It took three days of whining and complaining, but on the third day, Lizzie's mood lifted as she neared the completion of all her work. When it was done, she looked up and smiled.

'Mum, thank you. I didn't know where to start so I allowed the work to pile up. I'm good now and I don't want you to give up the career you've worked so hard for.'

I could feel tears gathering. 'Oh Liz, I'm so sorry. I should be here for you. This is where I belong.'

'Please, Mum. I'll never forgive myself and Dad will never forgive me if you give up now. I've witnessed the tears and sweat, not to mention the expense to get there. Go back to Tonga. I'll never let my workload pile up again. Thank you, but I'm fine now.'

'Liz, I wished I could get a flying job here in Australia. I'm trying but if you want me here, I'll stay.'

She cried too as we held each other. 'It will happen, Mum. I promise I'll complete my final exams. Go back to Tonga. I'll come over on the school holidays.'

My head was commanding me to go back but my heart ached for me to stay. I prayed that Lizzie would keep her promise and hopefully one day would forgive me. *So much sacrifice. I hope there will be some reward waiting for all these heartaches.*

The night before I went back to Tonga, I lay awake, torturing myself over what to do. Ken always sensed my uneasiness and he stroked my face. 'Shh! It's okay.'

'Do you want me to stay?'

'What do you want?'

'I want it all. I want my career and I want my family too. How can I choose?'

'Okay, if it's going to help, think about it. In a couple of years' time, the girls will have their own lives. What will you have if you abandon your career now?'

I realized then, not only did I love the excitement, fulfilment and the sense of achievement I got from flying but that I was still looking for that big pay packet that would free our financial circumstances. I was looking forward to the day I could help pay back my debt to the love of my life. So I reasoned with myself. *I must go back. At least Tema and Lizzie will still have one of us. If Ken had to go away and leave me with the kids, I'm sure he wouldn't bat an eyelid over it. Nothing is easy for a career mum.*

Elizabeth completed Year 12 and matriculated from high school, then she came to Tonga. I was so happy and looking forward to this one-on-one time with my firstborn. We had an amazing time reconnecting, and not just as mother and daughter. For the first time, I saw my daughter as an independent individual and a friend.

But when the conversation started up about her future and university, she was defensive. She didn't want to go to uni.

'Liz, you've made me and your father very happy and proud,' I said. 'Your high school leaving certificate is your passport to future education. I'm okay if you don't want to go to university. You have two options — you either go back to Australia after the holidays and find a job or you can stay with me here in Tonga if you want. But if you decide to stay with me, you're going back to school and that's not negotiable.'

'What kind of schooling would I be doing here?' she asked.

'A diploma in computer science.' My brother Paul was with the Ministry of Education of Tonga at the time. I knew his influence would get her into a course.

She brightened up at that. 'Yay! I'll get to see Uncle Paul every day.'

She was spoilt by my brother, which wasn't ideal, but I was happy she was with me. I knew my absence from Australia had affected her more than she'd let on but I hoped this would repair the damage in some small way.

At the end of 1999, the world eagerly awaited the arrival of the new millennium. There was much anticipation and fear that the world would blackout if computers failed to recognize the change from 1999 to 2000. If the world ended, I would be the happiest, as I had my family by my side — Tema and Ken had come to join us for the Christmas break.

We celebrated the end of the year at a block party in Nuku'alofa, where the esplanade was closed off to traffic. Ken, Elizabeth, Tema and I, with some of my extended family, met at the foreshore in Nuku'alofa, together with half the population. It was a hot night but the cool sea breeze made it bearable.

I'd never seen so many people in one place in Tonga. We had to stand the whole time as there was no room to sit on the ground. There was a band playing, people dancing on the spot, bumping into people with drinks. Then out came the loudspeaker. 'Ten, nine, eight, seven, six, five, four, three, two, one. Woohoo! Happy new year!'

Then there was silence. I felt Ken's arm squeezing mine but I said nothing. Surprise, surprise, the clock ticked over and nothing happened. The world still rotated on its axis, the clocks still ticked away and the oxygen still flowed freely.

'Happy new year, darl,' Ken finally said.

'Yeah! Happy new year. Happy new year, Liz and Tema. So glad you're here.'

I had no idea what the future held for us, but I was still enjoying flying in Tonga. Lizzie had already decided to stay with me, but Ken and Tema returned to Australia. It was Tema's turn for her final year at school. She had already accepted the fact that I wouldn't be there. If she had any reservations about my absence, she never voiced them.

The new millennium brought some good fortune. I was promoted to captain. The command training was gruesome, but the reward was well worth the sweat. When it came time for my final check to line, I was full of trepidation. I missed not having Ken with his encouraging and calming demeanour to steady my nerves.

The flight test consisted of three sectors in which I had to demonstrate competency as a captain. At the end of the third sector, as the last passenger disembarked, only then did the check captain say, 'Congratulations, Captain McLeod, well done.' He shook my hand.

'Thank you, sir. This is an unbelievable moment.'

'Believe it, you've done it.'

Being the first Tongan female pilot was one thing, but now a captain was unfathomable. How I wished that my biggest fan, my Ken, was there with me. He was my true captain, who steered our ship in the right direction.

My first flight as captain was to my home island of Vava'u. I was excited and nervous at the same time when I thought of the enormity of the moment. I was responsible for the lives of the 21 souls onboard. Remembering 20 years earlier when I'd heard the announcement being delivered in English by a white pilot, my dream was fulfilled as I picked up the microphone.

'Good morning, ladies and gentlemen, boys and girls. On behalf of Royal Tongan Airlines, welcome aboard. My name is Vaisiliva McLeod and I'm delighted to be your captain on our flight 801 to Vava'u this morning.' I had to fight back tears as those words spilled out with overwhelming emotion.

'For your own safety, please ensure your seatbelt remains securely fastened in case of un-forecast turbulence. There's a safety card in the pocket in front of you. Please familiarize yourself with the emergency exits and safety equipment of this aircraft. Flight time to Vava'u is one hour and ten minutes. The weather conditions enroute are expected to be smooth. Final baggage is being loaded and once the paperwork is finalized, we'll be on our way. I will update you with arrival weather into Vava'u later on in-flight but for now, with first officer Adrian, we invite you to sit back, relax and enjoy the flight. Thank you.'

As I finished my announcement in English, I switched over to my native tongue.

> Malo e laumalie 'a hou'eiki moe kainga, meihe Royal Tongan Airlines malo ho'omou me'a mai. Koau Vaisiliva McLeod 'a e finemotu'a 'oku fakahoha'a, ko ho'o mou Kapiteni ia oku faifatongia ma'a kimoutolu 'i he 'etau folau fika 801 ki Vava'u 'i he pongipongi ni. Fakatokanga'i ange ke fakama'u e leta ho sea ma'upe telia na'a hakohako 'etau folau. Vakai kihe kato 'oe sea 'i mu'a 'iate koe 'oku 'iai 'ae tohi fakahinohino kihe ngaahi naunau malu'i 'oe vaka ni telia na'a 'iai he fakatamaki e hoko. Koe taimi folau ki Vava'u koe houa e taha miniti hongofulu. Fakamatala 'ea 'oku 'alomalie pe mo tokalelei a natula. First officer Adrian mo au,'oku 'oatu 'ema faka'amu ke mou ma'u ha folau lelei. Malo 'aupito.

As I clicked off the microphone switch, there was no word to describe the elation I felt. I'd dreamed of delivering the announcement in my language and here I was, with another item ticked off my bucket list.

There were a few palpitations when all doors closed, the paperwork was signed and I got clearance to start engine one then two. Then it was down to business.

Upon touchdown in Vava'u, my family was there to greet me. This wasn't only a victory for me, but my family, my little village and all Tongan girls. I was so glad that my grandma was there to celebrate with me.

I couldn't go to my village to satisfy my family's need to show me off, but it didn't stop them from bringing their feast to the airport. There were floral leis and green baskets filled with local delicacies. My grandma danced, which was very embarrassing because there was no music. She was so proud and I allowed her to have her moment rather than scold her.

When we got back to Nuku'alofa, the ground crew congratulated me on my first day. Then I heard the load controller calling, 'Captain, someone is waiting for you in the arrival hall.'

'How much do they want?' I asked. 'I'm sick of people asking for money. They must think I shit out money now I'm a skipper.'

We both laughed as we walked into the terminal together. I was still adjusting my eyes from the brightness of outside, but there was no mistaking the silhouetted figure against the window. I dropped my flight bag and almost broke into a run. I completely forgot where I was as I threw myself into Ken's arms.

'You've got to stop doing this to me. You're going to give me a heart attack,' I said, the tears doing their thing.

Some onlookers were crying too, but some had shocked looks on their faces. I could almost hear the same criticism from long ago. *Why is this black girl throwing herself into the arms of this white man?* Being black was one of the demons I'd faced ever since I'd said 'I do' to this palangi god of mine 20 years earlier, but with Ken by my side and four bars on my shoulder, I was complete. 'We did it, darl. We did it, thank you.'

We had the best week together celebrating my command and dreaming of a bigger future for us.

Ken singlehandedly guided and supported Tema through her final year of high school, as he had for Elizabeth.

Tema came home from school one day and said, 'Dad, when I've finished Year 12, I want to take a year off to travel.'

'But not before you turn eighteen,' he said.

She grinned. 'Sure. My birthday's on the 30th of April next year and my flight is booked for the first of May.'

Liz and I came back to Australia for my baby's eighteenth birthday. We stayed two weeks to see her off on the biggest adventure of her life. We watched her, so excited, but when the time came to say goodbye, it wasn't easy for any of us. I watched with pride, sadness and a squeeze of my heart when I saw Tema and her dad embrace.

'Thank you so much for everything, Dad. You're the best dad in the world. I love you.'

'I love you too. Have a good trip and be careful,' Ken said. She let go of him and walked over to me but I was already a mess.

'I'm so envious of you, Tema. I would have loved to do the same if given the opportunity at your age,' I said.

'Don't be a greedy guts, Ma. You went on an adventure.'

That was the first time I felt that Tema, too, had been hurt by my choice to go to Tonga. 'Yes, true, I went on an adventure. But yours is bigger than mine. At your age, I would be pissing myself with fear. I admire your adventurous spirit.'

She looked between Ken and me. 'Where do you think I got that from? Both of you.'

'Bon voyage, Temaleti. Don't do anything I wouldn't do,' I whispered as I hugged her again.

'Sure, Mum. But you're boring. Can I still have a beer or maybe a cig occasionally?'

'Okay, maybe one.' We were both trying to make light of the misery of saying goodbye. 'I love you, Tem. Have a safe trip.'

'Love you back more, Ma.' With another squeeze, she left.

The big security door of Melbourne International Airport slid open and swallowed up her tiny figure. We stood there watching the closed door for a few minutes before walking away.

At the end of that year, Elizabeth graduated with her diploma certificate in computer science and she reluctantly returned to Australia with Ken to look for a job. In the new year, she moved into her own flat and was working, getting on with life in Australia.

With Tema in the United Kingdom and Liz moving on with her life, it dawned on me what Ken had said. *'In a few years they'll have their lives and what will you have?'* There were only two left now — Ken and Bitzy, our Border Collie/Kelpie. With my local salary, I couldn't support two households, so we couldn't afford to shut Ken's electrical business and have him move to Tonga if we wanted to keep our house in Australia.

Three years of separation was starting to strain our relationship but I couldn't see an end to our arrangement. I was depressed watching the pile of resumes I sent out to Australian airlines in my hunt for a job there, all to no avail.

We started to argue on the phone a lot. Afterwards, I went under the radar, refusing to take Ken's calls. He never handled it well when I gave him the silent treatment. He rang multiple times and left messages on my answering machine. I listened to them over and over just to hear his voice, but I didn't pick up or return his calls for days. I was miserable and missed him so much, but I didn't know how to deal with it.

How Ken put up with my childish ways, I'll never understand. *I wish he'd ask me to come home.* My head was stuck with thoughts of getting a job to support us in case Ken's health deteriorated and, if not, at least repay my debt to him. I felt I was playing roulette with our marriage but I was too proud to give in. He always turned up at Nuku'alofa airport when I had those moods. Everyone got used to the sight of a black female pilot wrapped in the arms of a white man.

I continued this behaviour while residing in Tonga. But eventually, he couldn't take it anymore.

'Liva, this has to stop. I can't keep running back here every time you have a hissy fit. If you want to continue flying in Tonga then you'll have to stop being childish. And if you've had enough, god knows I have. Let's pack up and go home.'

'But if I come home now, what have we achieved? The tears and heartaches of the past few years will all be for nothing. I'm broken inside, Ken. I think we need a holiday.'

So I planned a trip to the United States for the two of us. *There's nothing a holiday can't fix,* I figured. *Ken will forgive me.* It would be our first holiday by ourselves — no kids, no Tonga and no Australia.

The morning of our trip, I was up early because I was rostered to work before jumping on an Air New Zealand flight from Nuku'alofa to Auckland. I called Ken and he was up early too for his long drive to Melbourne airport. He sounded excited, which made me happy, given the discussion we'd had on his last visit.

I got back and signed off from duty in time to board my Air New Zealand flight, thrilled to being seeing Ken in a few hours. The flight was fully boarded and we were taxiing for departure, but as we lined up for take-off, the aircraft stopped for an unusually long time.

My heart sank. I knew there was something wrong. I kept checking my watch, knowing that Ken would be sitting nervously in New Zealand.

Then the crackling of the microphone as the announcement came through. 'Ladies and gentlemen, this is your captain speaking. We've just resolved a small technical issue and we'll be on our way shortly. Thank you for your patience.'

I scribbled a note and handed it to the flight attendant. 'Can you please pass this on to the captain?' I asked, feeling cheeky.

The note said:

> *Dear Captain, can you please advise Auckland of our revised ETA as I am connecting with another Air NZ service to Los Angeles?*
>
> *—Captain McLeod, Royal Tongan Airlines.*

During the flight, I had a visit from the captain. 'I've got some good news for you,' he said. 'Auckland advised us that they'll hold the flight pending our arrival. You'll disembark first and be taken to your gate. They've also got your husband.'

'Phew! Thank you so much.' Was it the note that worked or the emphasis of my status? I would never know.

We arrived and I was greeted by Ken's beaming smile together with the Air New Zealand airport crew. They rushed us through to the departure gate for the LA flight when one of the boarding crew called out, 'Captain McLeod, sir? This way.' He'd addressed Ken, who was in front. Ken shook his head, laughing, as he motioned over his shoulder towards me. 'Not me. Her. My wife is the captain.'

Here we go again, I thought. I was still in uniform minus my epaulettes, but even that was still not enough. My ticket was endorsed 'captain', but the boarding crew had assumed that Ken was the captain. *That's okay,* I reassured myself. *I'm used to it.* I brushed imaginary dust off my sleeve.

The LA flight was fully boarded and awaiting us. The flight attendant met us at the door and looked at our boarding passes. 'Sorry, Captain, this way,' she said, quietly directing her words at me. She then ushered us towards the pointy end of the aircraft as I started to giggle at the irony of this treatment. I knew exactly where she was taking us.

'What's so funny?' Ken whispered.

'They held a fully boarded aircraft for us. It's nice but embarrassing. Now they're putting us in business class. If only they knew the size of the aircraft I'm a captain of. It's hilarious.'

It was a privilege traditionally reserved for captains, who were predominantly men. *Who cares? Enjoy the moment, Liva.*

After our trip, Ken came back to Tonga with me for another two weeks before returning to Australia. I was relentless with my job hunting. I knew it was just a matter of time before some Australian airline got sick of my harassment and gave me a job.

I got close to securing an interview with a major airline. I'd gone through all the administration requirements and had been in conversation with the recruiting officer and she'd requested a photo ID and a copy of my passport. I was excited at the prospect of working for an

Australian airline. Not long after I submitted the required information, I received an A4 envelope with all my application documents, including my photo ID and passport.

The note in front simply said: We regret to inform you that your application has been unsuccessful.

Another headbutt on the wall.

What else could I do? I couldn't see an ending. In the beginning, I'd viewed Royal Tongan Airlines as a steppingstone, but I was marking time in one spot.

But never in my wildest dreams could I have predicted what was to come.

23

The fear and pain
of being apart

On Wednesday, 12 September 2001, I had an early sign-on at 6 a.m. and was sitting in my aircraft ready for the first flight of the day. It was still dark but was a warm morning.

I saw Mo, one of the other pilots yelling out as he walked towards my aircraft. 'Did you hear the news?'

'Nope, what did I miss?'

'Aircraft flew into the Twin Towers in New York. Apparently, more planes were deliberately crashed all around America in an orchestrated terrorist attack. We could go to war.'

'What do you mean aircraft flew into buildings?'

'It was a terror attack; it was like watching a movie, but it was real.'

'Oh my god! Has the world had gone mad?' was all I could utter. I sat in shocked silence, trying to decipher what he'd said as Mo walked off towards his aircraft.

As a pilot, the thought of jet aircraft being deliberately flown into buildings was unfathomable. *The people who committed these acts must have steel hearts* ran through my mind. As a pilot, I'd been programmed to do everything in my power to save myself, my aircraft and its occupants and keep them out of harm's way. My thoughts shifted to my family scattered around the world. I was in Tonga, Tema was in England, and Liz and Ken were in Australia.

I set off on my duty for the day with a heavy heart. I was in the remotest of the islands in the Northern group, Niuafo'ou. It was the last sector of my long day and the flight was fully boarded when there were some issues with the loading. The first officer went to investigate. He came back to my window and yelled up, 'A gun has been loaded in the cargo hold.'

'What gun?'

'It's a rifle — twenty-two.'

'What the ...? Get it off my aircraft.'

'But the safety catch has been removed and the—'

'But today of all days, seriously? I don't care who the fuck owns it. Get it off my aircraft.'

'It belongs to an off-duty police officer and he's a passenger,' the first officer said.

'Are you deaf? I don't give a hoot if he's the President of America. Get it off.'

He disappeared and a few minutes later he joined me at the flight deck. 'It's been off-loaded.'

'Great. Let's get the hell out of here before the storm comes and we have to stay on this mosquito-infested island. They won't see me but they'll have a feast on your white arse. You wouldn't want that.' *Who's the racist now?*

At the end of my day, all I wanted was to go home to Ken but that wasn't going to happen. My thoughts were preoccupied with Tema, as she was in the United Kingdom.

When I got home there was a message on the answering machine. I pushed 'play', knowing full well who it would be. 'Hi, darl. How are you? I guess you've heard the news. Hope you're okay. Give me a call when you're finished.' He sounded concerned and sad. I sat down on my bed beside the answering machine and hit 'replay' just to hear his voice again. The pain and fear of living apart were at the forefront. I picked up the phone and dialled my home in Australia.

Ken answered straight away. 'Yes, I'll accept the charge.'

'Go ahead,' the operator said.

'Hi, darl. Are you okay? That's terrible news. Did you see it on TV?' Ken said.

'No, I haven't seen it yet. I've just got home but I'm sure it will be on TV later.'

'It's very scary. Unbelievable how many aircraft were synchronized to crash at the same time,' he continued while I sat quietly, happy to just listen to his voice.

'I couldn't imagine what kind of pilots would do that. Have you heard from Tema?' I asked.

'They were fresh pilots specifically trained to commit the act. No, I haven't heard from Tema yet. I hope she's okay.'

'I'll send her an email.' Tema moved around a lot but she always let us know where she was. The last time we'd heard, she'd been at Sidmouth, in the south of England.

We spoke at length before he hung up. Then I curled up in a ball, hugging my pillow. *I miss you, Ken. I miss you, Lizzie, but I fear for you, Tema. Please Lord, keep her safe.* My prayer was answered when Tema called.

'Please come home, Tema. I know you'll be safe in Australia. I'll pay for your ticket and when it's safe again, I'll pay for you to go back if you want to.'

'Mum, I'm fine. I've already spoken with Dad. I'm far away from London and I feel safe here.'

Then I remembered that I didn't want her on an aeroplane. 'Okay, you're right. It's probably safer to stay put. Just avoid subways and airports.'

At the end of that year, I went back to Australia. I was talking to Tema again on the phone when she asked, 'How long are you staying home this time, Ma?'

This time? Those words punched me deep in my stomach. 'I'll be heading back after new year,' I said.

'Okay. Can I speak to Dad?'

'Love you and Merry Christmas. Here's Dad.' I passed the phone over.

She wants me to stay home. I could hear it in her voice. Maybe she thought it was time I came home and looked after her dad.

One day during my stay in Australia I turned on the TV and was shocked at what I saw.

'The Kingdom of Tonga, known as the "friendly island" has been wiped by Cyclone Waka. Vava'u group is reported as being the hardest hit, as the new year announced its arrival with ferocious wind gusts of up to 250 kilometres per hour,' the newsreader said.

I stood with my mouth open, staring at the screen. Sheer devastation.

Cyclone Waka was a category four and had passed my beloved Vava'u on 31 December. It only claimed one life, but the damage was recorded at $54 million. What's more, I couldn't contact my family in Vava'u.

'Dear Lord, look after my grandma,' I prayed.

When I got back to Tonga in mid-January 2002, half the roof of my rental house in Nuku'alofa had been peeled off and there was a lot of water damage, with fallen trees and lots of debris everywhere. I had no power and the house stank of rotten food from my dead refrigerator.

My sister Joyce came around to see the damage. 'It made a mess, didn't it?'

'Yes,' I said. 'Everywhere.' I knew that most of the damage was on my home island of Vava'u and was eager to fly over and check. The phone line was down and there was no word from Grandma.

'Joyce, do you think you can work on getting the power back on while I'm at work?' I asked.

She nodded. 'Sure. It'll be back on before you get home.'

'Whatever, Joyce.' No way that would happen. We'd be lucky if there was power anywhere for weeks!

My first flight to Vava'u after the cyclone was a sight I'll never forget. When the islands came into view, they were unrecognizable — the familiar green dots of islands had been replaced with brown dots. Houses had been flattened and trees uprooted. When I flew over my

I was flying for Aeropelican, NSW. 2004.

Inside the Royal Flying Doctor's aircraft, the Beechcraft Super King Air 200. 2005.

My village people helping out with the food for the wake for my grandma's service. 2004.

Happy times with friends: Maria and Keith Stephens during one of our annual golf trips. Howlong, NSW.

Royal Flying Doctor days. 2005–2006.

On duty – Boeing 737 in 2007.

The flight manager Lilian came up for a visit to the flight deck during the flight. Lilian was a Samoan and I was very proud to be looked after by another island girl. Part of their duties were to check on us pilots every 20 minutes.

The view from my office at 37,000 feet, as the sun comes up on the coast of Los Angeles at daybreak after 14 hours of flight from the east coast of Australia.

There was so much love as father and daughter, Ken and Temaleti, embraced before Ken handed Tema over to Andrew on her wedding day. The last of his duties to both his daughters. 2011.

Tema and Andrew tied the knot at Montalto Vineyard, Mornington Peninsula.

At Abu Dhabi airport, Etihad was promoting a flying nanny to look after the kids in flight. Being a nanny myself, I couldn't resist this pose. 2013.

My McLeod family. Ken, Dad, Bruce, Linda and Mum on her 80th birthday.

I couldn't be any prouder than when called 'Nanny' while in uniform! I had just arrived from a trip and ran into Harlem and Loxy (Andrew and Tema's kids) on their way out on holiday at Melbourne Airport. A lovely surprise.

I love this photo of us. Elizabeth and Tema as young independent women with their own families. At Portsea, 2014.

Nanny on duty. Malakai, Harlem, Loxy in the hug-a-bub and Grayson in the pram.

Ken was in a coma but he loved his shave every day, so I continued to provide his personal grooming instead of the nurses. 2015.

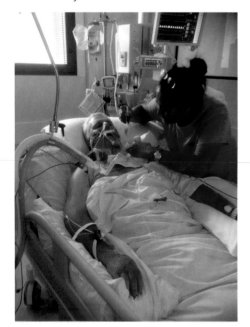

In my traditional mourning costumes when my father passed away. 2017. Only three years later I watched my daughters dressed the same way for their white palangi father.

Ken had been in a coma for several days, but when he woke up he didn't forget it was our 35th wedding anniversary. He assigned a friend the task of getting me flowers and an anniversary card.

With the crew at an LA hotel getting ready for the airport. 2017.

Inside the engine nacelle of the Boeing 777. You get to appreciate the size of the aircraft when you feel like you've been swallowed up whole. 2017.

A happy family snapshot of our brood in our garden. Back row — Andrew and Tema, Paul and Liz. From left to right: Malakai, Eleanor, Leilani, with Lox on my knee, Harlem, Grayson on Ken's knee, and Orlando on Lizzie's lap. 2017.

Outdoor dining at the Nautilus restaurant, Port Douglas, QLD, 2018.

I was departing from Brisbane International airport and my sisters happened to be there and turned up to surprise me. Joyce and Maumi were so proud. 2017.

My grandparents' memorial head-stone that Ken and I erected on Mother's Day, 2018, which happened to be our last trip with Ken to Tonga.

Ken's 70th was his last celebrated birthday. It was monumental to share this with our seven grandchildren. 2019.

My Ken, Ken jr and Kenny boy. 2018.

Elizabeth and Temaleti in Tongan traditional mourning costume to pay their respects to their father. They were prepared by my sisters who were able to be with us. 2020.

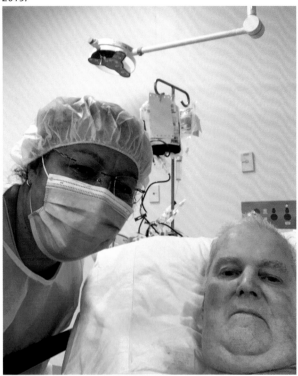

The last time that Ken was admitted to hospital. I was finally allowed to see him after a whole day of distress and I will never forget how happy he was to see me despite tight security brought on by Covid-19. 2020.

Seventy white roses for each year he lived. Ken's send-off at The Sanctuary chapel, Bunurong Memorial Park. 2020.

The island girl in me with a Sei (a flower in the hair). 2021.

Going solo. My pride and joy nowadays. These little souls kept the smile on my dial after Ken departed. 2020.

village, I felt sick. It looked like a pile of matchsticks. 'Grandma, I hope you're okay,' I whispered under my breath.

'Ladies and gentlemen, we're going to have one lap over my island. Look out and if you see Grandma, please wave,' I announced on the PA. I slowed the aircraft and circled the rubble beneath me, where Grandma's house should have been. I was rewarded when I saw people waving. I couldn't make out who was who, but I knew Grandma was amongst them. A sigh of relief escaped my mouth. *They are safe. She is safe.*

I took the next couple of days off and went to see Grandma. The drive from Vava'u airport was sheer desolation. When I arrived at my village, it confirmed everything I'd seen from the air the day before.

'Oh no!' I whispered, with my hands on my mouth. My grandma's house had no roof and what was left standing leaned like the Leaning Tower of Pisa. My uncle had erected a temporary shelter from tins and coconut leaves. There was no power or running water and it would be months before utilities were restored. The village's underground water system had been destroyed. The storage tank was resting some 100 metres away.

With no running water, the villagers had opened an old underground well as an alternative supply. It took me right back to when I was a young girl. One of my jobs had been to fetch water by dropping a bucket attached to a rope, pulling it up by hand.

Grandma had aged so much from when I'd seen her last only a month earlier. All the comforts we'd provided for her were gone.

'Nane, the days of you suffering this way are over,' I said. 'I'm taking you with me to Nuku'alofa until we can fix up the house. You can't live like this. You're not young anymore.'

The next day I took her to Nuku'alofa with me. There was no pension or government help in Tonga. I had to take charge.

When Grandma and I arrived at my house in Nuku'alofa, I was shocked to see that the power to my house had been restored. Amazing! Soon after, Joyce came over, looking satisfied with the results of her efforts.

'How did you manage that in two days, Joyce?' I asked.

She winked at me. 'A bottle of rum speaks louder than money. You know alcohol is like gold, very expensive and almost impossible to get.'

'Oh, god. Sorry I asked.' I'd forgotten about that aspect of life in Nuku'alofa. Bribes were sometimes the most effective form of currency.

In 2002, Royal Tongan Airlines acquired its first Boeing 737. Suddenly, flying a jet became a possibility. There was new hope for what might be ahead in my career. *How exciting would it be,* I hoped, *the first black female pilot from Tonga to fly a jet?* But it wasn't that straightforward. I still had to battle while I watched my male counterparts progress. *Your time will come. Be patient, Liva, you're here to stay.*

The B737 was quickly replaced by a B757. This aircraft was wet leased (an aircraft lease, complete with crew) from a foreign international airline. The arrangement was for the Royal Tongan Airlines' crew to be trained up and eventually take over.

Two male pilots were sent first for the type-endorsement in the B757. I was advised I would be in the next crew to go. My passport was taken for a visa application. Disappointingly, after a couple of weeks, my passport was returned with no visa and one of the male crew was sent in my place. No explanation was given but I was no idiot either — I had no place in this male-monopolized field. Feeling demoralized, I pretended it didn't hurt, but it hurt like hell.

'This is the country of my birth and yet I don't belong,' I whined to Ken on the phone. 'What hope have I got of finding a job in Australia when my own country's airline rejected me?'

'Good things come to those who wait,' Ken said. 'Have faith and believe in yourself.'

I closed my eyes and thought of my school motto: Esto Fidelis — Mo'ui 'aki e tui — be faithful. I couldn't quit now. I was bitter but had to work hard to overcome these hurdles. Ken wasn't around to comfort me so I had to toughen up and soldier on.

24

The gift of a second chance

Ken had continued his monthly visits to the cancer hospital, sometimes with me when I was able, and other times solo.

In March 2003, he visited Dr Wolf and I was awaiting the report of his review. It was late and I must have dozed off and thought I was dreaming when the phone rang. I fumbled the phone and nearly dropped it. I heard the familiar peep of the international tone as I saw the time — it was after 9 p.m., with a mental calculation it would be 6 p.m. in Australia. It could only be Ken.

'Hi, darl. How did you go with Dr Wolf today?'

There was silence.

'Ken, are you there?' Immediately I sensed that this was no normal call. I steadied myself for the blow.

'Yeah, I'm here, darl. Dr Wolf told me that my cancer is back and I need to have chemotherapy again.' There was such misery and despair in his voice.

I'd enjoyed our last thirteen years and had almost fooled myself that Ken was cancer-free. I gulped a mouthful of air and exhaled into the phone. 'Oh no, no, no. I'm so sorry, darl. I'll catch the next flight home. I'm so sorry you had to hear that alone.'

I wanted to hold Ken and, mostly, I wanted to be held too. I'd been punished for my selfishness at last. 'Please God, please Ken, forgive me.' I hung up the phone and cried myself to sleep.

The next day I caught a flight home. Home! Where my heart was — with Ken in Australia. That was where I belonged. Ken picked me up from Melbourne airport. He looked happy that I was home. I burst into tears as I held him. *You're not going anywhere, Ken,* I thought, *I'm not ready.* I inhaled his familiar sweet smell, felt his heartbeat and hoped he felt mine too.

'We've walked this walk before, we can do it again,' I whispered.

'Of course. I've been so lucky to survive this long, I'm not done yet and you're not going to get rid of me that easily.' He pushed me away so he could look at my face then he tugged my flat nose.

'Too right. Let's do it,' I said as we walked out of the airport hand in hand.

I was glad to be home in time for the meeting with Dr Wolf the next day to discuss the options for Ken moving forward. We both had a restless night, so we decided to leave early to get to the Peter MacCallum Cancer Centre. During the one-and-a-half-hour drive, we hardly said a word to each other. We were both lost in our own thoughts.

We were in the waiting room when Ken was called and we were ushered to the familiar room of Dr Wolf. We waited for a few minutes before the door opened and were surprised to see Dr Wolf was accompanied by another lady as they entered.

'Hi, Ken. This is Katrina, a clinical trial nurse and you might as well get acquainted as you'll be seeing each other a lot in coming months,' Dr Wolf said.

'Hi, Katrina. Pleased to meet you,' said Ken. 'This is my wife, Silva. You might as well get to know her as she'll be seeing you a lot in coming months, too,' he added and we all laughed, breaking the heaviness in the room.

'Ken, there's a new procedure called an autologous transplant, which you can benefit from,' Dr Wolf said. 'In simple terms, it's stem cells transplanted using your bone marrow instead of someone else's. Like any procedure, there are risks, but we believe the benefits will outweigh those. If you agree, Katrina will explain the procedure. There's also some paperwork to be completed.'

'Thanks, Max. The cancer will eventually kill me anyway, so I might as well die trying,' Ken said. *Aw, Ken, how heroic was that comment?* I was numb and speechless.

Dr Wolf left while Katrina helped us navigate through the paperwork.

'There will be six months of chemotherapy before the transplant. Providing you respond to the chemotherapy, we can start to harvest your stem cells then,' Katrina explained. 'Once we've collected enough stem cells, you'll have what we call "high-dose chemo". After that, we'll restore your bone marrow with your stem cells.'

I tried to digest everything and knew that Ken didn't hear one word. It was made obvious when Katrina asked, 'Have you got any questions?'

'Where do I sign?' Ken asked.

Katrina directed him to the dotted line on the authorization form and looked up at me. 'If you have any questions, Silva, you can always call me.'

Throughout the next phase of Ken's fight, our fight, I was by his side. It gave me great comfort and I was sure he loved me being there. *Together, in sickness and in health, for as long as we both shall live.* We could weather the storm ahead.

I'd become complacent, thinking Ken would live forever, but it was inevitable that my time with Royal Tongan Airlines had to end. I felt as if Ken's illness was like a light bulb moment telling me it was time to go home.

While Ken was recovering from his six months of chemotherapy, he was well enough to accompany me to Tonga to finalize my work commitments. We went to the Royal Tongan office to hand in my resignation after nearly five years. Walking out of the Royal Tongan Airlines building with Ken beside me made it easier. No tears, just grateful that I got to live my dream. Squeezing Ken's hand, I knew it was the right decision.

We flew to Vava'u to say goodbye to Grandma, as my departure was sudden. We stayed one night. It was hard leaving Vava'u and Grandma but I was faced with a much harder dilemma — my future with Ken was cloudy. I kissed Grandma goodbye, not knowing when I would see her again. 'I'll be back soon when Ken gets better. Wait for me, Grandma.'

'I will be here but please, Liva, look after Ken. I wish I could trade places with him. Give Lizzie and Tema my love.'

I walked away without looking back. I seriously doubted I would see Grandma again.

Glad to be home in Australia, feeling free, without distractions, we focused on the next phase — the transplant. In January 2004 Ken was admitted to the cancer centre, where he stayed for nearly six weeks.

But first, he had to survive two high doses of chemotherapy. During the administration of his first high dose, Ken went into a seizure and shook violently. He looked like he'd been exorcised as he convulsed and appeared to be lifted above his hospital bed. The sounds of doctors and nurses' footsteps was deafening as they arrived at his bedside. I watched in disbelief as Ken was wrapped in a silver foil blanket. He looked like a spaceman.

I was terrified and crying at the same time. 'Oh no! Please tell me this isn't happening. Why? What's with the space blanket? Where's my God that I pray to every day?'

The intravenous drugs were disconnected and they wheeled Ken out of the room.

'He'll be all right,' said a young doctor I'd never seen before. His hand was on my shoulder and they were the comforting words I needed to hear.

'Where are they taking him?'

'Ken is being taken to the theatre to remove his chemo port. We think it has an infection and it flushed through with the chemo into his bloodstream. He won't be too long.' A chemo port is a small implantable reservoir attached to a vein. It allows chemotherapy to be admitted directly into the port rather than a vein, eliminating the need for needle sticks.

A couple of hours later Ken arrived back in the ward with a cannula in both arms. He was asleep but stabilized as he continued with his high-dose chemo.

I found solace inside St Patrick's Cathedral, next door to the hospital. When I was there on one of my dark days, I could hear my grandfather's voice, 'There will be sunshine after rain, fair weather after storm, comfort after difficulty and dry land after sea-drift.' I emerged feeling calmer. I returned to Ken's bedside to find him fast asleep. He looked so peaceful, so I left him and went home for some rest.

He came through with flying colours and was ready for the stem cell transplant, which also went as well as expected.

'Ken behaved well during transplant,' Dr Wolf told me, 'but afterwards, he was a bit nauseous, which is normal. The transplant puts him at a very high risk of getting infections. With new bone marrow, he will have to be immunized again, like a newborn baby. I'll advise his GP to schedule those. His immune system is non-existent for now, but he'll get stronger.'

Tema returned from the United Kingdom upon hearing of her dad's downturn. When I saw her come through the security double door at Melbourne airport, it was hard to contain the emotions. It had been two years and I hoped her arrival would lift Ken's spirit.

As we drove to the hospital, I updated her on her dad's condition. She sat quietly, which reflected her mood.

'Mop your face up. We're here,' I said.

My reaction at the airport was repeated by Ken when his baby girl walked in. Tema quickened her steps with outstretched arms to her father. Ken reached up with both arms to hug her. There was so much love in the room.

'Aw, Dad, so good to see you. How are you feeling?' Tema finally said.

'I'm really good now. Did you have a good flight? How was your adventure?' Ken seemed to have so much energy all of a sudden. Tema's homecoming had definitely made an impact and I was grateful she could distract him from everything else.

Five weeks post-transplant, Ken was discharged from hospital and coped well at home. I was just happy to be with him, supporting him as he had always supported me.

In April, we were awoken early one morning by the angry sound of the telephone ringing. I glanced at the bedside clock. It was six. I bolted upright. A call that early could only be from Tonga.

'Hello?'

'A collect call from Lopeti, Tonga, do you accept the charge?' the operator asked.

'Yes, yes, put him through.'

'Liva, it's Uncle Lopeti.' My heart stopped beating for a second at the heaviness of his voice. 'Grandma Nane passed away in her sleep.'

'Oh no! Oh my god, does it have to be now?' I screamed.

'Please don't cry. It's okay, we understand your situation. You don't have to come. Grandma would want you to take care of Ken. I'm only letting you know.'

'I asked you to wait for me, Grandma. Oh no. I wanted to kiss you one last time. I'll find a way to come and say goodbye.' I begged my uncle to hold the funeral.

'Liva, it's alright. I'll call you later. Take care and love to you both.'

The phone clicked and I was left to stare at the dead phone.

Ken had heard the conversation and I felt his hand stroking my back, which made me cry even more. He reached over and took the phone from my hands.

Once I had no more tears, he said, 'You know you have to go. I'll be fine. You need to go and say your goodbyes, our goodbyes.' Those words managed to find some fresh tears. *Goodbyes!* That was final. She was the matriarch of the family; it was the end of an era.

'I am sorry, Ken, but I have to go and see Nane off.'

'It's okay, I'm sorry I can't come with you. Send my love to Grandma and everyone, and please you take care of yourself. I need you back.'

Arriving back in Vava'u was the weirdest homecoming ever. I looked around but Grandma was nowhere to be found.

When I arrived at my childhood home, there was a sea of black-dressed villagers everywhere. It reminded me of Grandpa's funeral sixteen years earlier. At least they were together at last.

Grandma was to be reunited with Grandpa Tai in the same grave. This might sound backwards but that's my life, my culture, my tradition; so unique and I'm proud to share. We opened Grandpa's grave to make room for Grandma. I wasn't sure about the feeling I had. I was pleased to see my beloved Grandpa once again, even in dust. *He'll be Grandpa in a different form.* I was curious even though it was a bit spooky at the same time.

Culturally, the grandchildren formed a guard of tapa cloth around the graveside. When the concrete lid of the grave was opened, it revealed a rotten coffin, but it was unmistakably my grandpa lying there.

The oldest grandson, who'd been named after my Ken, went into the vault to lift up Grandpa's remains. I sat cross-legged at the graveside with a huge tapa cloth to receive the bones from Ken junior. I then bathed Grandpa's bones with our traditional scented coconut oil under the watchful eyes of the village elders. I had so many mixed feelings as I performed this sacred task, traditionally given to granddaughters, but the others had freaked out and I was left with the job. It was the first time for me and I was honoured to do it.

I completed the oil bathing ceremony and carefully wrapped Grandpa's remains in the prepared tapa cloth and handed them to Ken junior to be placed back in the corner of the crypt, making room so Grandma's coffin could join him. I smiled at the irony of such a scene, seeing Grandpa in the naughty corner just the way Grandma would've liked it. The grandparents who'd sacrificed so much for me and accepted and loved the white foreigner of my choice were finally reunited.

What would Ken think of this tradition? He would never understand but he would respect the ritual as part of my culture.

Some years later, my sisters and cousins asked me, 'Weren't you scared doing that bone cleansing thing with Grandpa?'

'Really? Why? He was my grandpa and I was blessed with that task; I was glad to do it rather than having a stranger touch him.'

I often replay that scene in my head and am in awe of my rich foundation that has such respect, even in death. I was so proud to dig deep into the Tongan in me. Despite the white cultural influence of Ken's world, I couldn't be any prouder of my heritage.

I stood at the cliffside cemetery of my ancestors all alone, saying goodbye to Grandma. The sun beat down and even though it was a hot day, there was always a chill as the sea breeze rose up the cliff face and swept across the small graveyard.

There it goes. Dust to dust, I thought as the handful of dust hit the coffin. The chilling sea breeze gathered up the spirit and descended to the sea. I looked up to see two white doves sailing across. *Bye, Grandma. Bye, Grandpa. Thanks for everything.*

It hurt a lot to lose Grandma and yet I couldn't get back quick enough to feel my Ken's arms around me and to hear his voice telling me that all would be okay, just as he'd done when I'd lost my mum and grandpa.

But now, Ken needed my arms around him instead.

Ken's electrical business was put on hold while he was recovering. But as long as we had each other, that was all it mattered. Wrong! The bills didn't take sick leave. We were both unemployed with no income and whatever cash we had was quickly depleted.

'We can't both stay home with no job,' I said when Ken started to feel better. 'I'm the healthy one so I'd better look for a job. I don't know what, but I'll find one.'

While looking for a job, I went to Centrelink for the interim. I'll never forget how that place made me feel. I had never been to a Centrelink before so it was a whole new experience. I walked in, unsure of what to do and was very conscious of being the only coloured person in there. Queuing up for the dole made me feel the lowest of the low. I was overwhelmed with shame and guilt. There was nothing wrong with me. If only someone could give me a chance, I would prove I could do anything. But I had doorknocked at shops, sent emails, to no avail.

Centrelink enrolled me in an aged care course, as there was a demand for workers. Once I'd obtained my Certificate IV in aged care, I was employable at last. I got a full-time job in a low-care facility 20 minutes from home. I didn't care what I did as long as I didn't have to go back to Centrelink.

It was hard to look around the aged care facility and see these people; all of them used to have a life and all had a story. I felt sad that they'd been put away like this — so unlike Tonga, where family took care of the elderly. But my life was enriched by knowing these people. One lady I cared for reminded me of my grandma. She was blind but I loved her spirit. I told her about my flying and one day while I was helping with her shower, she said, 'You're way too smart to be stuck with old people like me. Wouldn't you rather be up there?' She pointed upwards. 'But I appreciate you.'

She didn't see me smiling. Those words meant more to me than she ever knew.

Perhaps circumstances had sent me there. I'm a true believer that everything happens for a reason. Without a doubt, being a carer for the elderly helped shape me. I hope that when I reach my expiry date, I can proudly say that I have contributed in some small way to the world we share.

But as rewarding as the job was, I missed the sky. I missed the adrenaline rush I got from lifting off and watching the ground disappearing from under me. I missed the smell of kerosene from an aircraft's engines. I missed the sense of achievement when I returned the aircraft safely back to the ground. I missed going places.

It was difficult to explain my love for flying to people. Ken was the only other person who understood and was never jealous about my other love affair.

I could hear the sky calling.

25

Returning to the sky

Ken's transplant was a huge success and he recovered fully. His hair grew back, along with his appetite, and his energy returned. We were back to monthly visits with Dr Wolf, and Ken started to get electrical work again.

I was constantly thinking about flying again. After a nearly twelve-month hiatus, I started the arduous task of applying for flying jobs. It went nowhere. I realized that, although I was applying for lots of jobs, nothing beats making face-to-face contacts. So I purchased a round trip Melbourne–Sydney–Melbourne ticket for the same day. But how could I tell Ken what I was planning? What would he think about me leaving him again?

When I got home from work at the aged care facility, I found Ken watching TV.

'Hi, darl,' he said, but didn't get up to meet me.

'Hi,' I said walking up to kiss him. I sat down on the floor beside him and the pain from my back and feet from standing all day was enough to turn on the tap. 'Ken,' I looked up to his face, 'I want to go back flying, please? I'm hurting and I don't want to do this job any more. My wings have been clipped for way too long.' I couldn't read his face and I looked away.

Then I heard his voice as he stroked my head. 'You know, I've always said that it's better to let you go and be happily married than stopping you and having to live with a miserable bitch. My view hasn't changed.' He kissed the top of my head. 'I'm happy you're returning to the sky. You've worked too hard to throw it away.'

Those words were like an angel's voice.

My flight arrived in Sydney at 8.30 a.m. From there it took another two hours to reach my destination: Newcastle airport. When I arrived, I was so excited — the smell of kerosene in the air awoke so many senses, the types that only a true love affair could evoke. A Twin Otter had just touched down, with another one lining up for take-off, and I wanted more. The sensation of being weightless like a bird filled my being and I couldn't stop smiling.

I made my way into the building and nearly collided with the blonde receptionist I had spoken to a thousand times in the past. 'Yes? Can I help you?' she barked with the air of importance.

'Hello, can I please speak with the chief pilot?'

Before she could answer me, a middle-aged man walked out of the office. He was short but had a smile on his face. 'Hello, can I help you?'

Give it your best, Liva. You only get one shot at this. 'Hi, my name is Silva. Sorry if it's not a good time but I'm looking for a job. Every time I try to reach you, your blonde protective armour at reception won't put me through. So I flew in from Melbourne and drove up here in the hope of meeting you.'

He laughed but I wasn't sure whether he found me funny or pathetic. 'This isn't a good time. What's your name again?'

'Silva,' I said. *God, he's forgotten my name already. Just as well I didn't say Vaisiliva.*

'Wally Smith. I'm in the middle of a CASA audit.'

My stomach rose up to my mouth. That was a Civil Aviation Safety Authority audit. This was *so* not a good time.

'But if you have a one-page resume I'll have a look at it when I'm able.'

I couldn't fish it out fast enough from my backpack and handed it to him. 'Thank you and I hope to hear from you soon. All the best with the audit.'

I left disheartened. *Why should he hire me? I wonder whether there are any female pilots in his team, or coloured pilots, for that matter.* I'd wanted to chat a bit longer but didn't get a chance.

So it was back to Melbourne, to my aged care job.

One week later, I was making the bed at home when the phone rang.

'Hello?' I answered.

'Hello! Silva, it's Wally Smith here, chief pilot, Aeropelican. I may have a job for you, but I wouldn't uproot the family to come here. If you want it, it's yours. When can you start?'

Huh! If I want it. What planet is he from? Of course I want it. 'Thank you so much. I'd love to, but can I have two weeks to give my current employer a chance to find a replacement for me?'

'Okay, after Christmas then. Let me see, how about 29 December?'

'Sounds great. I'll see you then.'

I'd landed my first airline job in Australia. Yippee! I ran around in a circle, so thrilled. I closed my eyes and gave thanks to the Lord first, then I rang my biggest supporter.

He answered on the second ring. 'Hi darl, guess what?'

'If you're pregnant, you certainly have some questions to answer,' he said. We often joked about that, as he'd had a vasectomy.

'Ken, be serious. I've been offered an airline job with Aeropelican.'

'Wow! Well done you. I'll be home shortly.'

He arrived with flowers 'picked from the cemetery' again. 'I'm so proud of you. You've never given up. Heaven knows how hard you've tried. You deserve it.'

'I think I enjoy chasing the most. Now I've got it, I'm not too sure whether I want to move away from home again.'

'There you go again. Make up your bloody mind.' He looked annoyed.

'Christmas is coming and I have to organize where to live in Belmont, Newcastle.'

'Don't overthink it, Liva. Go and try. At least you're in Australia. Don't like it, you can come home. Too easy.'

It was just the encouragement I needed.

Unlike the job in Tonga, this time the separation was a bit easier. Ken drove me to Newcastle, but then had to return to his business. The painful pang of goodbyes re-surfaced. I'd been kidding myself to think it would be easier. I couldn't believe I was putting us in that same awful situation once more. I never got used to that, yet I couldn't stop.

I wonder whether it's the same feeling as a drug addict or an alcoholic, the euphoric feeling of being weightless like a bird. I've proven I can be somebody, not just an island girl. Wearing my pilot's uniform endorses my accomplishment.

Belmont was a small airport and it reminded me a lot of the airstrips I'd operated from in Tonga, except my passengers were all white people and all spoke English. But it was my reality and I was the only female pilot and of colour, and very grateful.

Ken and I continued our long-distance marriage, with him visiting as often as he could. I had to make a few trips home during 2005 as we were organizing a special event. Elizabeth had decided to tie the knot at the end of the year.

One of my brothers, his wife and my sister 'Ana came to Australia for the occasion and they brought with them a bit of my Tonga. The night before the wedding, we were going to have an early night when 'Ana said, 'It doesn't feel like a wedding. It's more like a funeral. So quiet. What's going on? I want to dance, I want to sing, I want to be happy. Gosh, this is boring.'

Before we knew it, Tongan music could be heard from miles away as she started to dance and make a lot of noises. It didn't take long before we all got up and joined in the fun. Except Ken. He operated the video camera. That was his excuse, anyway.

Lynette and Amber thought it was amazing, especially Amber. 'This is crazy,' she said. 'I've never seen anything like this before. 'Ana, when I get married I want you to do the entertainment.'

'Don't worry Amber, there's already a special number reserved for your wedding day,' she replied.

The next day, we gathered at the back beach of Portsea for Elizabeth's sunset wedding. Sure, the sun was setting, but the wind was blowing and it was a cold evening.

As the vintage MG rolled up, Ken got out of the car. He looked so handsome in his white Hugo Boss trousers and his dark striped shirt. He held his hand out and Elizabeth took it as she stepped out of the car. She looked so beautiful.

Tema and Amber, her bridesmaids, walked ahead, followed by father and daughter. It was something I'd once thought unachievable. But there was Ken, well enough to walk his eldest daughter down the aisle on her big day.

For the service, 'Ana and my brother and his wife appeared, armed with mats and tapa cloth. They laid them out on the sand for the wedding party to stand on, oblivious to the inquisitive looks from our Australian friends. I was about to scold 'Ana but she cut me off. 'Don't speak to me, Liva. You know nothing. One day Liz will be proud when she looks back and sees evidence of her heritage.'

'While in Australia you do what Australians do and she's Australian,' I protested.

'You can take the girl out of the island but never the island out of the girl. Remember that.'

As my time with Aeropelican approached two years, I could see the strain of Ken and me living apart once again.

'How long do you think you can stay here, Liva?' he asked when visiting me one day.

'I'm working on it. I'm trying to find a job in Melbourne,' I answered, annoyed at the question.

'And if you can't find a job in Melbourne then what?' he said without looking at me. He looked sad; he didn't know I was watching him.

'Well, then you move up here,' I blurted out as if I'd been rehearsing the words. And I had.

I waited for his outburst, but it never came. I took advantage of his silence. 'Why don't you close the business and take a break and see if we might like it here?'

'That would be possible if you were earning enough to cover the expenses of two homes,' he said sarcastically.

Ouch! I didn't see that coming. Serves you right, Liva. Our home was our rock, just like Ken — always there, always safe and secure. Ken would never gamble with that.

He returned home and left me with another heavy heart. But the anguish was always short-lived. The sky was my go-to place that gave me comfort and happiness when I was left on my own.

There weren't many options for an airline job in Melbourne. *Why not use my flying for something more meaningful?* I asked myself. The Royal Flying Doctor Service would tick that box. I'd tried for a job with them in the past with no luck. But I was used to being knocked down and I always got up. I started calling the head office again and again.

After work one day, I arrived home feeling down and lonely. I swung my flight bag into the corner of my room and laid down on my bed with tears of frustration.

'Oh Lord, don't abandon me now. I just want to go home. Is that too much to ask? I beg you not to throw away all my hard work. In the name—'

I jumped up when my phone blared from my flight bag. I thought it was Ken at first, but I didn't recognize the number on the screen.

'Hello?'

'Silva, It's Dave, chief pilot, Royal Flying Doctor. I hope you're sitting down. I have some good news for you.'

I was still crouched down at my bag in the corner so I sat cross-legged on the floor just like a Tongan.

'You can start packing. You're coming home and you'll be based in Essendon, Melbourne.'

'Are you serious?'

'Yes. How long do you need to give notice?'

'I'll need four weeks.'

'Okay, your starting date with us will be 29 May. You can give notice now and I'll send your contract with all the details. If you agree, you can sign and send it back. Is there anything else you want to know?'

'No, thank you.'

I was still on the floor cross-legged as I dialled the number I could call blindfolded. I could almost hear the sigh of relief in Ken's voice. Finally, I had everything: a job doing something I loved and staying at home with Ken.

26

Royal Flying Doctor Service

Arriving home was sweet, unlike when I'd returned from Tonga when it had been clouded by sadness and uncertainty with Ken's illness.

I started my new job with RFDS but quickly realized I needed accommodation closer to the airport. The one-and-a-half-hour daily drive was too much. We found a home away from home in Essendon. It was only a one-bedroom apartment but it benefitted both my job and when Ken attended the cancer centre.

I only stayed in the apartment when my roster dictated an early morning start, otherwise I managed my duties from home. On average, we spent about three nights in the city. Ken continued his electrical business and it was surprisingly easy to manage our work commitments.

I arrived at the apartment after work one day and, to my surprise, Ken's truck was parked outside. I started to panic. I barged in, eager to find out what was going on. He was sitting on the couch staring with a red face at a blank TV.

'What's the matter? Are you okay?' I asked, rushing to his arms.

'We lost Bitzy,' he said, tears rolling down his face.

'Oh no. Ken, I'm so sorry.' Bitzy, our beloved Border Collie/Kelpie, had been a constant companion for Ken while I'd been gallivanting around the world. I'd only seen Ken with tears when he proposed but this was an exception. I let him be and was thankful to be home to comfort my darling while we grieved together.

In October 2006, we caught the train to the city for Ken's monthly review. It was two-and-a-half years post-bone marrow transplant and Ken was in good health. There was no sign of any underlying issues.

As we walked from the station to the cancer centre, Ken was panting as if he had shortness of breath. Then he grabbed his chest and started to rub it. 'Feels like I have asthma. It's hard to breathe,' he said, hanging on to the fence of St Patrick's Cathedral.

'Gosh, Ken, you have to keep walking. This is embarrassing. If you looked after yourself you'd breathe easier. The hospital is just around the corner. Hanging on to the cathedral's fence isn't going to help you,' I said, ashamed of the attention we were drawing.

But I'd underestimated his discomfort, as he said, 'Piss off then and leave me alone.'

When we got to the hospital, much to Ken's disgust, I reported it to Dr Wolf.

'What time was this?' Dr Wolf asked.

'Near enough to eight o'clock when we walked from the train station.'

Dr Wolf walked out of the room without saying a word but within minutes, doctors and medical staff filled the room with all sorts of medical equipment. Blood was drawn, ECG machines hooked up and a blood pressure machine attached. It happened so fast, and before I knew it, Ken was transferred by ambulance to St Vincent's Hospital.

'Ken has the classic symptoms of a heart attack,' Dr Wolf explained to me, still at the cancer centre.

Did someone just pull the rug from under my feet? I thought. But then I saw myself from outside in. *That poor black girl, sitting there, all alone. Don't be so pathetic. Get up and go find your white fella.* That thought empowered me and I decided to walk, as the city traffic was crazy. I don't know how I got to St Vincent's before Ken, but I remember praying and crying all the way.

Ken was taken straight to theatre for open-heart surgery. How quickly my day had turned ugly. I called Elizabeth to let her know.

'Oh, Mum. Are you okay? I'm on my way. I'll pick Tema up and fill her in.'

But I wanted to be the one to tell Tema, so I dialled her number and repeated what I'd said to Elizabeth.

They walked in together and I could tell they'd both been crying. We hugged as I tried to keep it together.

We waited all day in this tiny little waiting room with no news. At 5 p.m., we finally got a briefing from the surgeon.

'The operation was a success. Ken has had five by-passes.'

'What? I've never heard of five, only bi, triple and quadruple. What do you call five by-passes? Trust Ken to take an extra one,' I said with a relieved giggle.

The surgeon laughed. 'Sorry, it took longer than anticipated. We took veins from his arm and leg to mend the damaged arteries. He's still asleep but you can see him, one at a time.'

I wasn't prepared for what I found. Ken looked like a corpse. There were tubes going everywhere but what struck me was the absence of any life emanating from his face. I knew he was alive though and that was enough.

He didn't know I was there, but I knew he would feel my presence. 'Ken, stay with me, we're not done yet,' I whispered. When I kissed him, the coldness matched the lifeless corpse and he gave no signal that he'd heard me.

I went out and took Lizzie in first for a few minutes. She cried but remained quiet. When she left, I brought in Tema. She took one look at her father and crashed to the floor like a sack of potatoes. Luckily, I saw it coming and supported her.

Ken spent ten days in hospital, followed by a long rehab program. The advantage of working for RFDS was that they were empathetic and flexible with the time I needed off. I took three weeks to nurse Ken back to health. His resilience was something to be envied.

Ken made great progress but wasn't strong enough to be on his own, so I took him to the city apartment where I could go to work and still look after him.

The Royal Flying Doctor Service turned my flying into something deliciously meaningful. It was a match made in heaven, with my fantasy (to be a pilot) and my dream (to be a doctor) and together it took my career to a different level, not to mention how rewarding it was to be part of an elite rescue team. My rosters required me to stay at the airport two consecutive nights every ten days. If I was lucky, I slept all night, but if there was an emergency, I had to be up and ready with a flight plan and in the aircraft in 20 minutes.

I emerged from our sleeping quarters stressed to my eyeballs on my first midnight emergency.

'Hello, Silva,' said the controller. 'Is everything okay? You're late.'

'Well, no. Everything is shit. There's no way I can be ready in 20 minutes. I need 30 minutes.'

'Thirty minutes?' he said.

'You're forgetting I'm a girl. I have excess baggage. By the time I put my bits, hair and my face on, there go my 20 minutes. Busted before I check the weather and get my flight plan, let alone getting a coffee to wake me up.'

For the first time ever, being a girl worked in my favour. Every time I got a midnight rescue mission, the controller would stipulate that I had 30 minutes.

The flying aspects of RFDS were something I treasured. I would become airborne and head towards a destination, only to be told mid-flight to change direction.

The nature of the emergency dictated what type of medical team was required. For instance, premature babies and infants required a NETS (neonatal emergency transfer service) team consisting of a doctor, nurse and paramedics. This service is like an intensive care transfer for newborns. Adult emergencies required a PETS (patient emergency transfer service) team. I felt privileged to be part of such a lifesaving service and it opened my eyes that I wasn't alone in my battle with Ken's health. Everyone had their own battle.

It all came to the surface when one night I picked up a female patient from country Victoria. She'd had a brain haemorrhage and was in a critical stage. The PETS team was required.

We arrived at the remote town of Swan Hill in the middle of the night. It was cold but I elected to stay with the aircraft and the team went to pick up our patient from the local medical centre. They arrived back within a couple of hours and we were loading our patient into the aircraft when I noticed an elderly man with a long white beard hovering around. I assumed he was the husband or partner. His shoulders were stooped, mirroring the defeated look on his face.

'You can say goodbye now,' I heard the paramedic say to him.

The look of despair on his face will stay with me forever. He edged closer, looking scared to touch her. He bent over and I saw his lips and beard touch the woman's face as he kissed her. Then he stepped back from the stretcher and the paramedic pushed the patient into the aircraft.

This was the hardest part of the job. I shed more tears at home as the scene unfolded in my mind's eye while I was telling Ken. *I'm so glad I can look after Ken when he gets sick. I don't want him to be like that husband, alone with despair. It's in my DNA to nurture and care, not the other way around. That's what a woman does, it's expected and it's my job. Maybe I look like that man when I'm in despair.*

Flying in Melbourne in winter was always challenging. The Beech 200 aircraft was a single-pilot operation. It was a sophisticated machine and an absolute pleasure to fly. It was fast, pressurized for comfort, allowed for high altitude flying and yet could land in a paddock or on a road.

I was en route on a mission to the highest altitude airport in Australia — Mount Hotham — to uplift a skier who'd broken a leg, when my windscreen cracked mid-air.

'Oh! Shit, shit, shit!' I mumbled into my microphone, forgetting the paramedics could hear me through their headsets. Expecting some reaction from the back, I heard nothing.

I couldn't see a thing. Safe operation of the aircraft is accomplished by reference to instruments, but I needed to see for landing.

After a long minute or so, a voice came through. It was a nervous paramedic. 'Are you okay, Silv?'

'No, I'm not. Standby one.'

The mission was abandoned. I broadcast an urgent call for clearance from air traffic control as I steered my aeroplane back towards Essendon airport. A plan was in place, autopilot engagement was confirmed. I edged over to the other pilot seat where that side of the windscreen was not affected. Only then, I briefed my quiet paramedics and continued safely back home.

The dynamics of rescue operations kept my heart rate up continuously. We operated anywhere we could land an aeroplane. It could be a road, paddock or private airstrip. I remember approaching a remote strip in the middle of the night and it was very windy. The airport didn't have runway lights. Normal procedure was that the emergency crew on the ground would light oil/kerosene lamps along the runway in time for our arrival. The crosswind was so strong the nose of the aircraft wasn't pointing at the runway. This method was to allow for wind drift.

A voice came through my headset. 'Are you happy, Silva?'

'Yep.'

At 800 feet, a shaky voice came through. 'Still happy, Silva?'

'Yep.'

At 500 feet, half the lights on the runway extinguished.

'Now I'm not happy,' I said, as I powered up and the mission was abandoned.

There was never a dull moment flying with Royal Flying Doctor Service. One of the highlights of my time there was when I was called to uplift premature twins from a remote area. The team arrived back at the aircraft with our VIPs snuggled together in a special humidicrib made for air transfer. They looked cute — without a care in the world yet vulnerable at the same time.

I was lingering around the humidicrib, amazed at God's creation, when the doctor handed me something.

'Here, Silva.' He shoved a pair of gloves into my hand. 'Go on, have your fix and stop drooling. You can give them a pat.'

'Oh! Can I touch?' I said excitedly.

'Of course. Hurry up before I change my mind.' He turned his attention back to other equipment.

I smiled. Their tiny little bodies were so soft and warm but fragile. I stroked their thumb-sized arms with my index finger.

You two are so lucky. Look at all of us flying here in the middle of the night to rescue you. The babies on my little island have no help. Sadly, they'll never make it. I'm so glad I'm part of your journey.

I told Ken about my day afterwards and he was the only person in my world who understood the pain I'd experienced. The thought of my Vava'u with its primitive medical system will always pain me. My people will never get to experience the world-class medical service that Australians see as their god-given right.

My next mission was to pick up a patient with renal failure from the small town of Robinvale. 'Hey Silva, our VIP is Tongan,' the paramedic said.

It made sense because a lot of Tongans were fruit pickers in Mildura, northwest Victoria, and Robinvale is only an hour southeast. I'd never envisaged that one day I would be helping one of my people in this way.

He was absolutely astounded when I said, 'Malo lelei.' Hello.

'Are you the nurse?' he said.

'Nope, I'm the captain, so you'd better hang on tight.'

'What's your name and where you from? We might be related.'

'Silva McLeod from Vava'u.' I'd already checked the patient's name and it wasn't a name I recognized. With McLeod as my name, he probably didn't believe me.

'Were you a nurse before you came here?'

'Yep,' I said, laughing. It was easier to just agree.

I didn't think he got it, but I'd developed a thick skin over the years and his comment went over my head. I've been called a security guard, a flight attendant and now a nurse. After all, island girls weren't meant to fly. That instructor from long ago had told me so. The sky was still not pink. *That's okay,* I thought, *I forgive you. I can be a nurse for a night.*

Being the new kid on the block, I had to work on Christmas Day. I was rostered for a 1 p.m. shift, so I cooked a small roast pork with all the trimmings for lunch with the crew at the airport. I wasn't an island girl for nothing. I arrived early and luckily enough, we had a small window to enjoy a rushed Christmas lunch with the paramedics.

My first job was a small boy who required emergency uplift from Kerang, a small town in northern Victoria. Just to make the day happy, I wore a Santa hat with small flashing lights. We often took small stuffed toys that had been donated by volunteers, and I was in the Christmas spirit, armed with a little stuffed teddy for the occasion.

I watched as this little boy's face lit up when I came out with my Santa's hat flashing and my best Tongan Santa's voice. 'Ho! Ho! Ho! Merry Christmas!'

It was worth the effort as the mother said happily, 'All my son wanted today was Santa. Thank you.'

'Well, I'm the special Santa. I come with a teddy and I will fly you to Melbourne in my special red plane too. Ho! Ho! Ho!' I winked at the little boy who clutched the little handmade teddy I'd given him. It was one of those special moments that made working on Christmas day very pleasurable.

On a quiet day in early March, I went to answer the phone, thinking it was a mission. 'Hello, Royal Flying Doctor Service.'

'Hello, can I please speak to Vaisiliva McLeod?' The female voice sounded very businesslike.

'Yes. Speaking,' I answered cautiously. I was worried because no one calls me by my full name.

'I'm calling from Virgin Blue Airlines. My name is Carmel and I'm from the recruitment department. Are you still interested in a job with us?'

'Are you kidding me? Of course I'm interested. This isn't a hoax, is it?'

'No Vaisiliva, this is not a hoax. I would like to invite you for an interview if you like—'

'Sorry, to interrupt you; how did you get my details?' I was still sceptical.

'Your staff CV was on the employment database. Could you please update it after this, but in the meantime, we can book a date for your interview, if you like.'

'Sure.' I was dumbfounded as I hadn't updated my staff CV in two years.

I hung up but stood staring at the phone, trying to digest what she'd said. I was content with my career at the RFDS and was not actively looking elsewhere. As far as I was concerned, I'd accomplished every expectation in my flying career when I'd joined the RFDS. But here I was — I'd been offered an interview with one of the major airlines in Australia.

As always, I called Ken.

'Wow! That came from nowhere. What are you going to do?'

'It happened so quickly and I've agreed to an interview. I think I'll have to do it.'

When I got back to the apartment, my heart skipped a beat as I saw Ken's truck. I was so glad that he'd come over as I needed to hear his thoughts, see his face and read his body language.

He opened the door and it was obvious he was excited. He gave me a bear hug that nearly winded me.

'Ken, my heart tells me to stay with RFDS, but my head screams at me to go for it. What shall I do?'

'Look, it's only an interview. Aren't you excited to see what it's all about? You don't even know whether you have what airlines are looking for. You already have your dream job, so see it as an experience, a bit of fun.'

'Oh Ken, you always filter my head and open my heart. I feel better already. I didn't tell my boss as I feared being tagged as disloyal and I don't want to burn my bridges.'

'Liva, don't think you're indispensable. What will be, will be. Let's go out for dinner. I'm hungry.'

But my inner self kept asking whether I was taking on something beyond my capabilities. I'd been flying turboprop aircraft to this point. Could I now embark on a jet career?

Despite my uncertainty and with Ken's support, I catapulted forward with preparations for the interview. Ken accompanied me to Brisbane, where it was held. When I faced the interview panel of three men, every little bit of confidence I had deserted me. The questions were relentless. Just when I felt relaxed and thought I was in control, the HR personnel asked, 'What was the hardest thing you've had to do throughout your career to get here?'

Really? Have you got all day? I was scared that once I opened my mouth, old wounds would burst open again. *Deep breath and let it out.*

'When I left my husband and our two girls to fend for themselves in my selfish pursuit of my flying career overseas. There's no greater sacrifice than that. I carry that sadness and guilt with me always.' My voice trailed off as it threatened to betray me.

There was dead silence in the room. I wasn't sure whether I'd answered the question as intended but I couldn't take it back.

I managed to suppress the stinging at the back of my eyes. *I can't show weaknesses if I want to fly a Boeing 737.*

Day one of the interview process was over, but the flight simulator assessment was still to come. Four of us were in the simulator session. I was the only woman. How intimidating was that? The check captain walked in with an air of arrogance, all puffed up and looked straight into our eyes. 'I don't want anyone talking. I don't want to know where you come from or what you've done before.'

What an arsehole.

'When you've finished, you'll walk straight out that door,' he pointed to it, 'and do not engage in conversation with one another until you're out of the building.'

Yes sir. Okay! Got it, loud and clear. I wanted to run and never return. *Goddamn, this is not good. Ah well, the worst that can happen is failing.* Grandpa's infamous saying resonated loudly in my ears. 'You only fail when you quit. Do you hear me, girl?'

When the first candidate came out from his sim session, he looked red and disheartened and made no eye contact with any of us. He gathered his bag and left the building.

'Silva. Next,' Captain Puffer Fish yelled out.

Okay! Showtime!

I'd never seen a Boeing 737 cockpit before, only in magazines and on the internet. A quick scan and I recognized the controls I needed to fly a plane and ignored the bells and whistles I didn't understand.

I was positioned on runway 16 in Melbourne, as per the brief. I took off and completed the aerial exercises. Everything went well. I came back to land, but where was the runway? Shit! *What should I do? Better do something, Liva. You can't continue.* I lost it and squealed in my high-pitched nervous voice, 'Going around. Shit! I don't know how to go around in this thing. Handing over.'

Seriously? What the fuck was that? I don't belong here. I want to go back to my comfort zone with my beloved King Air at RFDS. This beast is way out of my league.

'Oh, I meant to remove the cloud base. Sorry about that,' Captain Puffer Fish said.

Yeah, right. Whatever!

'You're 500 feet runway 16 Melbourne, fully configured. All you have to do is land the aircraft,' he continued.

I was already in stress mode with smoke coming out of my ears. I smacked that piece of tarmac in front of me, glad to be on the ground again, if you could call that a landing. Now I knew why the first candidate had looked the way he did when he'd come out.

I left the simulator centre feeling deflated, happy to put as much distance between me and that building as I could. I was meant to wait for Ken to pick me up but I wasn't hanging around there, that was for sure.

The pressure of the last few weeks had been all for nothing. Tears of disappointment at my performance poured without shame. Then I started to giggle, remembering what my father-in-law had said numerous times. 'Do you know your problem, Liva? Your bladder is too close to your eyes.' But Grandma Nane had always said, 'Those who shed tears, their hearts are full of love.' I think I like Grandma's version.

When Ken got to the sim centre I was nowhere to be seen. 'Where the hell are you now, Liva?' he said when I answered my phone.

'I'm walking.'

'Where?' He sounded worried and pissed off at the same time.

'I don't know where I am. I came out of the building and turned right and kept walking. I thought you would see me.'

'I probably didn't come that way. Stop wherever you are. I'll find you.'

He found me. My mentor, my rock, hopped out of the car and held me while I convulsed on the curbside.

'Ken, I always felt that being an island girl, I had to prove above and beyond to be recognized. I put so much pressure on myself and I can't help that. It's only you I can be an idiot with and you never judge me.'

'I love you and I don't know how else to tell you that you're stupid to think like that. It's all in your head. Come on, get in the car.'

If Virgin Blue offers me a position, that would be great but if not, I gave it my best shot and will still be the happiest pilot ever to serve out the rest of my flying days with RFDS.

I was approaching my 46th birthday and was by no means old, but in the aviation world I was almost expired material. I wished the old saying that wine tastes better with age was true for me.

I was at home on my day off one Friday when the phone rang and startled me from my breadmaking session. I noticed it was a Queensland number.

'Hello?'

'Congratulations Vaisiliva, you've been accepted ...' I didn't hear the rest, my legs had gone to jelly. 'Are you still there? We're delighted to offer you a first officer's position in the B737 based in Brisbane.'

I cringed when I heard Brisbane but, heck, I'd been everywhere so that didn't pose any problem. 'Thank you very much. I'm honoured to be part of Virgin Blue.'

I sat down and looked up at the sky as I'd done many times in the past and gave thanks to the dream dispatcher. I called Ken but he didn't answer, so I left a message.

Oh Lord, I hope that soon I'll make enough money so my Ken can retire. He's done so much for me and now it's my turn to take care of him.

Without him, I wouldn't be where I am today. Please give us a few more years. 'Lord hear my prayer.'

I was lost in my thoughts and didn't hear when Ken came home. He startled me out of my reverie, armed with a bunch of yellow roses. I looked up to the familiar loving face I craved.

'Congratulations!' He beamed as he hugged me. 'You did it. I'm so proud.' I was overwhelmed that the last fifteen years of study, sacrifices and living apart had finally paid dividends.

We were both happy as we chatted about this life-changing news, but when I told him of my Brisbane base it was met with silence.

To leave the RFDS was insane. The job meant so much to me. But I was so close to a bigger pay packet, which would secure us financially. Ken could retire and I would take care of him.

There was no turning back.

27

The Virgin granny

It was a summer morning and Ken and I were having breakfast when Elizabeth turned up at our home, unannounced, with a grin on her face like a split coconut.

'Ta da!' She pulled something from her pocket. 'I'm pregnant.'

I had never seen a pregnancy test before, but it was a no-brainer to figure out what it was. I jumped up and gave her the biggest hug ever. Ken, maybe a bit shocked, was slow to join in.

'Oh my god, we're going to be grandparents!' I screamed with delight.

Ken's health issues were all but forgotten, I had the perfect job and another generation was on the way. Life couldn't be better.

'I'm going to be a grandma. I'd better start doing what grandmas do,' I said to Ken.

'And what's that, darl?'

'Knitting.'

That was exactly what I did. Apart from flying the plane and rescuing the world, I had a new job title — granny. I started my role by knitting a baby shawl.

My starting date with Virgin Blue was scheduled for September, four months since my interview. My B737 endorsement was conducted at the Qantas simulator training centre in Melbourne.

It was a giant leap from turboprop to jet aircraft. The training was tough; it was cruel and it was torture. But it was another mission accomplished.

Much to my delight, I ended up being given a Sydney position, which was more desirable than Brisbane. I commuted for a while until a Melbourne base became available.

I arrived in Melbourne on 2 October 2007. I was deep in thought as I wandered through the terminal towards my car when I received a call from Ken. 'Hi, darl. Thought you might want to know Liz is in labour at Frankston Hospital.'

'Oh! Okay, I'll go there first.'

'I'll see you there.'

I arrived at the hospital, striding in with purpose and perhaps too quick for a granny. *What should a granny be like?* I smiled at the thought. I entered the room and saw Lizzie with a baby in her arms and I couldn't hold back my tears. It was beautiful to see both mum and bub were fine. She looked smitten, and so she should. *Did I look like that, holding Lizzie many moons ago?* I walked over to the bed where Liz sat with her bundle of joy and opened the little bunny rug to reveal his gorgeous little white face and a mop of black hair.

I hugged Lizzie. 'Oh my god, he's perfect, just like his mama.'

'Malakai Blake Montgomery, meet Nanny,' Lizzie said, handing over her son.

'Aw, a Tongan name? I love it. Malakai, I love you and you look just like Nanny.'

'Don't get a big head, Mum. I just like the name Malakai,' Lizzie said.

'Oh! Pa's not here yet?'

As if he'd heard me, Ken walked in with a big grin on his face as he saw me with Malakai in my arms. He took the baby with such ease, just like all those years before with Elizabeth. Ah yes, he was smitten too.

I looked at him with Malakai, remembering that I'd been sad I couldn't give him a son. Now he had a grandson.

It was surreal that I'd been blessed with the birth of our first grandchild and, subsequently, the birth of my airline career. I giggled at the thought of my passengers hearing that a granny was their pilot.

I had been with Virgin Blue for ten months when I saw an internal advertisement for a pilot position based in Auckland with Pacific Blue. That was the sister company of Virgin Blue in New Zealand. It would be based on a secondment contract.

'I lodged my expression of interest for the pilot position in New Zealand,' I announced at the Melbourne crew room one morning.

'Huh, good luck with that. You're so junior you'll never get a look in,' one of the pilots said without looking my way.

'You have to be in it to win it, right? Did you apply, you jealous puss?' I laughed, but deep down, I believed him. *I'd like to know what makes him think he's superior and can muscle around with his cheap comments. Ego!*

It had been a while since the lodgement, with no news. I'd forgotten about it.

Ken and I took two weeks' holiday. While we were gone, I received a call from my base manager.

'Sorry to bother you on your holiday. Have you got a minute?' he said.

'Sure. I'm fishing in South Australia.'

'Nice one, but what would you say if I offered you one of the secondment positions in New Zealand?'

'Are you serious? I would give you a kiss right now.' *Not politically correct but that's how happy I feel.*

'Ha ha! You're funny, Silva. The contract will be in the mail but I'll see you next week. Enjoy the fishing.'

I was shaking my head in disbelief when Ken asked, 'What was that all about?'

'Virgin is offering me one of the positions in New Zealand, but Ken, there's no reason you can't close your business and come with me. It's only for twelve months.'

He scowled. 'Liva, you promised me this is it. Will you ever be happy?'

'Ken, this is a great opportunity to discover New Zealand properly instead of weeks here, weeks there. It would be like a working holiday. Please don't shoot it down. We still have a week to think about it. How cool would it be to fly the red jet to Tonga?'

I couldn't tell whether he was angry or just tired of trying to keep up with all my changes. I'd shifted the goal posts time and time again.

On our drive home, he said, 'I guess it would be fun to live in New Zealand for a year. I can organize my work and tidy up loose ends and won't take on any more jobs. I think it will work. I'll come with you, but what about my monthly appointments with Dr Wolf?'

'Whoa! Yes! It will be a lot of fun. Thank you, thank you, darl. Of course I can request for my roster to accommodate your monthly appointments. You won't have to miss any. I'll come with you.'

Thanks to the benefit of staff travel privileges, we were able to commute monthly to Australia for his medical appointments.

At last, I got to share my experience with the darling man I'd dubbed the wind beneath my wings. We spent two months in Christchurch and the rest of the secondment in Auckland. Ken and I got to explore both the North and South Islands of New Zealand. He accompanied me on a lot of my inter-island trips, where I sometimes had two to three nights' layover.

My first trip to Tonga in the big red jet, the Boeing 737, was something special. The flight was made up of 75 per cent Tongan passengers and I had the pleasure of making my PA in English followed by my native tongue version, just like the previous time I'd flown in Tonga. When we got closer to Tonga and I was transferred from New Zealand to Fuaʻamotu air traffic control, I couldn't help myself as I made my radio call. 'Malo lelei, Fuaʻamotu Tower, bluebird zero-six-one.'

It was met with silence before the air traffic controller responded with almost a question in her voice. 'Hm, malo lelei to you too, bluebird zero-six-one. Go ahead.'

'On descent passing FL290, cleared FL150.'

'Clear VOR/DME arrival. Runway 11. Call again 30 miles tango bravo uniform,' she commanded.

We were the only aeroplane in her airspace, so I knew very well that she was busting to know who I was. As if she could hear my thoughts, the radio crackled again. 'Is that you, Liva?'

'Busted!' I said. I could run but I couldn't hide. Being a female pilot who happened to speak Tongan, it hadn't been too hard to guess.

By the time I landed, every Tom, Dick and Harry was at the tarmac to greet me.

'The coconut radio never fails,' I laughed, then said to my captain, 'I will have to educate you on the three Fs.'

He looked aghast as he said, 'What?'

'Not like that,' I laughed. 'Family, food and funerals. Tongans do them like no one else. I will show you only two Fs today: family and food minus funerals. I'll be back.'

With that, I left to meet my family. As I stepped out of the aircraft I heard screaming. 'Hi, Liva! Liva!' I looked up to where the voices came from and saw my sister Selai and her family waving from the observation deck. Selai had moved with her family and now resided in Nuku'alofa. She was so proud, and as we hugged, she said, 'Who would think? I'm walking on air right now, Sis. I'm so proud of you. I wish Grandma and Grandpa could see you.'

'Yes, I wish too. So much loss. Please don't make me cry. I'm in uniform.' She had already prepared a box of food for me as she was aware of the quick turnaround time.

'All cooked with love, Skip,' I said, arriving back on the flight deck.

I was surprised that the crew had never seen some of these foods before, even though half of the Tongan population lived in New Zealand. We couldn't take the food into New Zealand so what we couldn't eat had to stay in the aircraft. Ken missed out.

I always requested to operate the once-weekly service from Sydney to Tonga. On one particular flight we were sitting on the tarmac in Sydney fully loaded but we were delayed, and we weren't quite sure why. Then the engineer said that we were waiting for the Tongan prime minister.

'Sure, whatever. I've been waiting for the president of America,' I mocked.

Then I looked up and there he was, the Tongan prime minister with his entourage approaching the aircraft. 'Oh! That's Fred,' I said.

'Do you know him?' the captain asked, giving me a surprised look.

'Sure. I used to know him when he was just plain Fred but now he's the Honourable Fred. We used to play tennis together when I was flying in Tonga.'

'Go on, then. Go and meet him,' he said, clearly disbelieving.

To his surprise, I got up and headed out of the flight deck just in time. 'Good afternoon Fred ... sir.' I corrected myself in time, greeting my prime minister as if he was still my tennis buddy.

'Well! Well! Silva, is that why you disappeared from the tennis circuit? I'm impressed. So good to see you. You've done well for yourself.' He beamed as we embraced.

'You did well for yourself too, I see. I hope you still have time for a game now and then. It's a pleasure to be of service to you, sir. What shall I call you?'

'You can still call me Fred, as always.'

'Welcome aboard. I've got work to do but I'll pop back once we're in cruise.'

I was busy but once we were in flight, I started to reminisce about my time flying in Tonga. 'I used to fly the royal family. I have flown the

King, Queen, Crown Prince, princess, members of the royal household and now my prime minister.'

When I got back from that trip, Ken picked me up from Auckland airport. 'Guess who I had in my flight today? My first VIP passenger in the red jet. Prime Minister Fred.'

'Whoever Fred is,' Ken mumbled. I often detected a hint of jealousy when I mentioned men I'd played tennis, golf or flown with, so I dropped the subject as we chatted about his next appointment in Melbourne.

We shared the rent of a penthouse at the Viaduct in Auckland Harbour with two other pilot friends. They loved having Ken there. It was a great feeling to come back after a trip and Ken was there waiting for me. It felt as if we were on a long holiday — no housework or gardening to do, not even bills to pay.

'Virgin Blue asked me if I would like to extend my secondment for another six months. How do you feel about that, Ken?' I asked over dinner.

'Although it's been an amazing long holiday, I need to be doing something. You can stay if you want but I might go back home to work.'

Ken was a worker and he'd allow me to achieve so much. 'Then home we go. I can't be too greedy, and yes, it's been a wonderful time having you here with me too. Your presence added a different kind of joy to my job — completeness. I know it must be hard for you and I do appreciate you.' I walked over and hugged my biggest fan.

In April 2009, we packed up and bid farewell to Aotearoa. We came home and Ken returned to his electrical business and picked up where he'd left off. Because I was on a secondment contract with Pacific Blue in New Zealand, I'd retained my Melbourne position with Virgin Blue flying domestically, so I went straight back to work too.

Ken was at work one cold winter's day when my phone rang and startled me. 'Hello?'

'Silva, this is Paul, flight operation manager for V-Australia.'

'What have I done to be granted such a privilege?' I asked cheekily. I'd flown with him at Virgin Blue.

'I would like to offer you a first officer's position on the B777 with V-Australia, Sydney base. It's short notice but the course is scheduled for 4 July and I would like an answer ASAP.'

Without second thought I said, 'Yes.' Again!

'Congratulations and good luck with your upcoming training. I could be your sim buddy. The training coordinator will be in contact to let you know the program.'

When I was a student pilot, I'd seen a picture in a magazine of the first Boeing fly-by-wire jet — B777. I'd been enthralled by its beauty. I'd enlarged and framed that photo and it had hung on the wall of my study since 1994. Never in my wildest dreams had I thought I would get to fly it. But V-Australia was Virgin Blue's international independent company and they were offering me a position on the B777.

Then I heard a car door being slammed. *Oh shit. Ken.*

'Oh! Hello, darl. You're home early.'

He gave me a kiss, put his lunch box away and went to the lounge room and turned the TV on.

'Would you like a coffee?' I called out.

'What do you want, Liva?'

I pretended I didn't hear him and made two coffees and joined him in the lounge.

'Ken, we need to talk. I've been offered a position in V-Australia, flying B777 long haul international—'

'What? You must be very happy about that. Are you going to take it?'

'Yes, I've accepted it already.'

'So why the serious look?'

'That's why I needed to talk to you. Sydney will be my base but I'm hoping it will be short-term.'

Ken's excited look was replaced by annoyance. I quickly raised my finger before he shut me out. 'Please hear me out. It will be hard for the first six weeks of my training. Commuting for long-haul will be easier than domestic—'

'Are you listening to yourself, Liva? You promised me no more separation. You know what? Do whatever you want to do.' He turned up the volume of the TV while I sat stunned.

'I'm sorry.' I got up to cook dinner. We ate in silence.

I couldn't sleep that night. My mind was in overdrive, trying to figure out a way to tell my boss that I wouldn't be taking the new position. In the middle of the night, I got up and walked into the study and stared at the cockpit picture of the B777 on the wall. *You'll always remain the mystery aircraft. So close, yet so far. I'll never get to fly you. I love Ken more.* I was startled as hands came around my shoulders. 'That's enough. Come to bed. We'll talk about it tomorrow,' Ken said.

The next morning, I got up with Ken for breakfast. I wanted to hear his thoughts.

'I've told you in the past I'd never stand between you and your dream. If that's what you want, of course I have your back. We'll make it work,' he said.

'Thank you. We've always made it work. We're a team, Ken. I could never do it without you and you know that. I need you on board 100 per cent.'

My love for flying had grown from the sheer exhilaration of being like a bird to a feeling of great achievement that I'd never thought would be possible for an island girl. I could explore the world with the other love of my life.

My first flight was from Sydney to Los Angeles with four pilots and fifteen flight attendants. Walking through Sydney International Airport, I couldn't have been any prouder — an island girl, and one of colour, was an international airline pilot responsible for the safety of over 300 people. The place was buzzing with people going on vacation and everyone was happy. *This is where I want to be, surrounded by happiness. Could someone pinch me?* After flight planning and briefing the crew, we made our way through security, passport control, duty-free shops, restaurants, coffee shops and finally arrived at the gate where the B777 was waiting for us.

God, she's big. I couldn't see her tail.

If I'd had any nerves before I arrived at the cockpit, they were nowhere to be found as I had no time to scratch myself once I was at the helm. Watching passengers coming down the aerobridge, I wondered how they could all fit. Three hundred and thirty passengers plus crew with fuel and cargo loaded; we then began taxiing for departure.

It was a typical September morning. The sun was shining but the temperature was fresh with a light wind. We reached the departure end of the runway, only to queue up. In front of us were an Airbus 380, Boeing 747 and other big jet liners. Our turn came when I heard the air traffic controller say, 'V-OZ one, runway 34 left, cleared for take-off.'

I released the brakes, advanced the throttle and set thrust, pushed the TOGA switch as the thrust levers moved forward, the engines spooled up, and the aircraft roared as it accelerated down the runway.

'Eighty knots,' the auto called out.

'Check,' I said, checking my airspeed.

'V one.'

'Rotate.'

I eased the huge aircraft off the tarmac and watched the ground fall away. Within seconds, all my troubles were behind me as I soared like an eagle. Australia was left behind before we'd reached altitude. This was the phase of flight I loved most — the power being applied, the speed, the adrenaline rush as I became weightless, defying gravity as I soared up, up and away.

The aircraft nose pointed northeast and there was only the ocean below and the sky above with the horizon ahead that we would never reach. That moment I was colourless, genderless and fearless. As I penetrated through the cloud tops, I thought, *If Heaven looks like this, then I'm in Heaven. I hope you can see me Mum, Grandma, Grandpa. Thank you, Ken, thank you, Lord, for the life I have.*

The fourteen-hour flight felt like fourteen minutes. We were transferred from Oceanic into American airspace. It was a nightmare as I tried to decipher what the air traffic controller was saying. 'V-OZ one, blah, blah, blah ...'

'What is it with that accent? Um, what did he say?' I asked the rest of the crew.

'V-OZ one, identified, 100 miles west of Ficky. At Ficky, cleared Leena four arrival, reduce minimum speed.'

The captain read back all the instructions as we were required to do. I was flying so I didn't have to deal with the radio calls. However, I still needed to listen to be compliant with the clearance.

Approaching and landing are the most critical phases of flight and it was intense on the flight deck. I soon heard, 'V-OZ one, runway 25 left, cleared to land.'

I lowered the huge aircraft onto the runway. I'd accomplished the unimaginable. The black duck had landed at LAX with its four runways.

There were aircraft everywhere. I cleared my head as I still had to navigate to our assigned gate. Once parked, with the brakes set and the engines shut down, I breathed. *Mission accomplished.*

In the arrival hall, I was coming down on the escalator, lost in my own thoughts, when I looked up at a photo of Barack Obama, the President of the United States, flashing his white teeth down at me, welcoming me to his great nation. It had been a year and a half since he'd been elected the first black president of the United States. I'd never dreamed I'd live to see that but there I was, staring at the evidence. I felt jubilant at being a black woman who'd just landed a B777 into the third busiest airport in the world. I'd harnessed my quixotic dream and finally captured it. Had he dreamed of becoming president from an early age?

By the time we got to the hotel, my head was so heavy, longing for the pillow. I'd thought working for the Royal Flying Doctor Service had primed me for red-eye flying but nothing had prepared me for how I felt now. But first, I had to let Ken know I'd arrived safely and wasn't floating somewhere in the Pacific Ocean.

I simply texted, 'The eagle has landed.' He never saw the funny side when I referred to myself as black, so I purposely didn't say 'black duck'.

'Rest well and we'll speak later,' the reply came back.

It was after midnight in Australia and I knew he would have been asleep, but he always texted back. I closed my eyes as I allowed exhaustion to take over.

I loved this aspect of my flying: seeing the world, different countries, people from all walks of life and cultures. Thanks to the B777, together with the love of my life we got to experience South Africa, North America, Europe, Asia and the Middle East.

In 2010, Ken and I moved out of our two-storey brick home of 30 years, a home that had been built with a lot of love and sweat. But we both loved our new home and it wasn't long before we were making more happy memories.

'How long do you think you're going to fly for?' Ken asked.

I looked at him, not sure where the conversation was going. 'I don't know but I'm way too young to be retiring. You can, though, if you want; play as much golf and fish all you like.'

'That's not a good look. Me retiring while you're still working.'

'Do I detect a bit of male ego here, Ken?' I teased.

I still loved my flying. It gave me independence, a sense of accomplishment, not to mention financial freedom. It enabled us to get Ken the best medical help whenever he needed it and we could indulge a little.

Not long after that conversation, Ken retired after 42 years in the trade. He joined the local golf club and played twice weekly. He made new friends. One of them was Doug, who was as passionate as Ken about golf and fishing. Doug had his own health issues and they were a constant company for each other. They had a lot of fun but, importantly, they understood each other's limitations.

At the end of 2011, I watched with pride as Ken walked Tema, our baby, down an aisle of grapevines on her wedding day. He looked more nervous than when he'd walked Lizzie six years earlier but still looked handsome, even with his silvery hair.

'Ana turned up once again, armed with her mats and tapa cloth. The surprise came when my niece Kelsey walked onto the stage dressed in Tongan costume, dripping in coconut oil, and performed a traditional Tongan dance.

Tema and her husband, Andrew, were going to Geneva via Abu Dhabi for their honeymoon. I saw this as an opportunity to pull some strings and surprise Tema.

The day before their trip, I asked Tema casually. 'How would you feel if I was your pilot on your honeymoon trip tomorrow?'

Tema looked stunned. 'What do you mean?'

'I mean, I swapped my roster around so I can fly you at least halfway on your trip to Abu Dhabi.'

'Wow! Oh my god! Mum, how many daughters out there can actually say that their mum flew them on their honeymoon? That's awesome. I can't wait to tell Andrew.' She lunged forward and hugged me with tears streaming down her face.

On the day of the flight, I arrived at Sydney international terminal to find it buzzing with people of different races, colours and languages. The PA system was blasting out in a language other than English. I was amazed at how times had changed from when I'd first arrived in Australia in 1981. *I would die if I heard the Tongan language through the PA.* I started to giggle.

I dropped my crew bag at the counter then went looking for Tema and Andrew. They had already checked in.

'When you're ready, go through and I'll see you at the gate. I have to go upstairs. I have work to do,' I told them.

I was so busy I didn't get to see Tema and Andrew until about two hours into the flight. However, the flight attendants kept me informed of their whereabouts. Much to their delight, they were upgraded to business class. Another perk of the job that I'm grateful for. It didn't take long to find them when I came out of the flight deck. I only saw them again an hour before landing.

We arrived in Abu Dhabi at midnight. The gratification I felt for transferring over 300 passengers across two continents was humbling. I was given the responsibility for their safety and I'd delivered. As the passengers disembarked, I could hear everyone saying. 'Thanks guys for a great flight.'

We weren't allocated a gate so we had to bus our passengers to the terminal. Tema and Andrew waited to ride with me in the crew bus. They were staying with me at my crew hotel before leaving for Geneva the next day.

Once in the privacy of our hotel room, I asked Tema. 'How was the flight? Did I do good?'

'You're fishing for a compliment, Mum,' she teased. 'But yes. Amazing! I've got to tell you, when you made your PA, I wanted to stick my head up and tell everyone "That's my mum". But it didn't sound like you.'

'Oh? How did I sound?'

'Very businesslike, "don't mess with me"-like,' she laughed. 'Seriously, I'm so proud of you. I feel very privileged. I'll never forget it.'

28

Tell death I'm not ready

New Year's Eve, 31 December 2013. I was getting ready for a trip from Melbourne to Los Angeles. As always, I was having a shower while Ken made a coffee. I made a final checklist of what to take in my flight bag and suitcase. Once satisfied, I sat down to enjoy my coffee with Ken before he helped me get my luggage to the car.

I kissed him goodbye. 'You can borrow another kiss for the new year,' I laughed as I gave him another kiss and another hug. As I drove off, I watched him waving in his dressing gown until I could see him no more. I loved the routine he'd created and dreaded the day I wouldn't see him wave to me again.

The drive to the airport was hideous. It took just over two hours to get to the staff car park. Every time I got to the airport, I felt the same excitement as if I was going on a holiday. Except this time I wasn't with Ken and I would miss the new year in Australia.

Upon arrival at Los Angeles, I texted Ken, 'Happy New Year, darl. The eagle had landed.'

There was no answer, no text to say, 'Rest well, speak tomorrow.' I assumed he was fast asleep and didn't hear his phone.

I called him the next day to wish him a happy new year, and still no answer. After multiple calls with no response, alarm bells went off. I hate inconveniencing friends when it was my choice to be an international pilot, but our girls lived hours away. I had no other choice but to dial the number I'd been staring at.

'Brian, can you please go around and check on Ken? He's not answering. I get the feeling it's not going to be a happy new year.'

'He's probably playing golf or maybe doesn't want to speak to you.' Brian was trying to make light of my concerns. 'I'll go around now and will call you from your house.'

He found Ken unconscious on the floor at home. As he had done numerous times in the past, he called the ambulance then FaceTimed me with an update and I walked him through our wardrobe to pack a hospital bag for Ken.

The disadvantage of being a long-haul pilot hit home. I was helpless on another continent and it could be days before I got home.

Three days after that dreadful FaceTime conversation with Brian, I walked into Frankston hospital ICU, grateful that Ken was still alive. Having multiple myeloma with a shit immune system meant that ongoing infections were part and parcel of Ken's life, *our* life.

When I walked in, his face lit up, then he broke down. I increased my pace with my outstretched arms ready to embrace him. He looked so vulnerable and alone.

Lynette was there as well. 'Ken's been watching that door all morning. He knew you were going to walk through any time,' she said.

As we hugged, the tears of joy, relief and fear all rolled out freely.

In a few short days, Ken recovered and was back at home. It was not a good start to 2014, but the arrival of Leilani Joyce, grandchild number four, was something to be celebrated. Leilani (meaning garland of Heaven) was a Tongan name and popular with the Polynesians.

'How lucky are we, Ken? We have two grandsons, Malakai and Harlem, and two granddaughters, Eleanor and now Leilani. What more could we want?' I said excitedly.

'God help us all,' he said but couldn't keep the smile off his face.

Six months later, on the night of 5 December 2014, Ken was again not well. Initially, I thought he had a cold but he started to feel nauseated. 'Ken, I think we better get the ambulance,' I begged throughout the night.

'No, I'm fine, I'm fine. We'll see in the morning.' By the early hours of the next morning, I knew Ken needed help. I didn't ask for his permission this time, I went ahead and dialled triple zero and the ambulance arrived soon after.

The paramedics checked his heart, blood pressure and temperature. 'Ken probably needs to see the doctor. We can take him or you can take him to his GP.'

Ken didn't look right. I moved up to our bed so he could hear me. 'What do you want, darl?' I whispered, stroking his head.

'I want to go to hospital,' he said in a weak voice. The look he gave me split my heart in two. He hated hospital and yet he was asking to go there.

They took Ken to the small local hospital of Rosebud. I cleaned up, had breakfast then followed. It was only a ten-minute drive. When I got there, Ken was still in the emergency department. He was in a cubicle with only curtains dividing him from the next bed.

'There you are,' he said, looking up as I entered.

'I told you I wouldn't be long.' I sat down beside his hospital bed. 'You look better already.'

'I wish I was feeling better.' He closed his eyes. I noticed some drugs were being admitted intravenously. The nurse told me they were antibiotics.

I hadn't been holding his hand for long when he tugged at me, signalling he couldn't breathe. I was shocked to see he'd gone blue. 'Nurse, help!'

I'd seen nurses and doctors move as fast as this before when Ken had been having chemo. I was so scared.

One of the nurses ushered me out. 'Mrs McLeod, could you please come with me? You should wait in the waiting room.'

But I'd seen that Ken wasn't breathing any more. The medical staff were frantically trying to resuscitate him.

There were a lot of people in the waiting room. I picked an empty chair far away from everyone else and watched the wall clock. *Oh Lord, just one more time. Please, please, please don't take my Ken away. Not yet. Please hear my prayer.*

After what seemed like a lifetime, a grim-faced doctor took me into a private room. So many questions were in my head but none came out. I rocked back and forth to stop myself from peeing.

'Ken went into anaphylaxis. He's alive, but we had to do CPR. He was gone for eight minutes,' the doctor said in almost a whisper.

I could barely hear what she said. *He's alive*, but I understood what she meant. 'Eight minutes? That's a fucking long time.' My heart hurt and the tears were uncontrollable.

The doctor tried to calm me. 'We had to put him into a medically induced coma to keep him alive. The air ambulance is on its way. Ken will be airlifted to a city hospital but I'm not sure which one. We'll update you on that, but we still have a lot to do before he's ready to be transported. I'll come and get you to see him as soon as I can.'

I tried to regroup, wiped the tears, then rang work to cancel my duty for the next day. I then rang Lizzie and Tema.

After that, I went in to see Ken, but of course, he was in a coma. There was a bit of blood on his pillow that I tried to ignore. I resisted the urge to go and change it but it wasn't the time or place to do that. He might as well have been dead for I didn't recognize him with all the tubes hanging from the lifeless body. *I've seen him in this state before and he still refused to give up.*

'Oh, Ken, my love, how can it be? I'm so sorry but you must get better. It's just another hurdle we have to get over. We've done this before, we can do it again. Please stay with me. Just stay, one more time.'

Ken didn't answer as I sobbed alone by his side, holding his hand, waiting for the squeeze that never came.

The helicopter arrived and they took him to yet another major hospital. I was advised later that Frankston was their destination. Eventually, I arrived at the now-familiar Frankston Hospital ICU. I was briefed by the physician who was looking after him. 'Silva, we won't know how much, if any, brain damage Ken may have suffered until he wakes up. He might have sustained some brain injuries and we want to prepare you for the worst,' she said.

'I feel confident of a full recovery, doc. Whatever state or however Ken is when he wakes up, we'll go home together as we came here.'

But if only she could have seen my insides. Terrified was an understatement.

For seven days Lizzie, Tema and I rotated in shifts at Ken's bedside, waiting for him to wake up. Finally, on day eight, our prayers were answered once again. I often wondered if God would eventually get sick of me asking.

'Ken woke up happy and singing,' one of the nurses told me, laughing. 'Does he sing a lot at home?'

'Ha ha! Never. Ken couldn't sing to save himself,' I said. Apparently, the nurses were being entertained with his version of 'Bye Bye Blackbird'. I'd never heard that song before, so I had to look it up on the internet.

Thankfully, the brain scan and MRI showed little damage to the nerve endings and it wasn't expected to affect his daily living. However, Ken had to learn to speak again and do basic chores like feeding himself, walking and so on.

He spent four weeks at a rehab hospital and in recovery at home. I took time off to help him get back on his feet. The recovery was long and arduous, but he didn't fail me, as he made a full recovery, enough to enjoy his golf and fishing again.

Sadly, we had to say goodbye to Ken's dad that year. I couldn't help thinking that for the life we'd lost, Ken had been spared.

Three days after Dad passed, we welcomed Loxy Silva, followed by Grayson Neil, both named after Ken and me. A couple of years later,

Orlando Harper arrived and made the final lucky seven grandchildren for us.

At this point of my life, I often told the boys at the flight deck, 'I'm the luckiest girl on earth right now. A grandmother to seven beautiful little souls, a wonderful career and a husband who loves me unconditionally.' Except I knew we were living on borrowed time as Ken continued to cheat death. 'Tell death I'm not ready,' he often said. But I knew sooner or later he would use up all his lifelines. Until then, we still had a lot of living to do.

One thing on my bucket list was to erect a headstone to mark the burial place of my beloved grandparents. It had been 30 years since my grandfather had passed and fourteen since my grandma, but the family couldn't afford to erect a headstone. Ken's health was deteriorating slightly but he refused to acknowledge it. He knew how important this mission was to me. He decided at the last minute to accompany me on my trip to Tonga. Once again, my selfishness overtook any common sense, as I hoped that a trip to Vava'u might reignite his will to live. The place of our humble beginnings had so many happy memories.

We arrived in Vava'u on Friday, 11 May 2018. I'd been back many times since I'd lost my grandma and yet I still looked for her. My uncle Lopeti (the only one still left in our village) was waiting for us at the airport.

'I'm sorry, Lopeti, but the days of Ken sleeping on the floor are over,' I said. 'I've booked us at a holiday apartment in town, mainly for Ken but I'll still come home.'

'Liva, I'm glad that you're still thinking of us and coming to visit. It's about time you took care of Ken. He's no longer the strong young man we used to know.'

'Thank you. I hope our people don't judge me.'

'If they do, let them, Liva. I gave up caring a long time ago. Be kind to yourself.' He gave me a hug; he knew the young island girl was still in me.

All the times I'd taken Ken back to Vava'u, he'd had to endure primitive conditions in my village. But with Grandma no longer there, I decided to get Ken comfortable. The apartment had a waterfront view and wasn't far from the hotel where we'd first met and fell in love. Sadly, the hotel had been destroyed by Cyclone Waka.

I elected Mother's Day 2018 for the blessing and unveiling of the headstone. Ken woke up not feeling well, but I shrugged it off, thinking it was the heat. 'Wouldn't you like to come to the Mother's Day service with me?' I said.

'No, darl. I'm so tired. You go. Come and pick me up afterwards, I'll come to the unveiling of Grandma and Grandpa's headstone.'

I attended the Mother's Day service without Ken at the very church where we'd been married 38 years before. A newer building. The beautiful singing was so powerful and evoked so many memories of my yesteryear. As I closed my eyes, I was again that young girl in my village when I still had a mum and grandma. The Methodist service was conducted by the village mothers of the church. The opening hymn was led by one of the older mums. The first lesson was read by another one and so it went. It was shared by young and old mums. After the service, mums, grandmothers and great-grandmothers were invited to be seated at the front and the children placed floral leis around their heads to symbolize the importance of their role as mothers. I was one. I wore a red rose to indicate that my mum had passed but if she'd been alive, I would have worn a white chrysanthemum.

As a child, I'd placed the floral lei on my grandma's head. How bizarre it was that I was back in my village as a mum and grandma, receiving a lei on my head from a young girl like I was once. *I've come full circle,* I thought. I opened my eyes and surveyed the room. Those who'd received a lei from me decades ago were no longer there. I closed my eyes again and remembered my mum, grandma and those of my village elders who were no longer with us.

After the emotional Mother's Day service, I picked up Ken for lunch and the unveiling ceremony at the cemetery. He didn't look well but he said he was fine to go. The unveiling was planned for late afternoon when the sun had gone down and it wasn't too hot.

It was a very intimate ceremony. Uncle Lopeti was the only child of Grandma and Grandpa there. The rest of us were grandchildren and great-grandchildren. Ken junior led the short service and peeled the cover off the headstone to reveal the black marble with a single photo of my beloved grandparents.

'Just how I remember them,' Ken whispered. 'That's very nice, darl.'

'Thank you, without you, it would never have happened,' I whispered back as he rubbed his thumb behind my neck.

Ken was tired and I took him back to our accommodation to rest, then I returned to the village to recap on our day with the family. I returned later to find Ken had been vomiting, which continued throughout the night. By Monday morning, he was feverish with a cold sweat. I had to take him to hospital. How ironic to take him to the very hospital he'd helped build all those years earlier.

Three nights of sheer terror in hell. That was how I described it. Ken was in a four-bed room. All the beds were occupied. The toilet was shared between about six wards. It was 50 metres down the hallway.

The shower wasn't working. Instead, each patient had their own bowl to wash with. The lack of sufficient funds for ongoing maintenance was obvious. Uncle Lopeti slept in his car outside the hospital in case I needed him. Indeed, I couldn't have gotten Ken to the bathroom without his help. Whenever I called, he raced in with a wheelchair.

'Where did you get that wheelchair from?' I asked.

He laughed and shushed me. 'Stop asking questions.'

Ken was grateful for my uncle's thoughtfulness and he didn't care where it came from either.

With no improvement by the third night, I needed to take matters into my own hands or run the risk of losing Ken on my island. *What am I going to do to get us out of here? This is where we began; let's hope this is not how it ends.* I reached for my work iPad, which had international roaming, and dialled our travel insurance in Australia. We were airlifted to Vaiola Hospital in Nuku'alofa the next day but not without more drama. Vava'u hospital couldn't process credit cards, so I had to finalize the hospital bill in cash.

The ambulance took Ken to the airport and I followed with Uncle Lopeti. This time I wasn't sad to leave Vava'u. I was glad to get out and seek help for my darling heart. We arrived at Nuku'alofa airport before lunch and the ambulance was there to collect us. It was a bit better equipped than the one in Vava'u. At least the stretcher had a cover and there was a blanket also. At Vaiola Hospital, Ken had a private room and a proper hospital bed with private amenities. Doctors and nurses fussed around him, getting him comfortable.

I didn't want to leave Ken alone in case he had a turn, so I continued to sleep on the hospital floor beside him. One of the nurses came in during the night for Ken's meds and saw me curled up on the floor.

'Aw, look at your wife, Ken. A white wife would be comfortable in a hotel room but she's elected to be on the floor by your side. You're a lucky man.'

'I know, I'm very lucky.' I heard Ken's voice breaking.

The next day we saw the doctor who'd tended to Ken when we'd arrived. She spoke very good English. 'The best thing for Ken right now is to get him home,' she said. 'He's got complex health issues that we can't help him with here in Tonga.'

'If you can stabilize Ken and get him well enough to travel, I'll take him on the first flight out,' I said.

'We've hydrated him and suppressed the nausea. We need to keep his fever down,' she explained to me before turning to Ken. 'You're looking much better than when you first arrived, Ken. I'll see you tomorrow.'

She came to see Ken on Monday morning, listened to his heart and looked at the report from the night before she asked, 'When are you planning to go back?'

'If you can release Ken now, we'll catch the Air New Zealand flight at noon to Auckland.'

She was taken aback as she checked her watch. 'Hm, okay, we'd better get moving then. At least get him to New Zealand.'

I looked at my watch. It was just after 9 a.m. 'Thank you, Doc,' I said, but she'd already hurried off to prepare the report for Ken's release.

Ken was loaded onto an ambulance by 10 a.m. and we were on our way to Fua'amotu airport. Familiar faces behind the scenes from my early days were still there and only too happy to lend a hand. Once Ken's paperwork had been processed, he was transferred from the ambulance to an airport cart then into an ambulant lift into the aircraft.

I was continually updating our girls in Australia. We were still on the tarmac in Tonga when I wrote a group text to say, 'I've got your father in the plane outbound for Auckland.'

'I'll meet you there,' Tema responded.

'Please ensure your mobile device has been switched off ...' the announcement from the flight attendant came through as I put my phone away. I heard the thrust being advanced and we accelerated down the runway. I looked at Ken's face but couldn't read what he was thinking. I reached for his hand and squeezed it. Feeling the lift-off sensation that I loved about flying and the clunk of the wheels being retracted, he gave me a little smile and only then could I sigh with relief. My worries had been halved. *Hang in there, my love. I'm taking you home.*

I didn't look outside to see Tonga being left behind.

It was a warm feeling when we stepped out at Auckland airport and saw Tema's beaming smile, though I could tell she'd been crying. She'd armed herself with a wheelchair while waiting, but Ken was already in one.

'Aw, great. Is that for me?' I joked while hugging her. She laughed and it broke the sadness of the circumstance, though it quickly returned as she hugged Ken.

We stopped in Auckland to give Ken a rest, then boarded a Virgin Australia flight the next morning. Ah! Familiar territory at last. I knew I could relax as the crew would look after my Ken. It was a full flight and we were seated in row three, close to the front of the aircraft. I had identified myself to the crew and they were aware of Ken's condition.

During the flight, Ken needed to use the bathroom. He took a couple of steps while I supported him from behind then, to my horror, he leaned backwards with his full weight on me. I was unable to support him; the only option I had was to fall with him. I sat in the aisle still holding him while nearby passengers started fussing around but the crew were there instantly. They worked quickly and efficiently and administered oxygen.

When Ken regained consciousness, it took a few seconds for him to take in his surroundings as he whispered to me, 'That was embarrassing. I'm so sorry, darl.'

'Hello, there. Don't be sorry. I'm not. If there's a place to do it, Ken, this is it. My airline, my colleagues and the company that's looked after me for over a decade.' And yes, the Virgin Australia crew stepped up for what they were famous for: caring with a capital C.

Upon arrival in Melbourne, I drove Ken to Frankston Hospital emergency department instead of calling an ambulance. That way I still had some control of where I wanted Ken to be. Not only that, Frankston was more convenient and the closest major hospital to our home, and they knew Ken's health history.

Ken was admitted into the infectious ward, given we'd just arrived from Tonga. It was a horrible reminder of when Ken had been suspected of having AIDS decades ago. I didn't care this time. 'You're safe now, Ken, in your beautiful, clean and comfortable world. I'll go home and have a sleep. I'll see you in the morning,' I said, bending over and kissing him through tears of relief.

'Thank you, darl. You go home and have a good sleep. Heaven knows, I've put you through hell. I'll see you tomorrow.'

When I got home I was hit with a wave of relief and elation that we'd made it home and Ken was being cared for. Sleep was welcomed and I was grateful for the safety and comfort of my home.

I was up the next day, feeling fresh and rested as I made my way back to the hospital. I was with Ken when the team of doctors came in on their rounds. I could pick out who was the ringleader. He was young with a non-Australian background like me. He was the only one who walked in without a notepad. The doctors accompanying were younger and one was wheeling a desk with a screen.

'Sorry, Ken,' the ringleader began. 'The results of your tests confirmed that you contracted dengue fever ... umm, where did you say you came back from?'

'Tonga,' Ken said.

'Okay. You have a bug as well.' *A what? We came from Tonga, not from planet Mars.* 'We'll keep you in for a few days for antibiotics intravenously then you can continue orally at home. All you need is plenty of rest and lots of fluid.'

'What? Dengue fever? It must have been the only mozzie in Tonga. I didn't see any. How lucky are we to have made it back to Australia,' I said.

'With Ken's complex health issues I'm glad you're back here too,' he said before leaving us in bewilderment.

At the end of 2018, it had been fourteen years since Ken's stem cells transplant. We were at the cancer institute for our routine monthly visit.

We were waiting in Dr Wolf's consultation room when he walked in. 'Hello, I can see you brought the reinforcement team today, Ken,' he said, smiling at me. 'Having the day off, Silva?'

'Hi Max,' we both said in unison.

'Ken, your blood test is showing an escalation of your myeloma. We've been watching it for the last few results and it hasn't stabilized. We need to have a bone marrow biopsy to confirm.'

My hand went automatically to my mouth. I reached out to find Ken's hand and squeezed it as if to draw the cancer out.

'You've kept me here this long, Max, I'm sure you still have some tricks left up your sleeves,' Ken said at last, as if Max was God. *Yes, Ken is willing to fight on.*

'See the girls at the desk and they'll schedule your biopsy and next appointment.' He shook Ken's hand. 'Good to see you, Silva. I'll see you next time.'

Ken began a new tablet treatment in the new year. It would be months before we would see a result, if any. He continued with his golf, but had long given up fishing; he was getting unsteady on his feet.

I returned home from LA early in April and found out Ken had had a blackout when he'd stepped out of his car outside the local newsagent. Fortunately, a lady who happened to be a retired nurse saw the whole episode and called an ambulance. She'd stayed with Ken and by the time the ambulance got there, Ken had regained consciousness.

I took extended leave from work to take care of my Ken. From then on, I watched helplessly as the love of my life started on a long, downhill, slippery slope, gathering speed as he slid.

'You should go back to work, Liva, I'm fine,' he said one day. 'It's not good for your flying to take time off for too long.'

'If you hurry up and get better, I will. I can't focus at work while you're falling all over the place,' I said. 'I need to be home. I want to be home with you.'

'I'm worried about you. Too much study to get back, but I kind of like it that you're home,' he confessed.

'Me too, darl, me too.'

As a result of his blackout, we were referred to a vascular surgeon. It was discovered that Ken had double blocked carotid arteries. It was back to the operating theatre for a vascular repair. He was in hospital for a few days then came home. He didn't look right but I was happy to take him home.

'I've had enough Liva, no more,' he said on our drive home.

'It's early days, darl. You're still full of anaesthetic,' I said, refusing to look in his direction.

'You don't understand, Liva. You'll never understand.'

'No. I know that, but I want you better. That I understand.' Tears rolled down at the defeat in his voice.

'Okay. Keep your eyes on the road. I don't want to talk about it anymore.'

When we arrived home, it was getting dark. I pulled up outside the garage so Ken could get out of the car with plenty of room. He got out and started to walk through the garage and I noticed he was swaying unsteadily. I jumped out of the car in a panic and ran towards him. I grabbed his arm around my shoulder while I hooked my other arm under his armpit around his body.

'Oh no! Here we go again,' I screamed. He was going down and there was nothing I could do to stop it. He saw a metal shelf and thought that could stop us, but the shelf wasn't secured to the wall.

I was first to hit the concrete floor, Ken on top of me, the metal shelf and toolboxes on top of Ken. For a moment I lay there, trying to feel all my limbs and get my bearings.

'Are you okay?' I heard Ken say.

'Yeah, are you?'

He didn't move. I wriggled my way out and screamed at the top of my lungs. 'Somebody help!'

I couldn't see Ken's eyes; they were full of blood.

Neighbours heard me and came to help. We put Ken's head on a pillow while I cleaned the blood off his face. He had a deep cut above his brows, so it wasn't as bad as it looked. The neighbours helped to get Ken into bed, then left.

Ken appeared okay but I took him back to the vascular surgeon the next day. I was helping him out of the car outside the surgeon's office when he went down, taking me with him again. The surgeon and his staff came running out to help. He took one look at Ken's black eye and shook his head. 'I can't send you back home. You'll have to go back to hospital while we figure out what's going on. You are a danger to yourself, not to mention your wife.'

Ken looked blankly ahead and said nothing.

The ambulance was called and Ken was taken to another hospital. He was admitted to ICU for four days, then a week later, he came home.

My darling's body was breaking down but I refused to see in Ken's pleading eyes that he'd had enough. I was all geared up for yet another battle, a battle that my inner consciousness told me I would lose.

29

Save the last supper for me

It had been a tough year, but I was still on a mission to get Ken better. *I'll never give up,* was what I thought.

It was the year that he would reach a milestone — his 70th birthday. I planned a surprise celebration to mark his special day in November 2019.

But things weren't good when he woke up one morning. 'I hope you're not planning anything for my birthday. I don't want anything and I don't feel like seeing anybody.'

I was devastated to hear him say that. 'I hope you'll allow me and the kids to share your special day, at least. If you must know, I've booked us at a resort close enough for the kids to come and spend the weekend with us, and if you get tired you can retreat and rest.'

I saw his face relax and he reluctantly agreed.

The day before his birthday, we boarded the car ferry to cross to the other side of the bay where the girls both lived. We took a leisurely drive to the resort I'd booked at Torquay. After checking in, we got to our room and found a birthday card and a bottle of red wine awaiting our arrival. But the days of enjoying a red were long gone for Ken. However, it was a lovely token and the girls enjoyed it on his behalf.

That evening, Ken was on a bit of a high and unusually energetic. I wanted him to save all that for his birthday the next day, but I was also greedy and wanted to enjoy that rush of energy that he rarely got these days. We had a quiet dinner at the restaurant, overlooking the beautiful golf course below and the ocean beyond. It was just the two of us and I'll treasure that for years to come. *You saved the last supper for me.*

As I had feared, Ken used up all his energy. On his birthday, I woke up and opened my eyes and Ken was just lying there looking at me.

'Oh, you're awake. Happy 70th birthday, darl,' I said and edged up to kiss him.

He kissed me back with an apology. 'Thanks, but I'm sorry, I'm not feeling too good. I don't think I can make lunch.'

'That's okay, no need to apologize, as long as we have you with us.' I reached over to the phone and ordered a breakfast tray for two and we shared that in bed.

The planned birthday lunch didn't happen. We changed the lunch venue back to the resort. The girls and their families came and we had lunch without Ken.

By mid-afternoon, he felt a bit better, and we took the cake up to the room as there were enough grandkids to make a heck of a party. *Look around you, Ken. This is the family we've created — two daughters, two sons-in-law and seven grandkids.* It was priceless to watch Malakai, Eleanor, Leilani, Grayson, Orlando, Harlem and Loxy all draped across the bed singing 'Happy Birthday' to their pa and helping him with his cake and presents. The girls presented him with a book they had made, *Seventy Years of You*. I looked in awe at the man I'd dared to marry many moons ago; his face lit up and, at that moment, I knew he was the happiest.

Elizabeth with Paul and Tema with Andrew opened the bottle of red and toasted Ken's birthday. The grandkids were delighted with Pa's chocolate birthday cake, which I'd ordered from a nearby chocolatier.

'The kids will be hyper after that much chocolate,' Ken said.

'Shh, not our problem,' I said.

The next day, Ken was a bit better and the kids joined us for a family breakfast before we came home.

'That's exactly how I wanted it, darl. Thank you. I may not feel well, but I really enjoyed and appreciated it,' he said on our way home.

'I couldn't let your 70th pass without acknowledging it. Thank you for making the effort, as I know it wasn't easy. I would've given you the world if I could. I love you so very much,' I whispered, grateful for the privacy of our car.

'Oh Liva, you have given me the world. I have had, we have had, a bloody good life, haven't we?'

We both sat in silence as the humming of the ferry's engine took over our space. My brain was in overdrive at the significance of his words.

We've had a good life. What the heck did he mean by that? Is he giving up on me? On us?

Four weeks after his 70th, Ken wanted to have the neighbours over for a Christmas drink in our backyard. It was our way of thanking them for all their love and support throughout what we believed had been one of our darkest years.

We started at 3 p.m. in the backyard but we finished up inside the house. The last person left at 9 p.m. and Ken lasted the night. He was saying goodbye, I was sure of that.

Like his birthday, we celebrated Christmas for the first time ever with just us, our girls and their families. Every year, our Christmas table had always been shared with either my extended Tongan or Australian family. It had been a tradition of mine that a trip to Queen Victoria Market was a must, where I bought the seafood and all the Tongan delicacies I could find. It was like a trip to the market in Tonga when I'd been a little girl. Grandpa had bought me butterscotch dumplings and a little bowl of fresh almonds in their shells, and I'd thought it was the best.

In later years, when Ken couldn't accompany me to Vic Market, I would buy six hot jam doughnuts and bring them home to share.

Hmm, I haven't been back to Tonga for a Christmas since I left in 1981. I wonder if it's still the same. Are they still singing carols in the village? Maybe one day when Ken gets better, we'll go for Christmas.

30

Liva, I am tired

It was 2020 and I wasn't optimistic about the year ahead, and I had good reason to feel this way.

At the end of January, my darling was admitted to the local hospital. He was anaemic and required a blood transfusion. On 25 February, he had a routine check-up with now Professor Max Wolf, and he was admitted to a different hospital in Melbourne. A bone marrow biopsy delivered the final blow.

Professor Wolf came in and sat at the end of Ken's bed while I tried to do the crosswords beside him.

'I'm glad you're here, Silva. The results of the biopsy show bone marrow failure. Possibly treatment-related.'

What are you saying? Did the high-dose chemo do this? I wanted to ask but didn't dare.

'Ken, you have a condition called myelodysplasia. It can develop into leukemia. You will require frequent blood transfusions.'

Fuck! Fuck! Fuck!

'Don't be too hard on yourself, Max. At least you bought me time and I had a bloody good time,' Ken said. 'I had a bloody good time,' he repeated.

I will never forget the resignation in his voice for as long as I live.

The message was delivered and Professor Wolf drifted out of our room, leaving us with our tears. Ken just hugged me while I sobbed. I wanted to climb into his bed and hold him for the night, forever, and never let him go, but I had to leave. I had to go home ... alone with my thoughts.

It was dark by the time I left the hospital. The drive home seemed longer than usual with so much going through my head. When I got home, it was quite late. I Googled the definition of myelodysplasia. It said, 'The survival rate for the highest risk category is nine months.' That was a good enough stat for me; it was worth fighting on. Ken was not in the high-risk category. Or so I thought.

Sleep overtook my body, but not for long. *The aircraft is on fire and it's broken in half, like the launching of a spacecraft. Ken is in the half that's still going even though it's on fire, while I'm trapped in the half falling back from the sky. I'm unable to help him. 'Ken! Ken!' I scream. I'm falling, falling ... towards the earth.*

I bolted upright, still screaming. My face was all wet but I wasn't sure whether it was from tears or sweat. I sat on our bed all alone, crying, and wanted to forget the horrible dream. *What the fuck does that mean?* I wanted to call Ken but maybe he was sleeping. I had to wait till the next morning.

I rang then and he answered on the second ring, which made me think he was playing with his phone as he usually took longer to get it.

'Morning, darl. How was your night?' I asked.

'I was in a lot of pain and had a fever last night. How was yours?'

'Okay, but lonely.' I decided not to tell him about my horrible dream. *He had a fever and I dreamed he was on fire. Oh gosh, what does that mean?* 'Do you need anything from home? I'll have some breakfast first then make my way over.'

'No, thanks. I'll see you soon. Drive carefully and I love you.'

He hung up before he could hear my reply, 'I love you more. See you soon.'

By the time I got to the hospital, Ken had had another blood transfusion. He always waited for me to help him with his shower and shave. After lunch, a doctor I'd never seen before visited. 'Hello, my name is Dr Chang. I'm from the palliative department.' *Where did that come from? I didn't know we were at that stage. I know what palliative means. End of life.* I lost all ability to talk.

'Everybody has different needs,' he continued. 'Rather than spending your days on a chair receiving blood, you might consider ticking off what's left on your bucket list, Ken.'

I couldn't believe how Ken sat there and nodded his head. *Didn't he hear what he said? Oh my god, darl, he's saying you're going to die. You're beyond repair.* I wanted to scream at him. *No. No way, not on my watch. Miracles do happen.* I still wanted to believe.

For the first time throughout our journey, I didn't hear Ken say, 'We'll get through this. We've done it before.' *Where is his fighting spirit, the one I admire so much?*

From that day forward, I felt I was fighting alone and I refused to hear or see the inevitable. There were days when Ken felt better, but there were days his pain was relentless. After ten days, he was transferred to another hospital in the Mornington Peninsula, closer to our home. 'Ken needs some rehab to help strengthen his failing body before coming home,' Dr Chang told us.

I volunteered to care for the white man who had given me the world. Once we were settled at home, we had visits from the home hospice nurses. They took over the care and pain management for Ken, together with our loyal family GP, Dr Simon Pilbrow. He'd been caring for Ken for the last 30 years, too.

Our home life was consumed by appointments and hospital visits. My career was on hold while I took full-time care of the love of my life. I slowly turned our bedroom into a hospital ward. In my mind, I was going to nurse my Ken back to life. But even the palliative nurses assured us that we were at the comfort care stage. *The what?* I was still praying for that miracle.

When Ken lost his appetite, I sourced the best supplement recommended by a dietician. I feared muscle wastage, so I massaged his frail body twice daily. I helped and encouraged him to do simple exercises every day. I organized for a physiotherapist to come twice weekly.

All this proved fruitless, but I was relentless. *There has to be a way.*

31

Flying solo

In spite of all the love and care I gave my darling, in the end it wasn't enough to keep him with me. Terrified he might slip away all alone on his last visit to hospital, I moved heaven and earth to make sure he got his final wish, as his pleading voice kept echoing in my ears. 'Liva, can I please come home?'

Covid was the barrier to our quest to get Ken out of hospital. 'Mum, how are we going to get him out? I'm coming with you,' Tema said.

'Watch me, Tema. Liz, you can stay and make some soup and light the fire to keep the house warm. Dad would like that.'

'What if they won't let him out? I hope you have a plan B so you won't be too disappointed,' Liz said.

'Thanks for your vote of confidence, Liz. Whose side are you on?' I scolded.

'Just saying, because you'll be no good to Dad if you fall apart when the hospital refuses to let him out.'

I hated it when she was like her father with her logic. Tema, on the other hand, just like me, wore her heart on her sleeve, ready to headbutt and trip over. 'Liz, I don't think that's necessary. Come on, Mum. Let's go and get Dad,' Tema said.

With Tema by my side, armed with a wheelchair and blankets, it was like déjà vu. Tema drove while I made some phone calls on the way. I called the hospital. Soon I was transferred to the Covid ward. 'Can I help you?'

'Yes, you can. Silva McLeod is my name. I'm Ken McLeod's wife and I'm coming to take him home.'

'I'll have to talk to the doctor in charge about that. We haven't received the result of his Covid test.'

'No, you don't understand, Ken wants to come home and you'd better get him ready. He doesn't have Covid, I'm in the car on my way and will be there in 45 minutes.' I hung up.

We arrived at the hospital at 10.30 a.m. Tema pushed the wheelchair with Ken's dressing gown and blanket on it. Outside the hospital, there was a queue lining up for the two officers who took names and temperatures.

We stopped at the Covid station to be screened and to answer some questions. Once I told the officer that we were there to take Ken McLeod home, she told us to wait. She then spoke to someone on the phone and before I knew it, security was there. 'Sorry, you're not allowed in. You have to remain in the car and the doctor will call you,' he said.

'No, you don't understand, we don't want to come into the hospital, we're here to take Ken home, out of hospital. If you won't let us in, can you bring Ken out?' I pleaded.

'They're still working on discharging him but you must remain in the car. The doctor will call you.' So Tema and I returned with our empty wheelchair and sat in the car.

At noon, Ken FaceTimed me. 'Where are you?' he asked. I stared at his face on the screen. He looked pale and zombie-like.

'I'm outside in the car park with Tema. They won't let us in.'

Tema leaned over and took hold of the screen. 'Hi, Dad. As soon as they let us in we'll take you home. Don't worry, Mum isn't going home without you.'

'I kept telling them I want to go home but they're not listening. I don't have Covid. You call them, Liva, you're more forceful than I am.'

'Hang in there, darl. I love you.' I ended the call. Both Tema and I burst into tears at the sadness on his face.

'Mum, he looked so sad. We have to take him home, I'm calling Andrew, he's a good negotiator.'

'Okay, thanks. Maybe a fresh head would be good. I'm too emotional.'

While Tema talked to Andrew, I called Lizzie to update her.

I knew that Ken had reached his limit when he called again and repeated the same thing. He sounded defeated, exhausted and fed up. He sounded drugged up as well, his words slurred. That was my cue — I wasn't going anywhere without him. We quickly went to get a sandwich and ate in the hospital carpark, afraid to miss the doctor's call that never came.

Andrew arrived and he too was getting frustrated with the bureaucracy. After numerous unproductive calls back and forth to the ward, I started to doubt whether I could take Ken home. I'd had enough of being diplomatic. I rang the ward again and demanded to speak to the doctor in charge, knowing it would be a different doctor for the afternoon shift. When the female voice came on, introducing herself as the ward doctor, I was beyond caring.

'I've been sitting here in the carpark since 10.30 a.m. and now it's 4.30 p.m. It's getting colder and very late to get Ken home. This is not a jail. Are you going to release Ken or shall I engage my lawyer and the media? This is bullshit. I was told that the Covid test result came back negative hours ago, so what is the problem?' I tried unsuccessfully to not yell but my voice was now escalating.

'We're just getting him onto the wheelchair,' the doctor said.

Oh! That was easy. So why did it take so long?

Finally, at 5 p.m., my Ken was wheeled out in a white hospital gown. He looked so lost but I knew he was happy to come home. I noticed he clutched something in front of him. It was his phone, the only possession he had. I was so happy to see him, I pushed all questions out of my mind. *Thank you, Lord.*

Once Tema and Andrew had transferred Ken safely into the car, I turned on the nurse who was trying to give me a brief. 'Seriously! What was the problem?'

'We had to take another Covid test,' he said.

'Why? I was told it was returned negative, but I could've told you that,' I said seething.

'Hospital policy dictates that two tests should be carried out.'

'There you go again. Fucking policy. Unbelievable. You people really know how to fuck with people's minds.' I snatched the script he had in his hand and stormed off.

I was just glad and relieved to have my Ken with me.

Andrew followed us in his own car to help with Ken's transfer to the house. It was Saturday, 6 June, and a very cold night. From there, we continued our battle to keep Ken comfortable.

For the last month, I found an alternative painkiller to Targin and Endone, opioid-based painkillers. Desperation drove me to marijuana. It was against our doctor's advice and against my ethics but I was on yet another frantic endeavour. At this point, I was prepared to cop the consequences, if only to give the love of my life a blissful couple of hours.

On our last few nights, we lay side by side and chatted into the early hours of the morning. Out of nowhere, Ken said, 'Liva, look at me. This is no life for either of us. It would be easier for me and you if I go.'

'Oh Ken, if only I could control your pain. I'll never complain. I'm happy to take care of you just to have your company. We can still share a coffee, a meal and have a laugh watching our funny TV shows.'

'I'm sorry, darl, but I've made up my mind.' He looked determined as he delivered his final verdict. The conviction in his voice was enough to rip my heart out. He was very calm, no faltering in his voice. *What about me? He's so heroic. I could only wish for a fraction of that.* Where was the strong white man I'd loved and married? We shared a lot of tears as we both realized the inevitable.

'How would you feel if I get married again?' I asked.

'I don't know about you, but I'll never get married again,' he said, sounding almost annoyed by the question.

'Answer the question, Ken. I asked how would you feel if I get married, not you?'

'Well, it's up to you, but I wouldn't,' he said in a huff.

'No! Hm! I think you're such a jealous puss,' I teased.

'Well, I guess you're still young. It's going to be a lonely life flying solo. As long as you're careful and make sure he's going to be better than me and treat you well, then you should,' he finally said in a serious voice.

'Hm, so you're willing to share me, but with conditions?' I laughed.

We then lay together for a while, caught up in our own thoughts, content to be in each other's arms.

I broke the silence. 'I'm scared.'

'Why?'

'Of making decisions by myself.'

'Huh! That's a lot of bullshit, Liva. All our married life you made all the decisions. And even on the rare occasions that I made one, you still went ahead and changed it. So don't give me that crap now.'

'See, you didn't know that I was only confident making those decisions because you were right behind me to either pat me on the back for a job well done or pick me up when I fucked up. The thought of making my own decisions without you is very daunting.'

He reached out and pulled me to his chest and allowed me to cry.

When I recovered enough to continue our conversation, I looked into his eyes. 'Together forever. I've sourced us a rock at Bunurong Memorial Park as our resting place. It's so close to the water that you could almost cast a fishing rod over. If the time comes, you'll go ahead and wait for me. Would you like to see the map of where it is?' He nodded, so I opened my phone and found the photo of our rock.

'That's nice. Thanks.'

'The chapel is also next door in case you change your mind.' I smiled.

'Very unlikely, but thanks,' he said sarcastically.

'Maybe I'll bring you home after cremation until I kick the bucket too, and the girls can put us both together under our rock.'

Once again Ken, the pragmatic man he was, turned on me. 'What would you do that for? You put me to rest and you get on with life. You have the girls and the grandkids, so stop this nonsense.'

'Get on with life? Listen to yourself, Ken. What life? When you're done, I'm done too.' *How can he be so calm and okay with it?* 'Can't you see what this is doing to me? I'm breaking. No, I'm shattered. Why did you bring me here only to leave me?' I sobbed.

'I hope you don't regret meeting me, falling in love, having our girls and the life we had. If I could give you the world I would. If I could stay with you I would. I have no regrets in bringing you here even if I have to leave you. Hopefully, with time, you'll find happiness again.'

'No regrets. You know I'm very grateful, thankful for the life we had but when I was young, in love, I thought we'd be together forever. Very childish I know.'

The moment was rudely interrupted by my alarm for his medication, but I was grateful for the soulful chat we had.

I gave him his meds and a few drops of his blue dream CBD oil. Then I watched him while he slept. He was ready to break away and allow me to continue navigating solo. He was so sure of what he wanted in life, even in the afterlife. He was in control to the end.

32

Until we meet again

I continued to nurse the love of my life under the watchful eyes of the palliative nurses. 'Ken, we're going to insert a little butterfly into your belly to help administer your pain relief when needed, is that okay?' the nurse asked on one of her visits.

A butterfly was a tube inserted under the skin for the admission of morphine. The two tubes were shaped like wings, hence the name butterfly.

'Sure,' Ken said, throwing his white sheet down.

I knew what those butterflies meant. The end of life was near. I had to prepare.

In my culture, when a person passes, their clothing must be in natural material with no buttons, metal or plastic. Traditionally, there's no coffin either — we wrap our loved ones in tapa cloth (made from bark) or mats (woven from pandanus). I could only control what Ken was wearing. Liz and Tema were in no position to help me fulfil those needs. Their understanding of my culture was shallow. Unless you live it, you can't feel the depth and richness of such ritual. Therefore, I spared my girls the agony and the sadness of facing the inevitable death of their father.

Covid restrictions were also in place. Modern technology, online shopping and the post office became my new helpers.

From our bedroom window, Ken could see who was coming and going from our front door. He watched when deliveries arrived and I collected the parcels and whipped them away.

One day curiosity got the best of him. 'What are you buying now?' he asked, sounding annoyed.

'Nothing.'

'There are a lot of deliveries to the door so how can it be nothing?'

'Well, if you must know, I had to source natural material for you as I don't have any sisters here to help me. Would you like to see?'

'No, thanks,' he said with an understanding look.

Since we'd brought Ken home from hospital both Elizabeth and Tema had brought their family to see Ken separately, then their husbands had taken the kids home while they'd stayed with us. They took alternate days to go home and see their kids. They both lived on the other side of the bay, which made the commuting a bit tricky.

The last time Tema ducked home she brought back Loxy. It was Tuesday, 16 June. The palliative nurse came for a visit to change the butterfly that hadn't been used. Ken was quite chatty.

'Silva, can I have a chat with you and the girls?' the nurse asked. We left Ken and we went and sat at the kitchen table. She opened up a plastic box and out came a demo butterfly kit. 'I wanted to give you a demo on how to administer medicine through the butterfly. Is that something you could do, Silva? You don't have to do it if you don't want to. If we're not around you can call the ambulance and they will come and do it.'

'Yeah, I can do it,' I said while Tema started to blub.

'Yeah, if Mum can't do it, I can,' Liz added. *Not that I would allow that.*

'How long do you think we have?' I asked.

'I don't think Ken is ready yet. I wouldn't say days but maybe short weeks away and definitely not months.'

After the butterfly demo, the nurse left. 'You heard the nurse, maybe this is a good time for you both to go home and take a breather,' I said to Liz and Tema. 'Don't think I'm pushing you away, but it's the logical thing to do.'

'You go, Tem. I'm staying put,' Liz told her sister.

So Tema and Loxy said goodbye. Ken knew that Loxy would be the last of his grandchildren he would see. He had tears in his eyes. 'Would you like to see the other grandkids?' I asked.

'No, I've already said goodbye.'

Throughout that night, Ken kept calling, 'Tema. Tema.' *Is he calling Tema our daughter or Tema my mum?* I wondered.

When he called Tema again, I turned his face to mine. 'Who am I?'

'Liva, Liva.'

'Tema's gone to take Loxy home. Would you like her to come back?' I asked.

'Yes.'

I believed he knew the time was very near and Tema was missing. Because the nurse had told us a few short weeks I didn't want to alarm Tema. It hadn't even been 24 hours since she'd left.

The next morning, on Thursday, for the first time, Ken refused to take his tablets and his supplements too. The palliative nurse came at 10.30 a.m. This time she attached a syringe-driven pump (a pump to regulate the morphine) to the butterflies already on his tummy.

'We'll start off with a small dose of morphine just to keep him comfortable and I'll swing by later in the afternoon for a review,' the nurse said before she left at noon.

We were surprised when Tema walked through our front door at 3 p.m. 'Oh my god, whatever's happened since yesterday?' She was shocked when she saw her dad.

He started to shut down. He didn't talk any more.

At 5.37 p.m., in the love and warmth of our home, Ken was surrounded by the love of his life, his girls, just the way he'd wanted. He kept his mind and his dignity all the way to the end. He opened his eyes and searched for me. 'I'm here,' I said moving up towards him. He locked them onto mine for the final time as he let out his last breath and closed his eyes again. I watched helplessly as the love of my life, my soul mate, my mentor and the wind beneath my wings took flight. *Till death do us part. Until we meet again.*

'Oh no, no. Darl, I love you. Always.' I held him and I cried.

'Oh, Dad.' I could hear the girls in unison as they sobbed.

The Tongan in me kicked in as I prayed. 'Our Heavenly Father, please receive thy Ken into your arms. He couldn't stay with me any longer. Please comfort him and take his pain away. You have called him to join your realm. You have gained an angel today. I won't complain, as you've blessed our little family with many happy years. But we love him and will miss him always. I thank you for the life we had. I thank you for the love we've shared. I thank you for the husband, the dad, and the grandfather we were blessed with. Please take care of him until we meet again. I pray in the name of the Father, the Son and the Holy Spirit. Amen.'

Thursday, 18 June 2020, is etched into my core and soul. The day that my heart was ripped apart and shattered into million pieces.

Once the girls had said their goodbyes, I sent them out of our bedroom and I had my time alone with Ken. I laid down and just held him. I didn't want to let go as I sobbed.

I heard the doorbell but I didn't move. The palliative nurse came back but it was all over. She too left me alone with my grief and sorrow.

I turned on the music on my phone: 'I'll Never Love Again' by Lady Gaga and Bradley Cooper. We both loved her music. I bathed and changed Ken into fresh clothes, making sure he looked his best. I was sad that he'd gone but happy with the way he'd left, surrounded by so much love.

Liz became the executor and she diligently followed instructions that had been laid out. She contacted the funeral director and requested that Ken be picked up at 6 a.m. the next morning. She advised Ken's brother and sister so they could break the news to their 96-year-old mum and be with her.

Just before dawn, the undertaker arrived as instructed. We said our final goodbyes. I'd never envisaged the extreme pain I would feel when Ken was wheeled out our door. He was leaving and he would never enter that door again. My legs went to jelly. I asked the driver to take a lap of our court as the three of us linked arms and watched the hearse disappear into the darkness. I didn't fail to notice a half-moon was up. *That's how I feel right now. Ken; you took the other half.*

I stormed into my bedroom and slammed the door shut as I buried my face in Ken's pillow, crying as I'd never cried before. Then the thought of Lizzie and Tema shook me out of my selfishness. What kind of a mother was I? The girls had just lost their father, too, and here I was neglecting my duty as a mum. I went out, seeking my girls, but they had gone into their separate rooms to deal with their own grief.

Ken had wanted his ashes to be buried at Bunurong Cemetery. The rock had become a laughing point towards the end, as when every visitor came I heard Ken saying, 'Apparently, I've got a rock.' The strength in him never failed to see things in a lighter spirit.

At the funeral home, I was surprised at the lack of choice of coffin/ casket. In my culture, a funeral is the last thing you would be penny-pinching on. Ken's was no exception. The flowers on top of the casket had to be meaningful, too. I ordered 70 white roses to represent each year he'd lived, white for purity and green foliage for life. The chapel was chosen for the serenity of its position, surrounded by water and with fountains visible through the windows. It was a heavenly sight.

I asked the girls to take me to a place where I could purchase the casket of my choice for their dad. I knew this decision was against Ken's wishes, but I had to satisfy the Tongan in me. 'Don't waste too much money on a coffin,' he'd said. 'I'm going to be cremated, not buried. Use that money to do the things you wanted to do but I held you back.'

Well, you're not here now, Ken, so I'm calling the shots.

This was going to be the last expense I would ever spend on my Ken, so I wasn't holding back. At over 6 feet tall, I made sure he was going to be comfortable, even in death. Once everything was in place, I was happy to move on to the next task.

It was time to go and see my aged mother-in-law, the loving nan of my girls. It was one of the hardest things I had to do. Life wasn't meant to happen this way, that a mother had to bury her son. Ken's sister Linda and brother Bruce and his wife, Brenda, were also there. This was my family, too.

I walked over and hugged Mum without a word. The grief-stricken woman looked every bit of her 96 years. She looked as if she'd been crying for days. Linda had been staying with her since the news of Ken's passing. But when I saw her hug the girls, I thought she was going to break up. She cried openly, shaking. She didn't have to say anything, her grief was bared for all to see.

'He's free of pain now,' Mum finally said, as if she was talking to herself. 'He hadn't been well for a very long time.' She sat back in her recliner and the girls sat on the floor holding her hands.

I was grateful to share this quiet time with Ken's mum and siblings. We shared some memories with tears and laughs over coffee. Then Lizzie drove us home to face the first night without my Ken. It was never going to be easy, but with our beautiful girls by my side, together we made it through.

33

'Ofa'anga folau a:
Smooth sailing, my love

I had three brothers, three sisters and Kelesi, my niece (Selai's daughter), living in Sydney and Brisbane. Once they heard of my loss, they all came to be with me. This strong family bond was something I was grateful for in my heritage, even though they were like a tsunami that swept through our home.

'That's why Ken loved us, we're happy people,' my loudest brother, 'Alani said.

We had a family meeting that night. Nuku, one of my brothers, was a Methodist minister and he led with a prayer first then a speech to represent the family. I felt very old, as these types of family meetings were normally held at the home of one of the elders of the family. I was the oldest of my siblings so it was hosted in my lounge room.

'A phrase we often hear, the number of people who came to pay respects after you've passed sums up the person you once were. That rings true today. Liva, we want to show you how much Ken was respected and loved by all of us, your family. In Tonga, we would bring mats, tapa cloth, pigs and cows but that would be useless here in Australia. We want to show you that you're not alone, we want Ken to know you're not alone. Please accept this gift we've put together and we hope it will help in some small way,' Nuku said.

He handed over an envelope, which I opened later, finding a significant amount of money in it. Ken had loved my family and they came to pay back that love and respect. I knew that Ken wouldn't have accepted that gift, but I had no choice but to say, 'Thank you.'

I had been unaware that my Tongan family were coming and the funeral program was already arranged and printed. Out of respect to my minister brother, I quickly arranged a Tongan service with my family at Rosebud Funeral Chapel the day before. Rosebud Chapel was where Ken was kept until his send-off.

I went early to check on Ken because I knew my family would want to say goodbye. He looked so handsome, even in death, as if he was just sleeping. The funeral director brought him into the chapel and lit the tall candle for us, just in time, as my siblings poured in. Ken would have been impressed — they were on time.

Elizabeth and Tema walked into the chapel draped from head to toe in traditional mourning mats. They showed their respect for their father in Tongan style. I couldn't have been any more proud and thankful for my sisters, who had prepared them, and for their understanding approach.

We all sat around Ken. My brother 'Alani moved his chair right up next to him and rested his arm on the casket. The rest of my family were almost in a huddle, singing Tongan hymns. It was hard to keep my emotions intact when 'Alani started up one of my favourite Tongan hymns and the rest of my siblings joined in.

> 'Eiki koe 'ofa 'a'au, koe moana loloto
> Pea ngalo hifo kiai, 'eku ngaahi angahia
> Lord, thy love is like the deep ocean
> And my sins are lost, in the depths thereof.

Ken may not have cared about the lyrics but he would've loved the singing and it felt special.

Reverend Nuku led the small but intimate service. Apart from a prayer, the rest of the service was informal as we shared memories of Ken visiting Tonga. We cried and laughed and 'Alani said, 'Ken was a Tongan trapped in a white skin.'

The next morning, the day of Ken's send-off, Tema drove my sister 'Ana and me to Bunurong via Rosebud Funeral Services. I had requested to see Ken for the last time and to tuck him in before they transferred him to Bunurong. Tema gave me a small wooden box that contained letters from her and the kids to give Ken. I placed it in his hands. I printed a picture of me that Ken had had on his screensaver and placed it on his chest. It was one of the rare pictures of me standing inside the engine nacelle of my other love, the Boeing 777. I said a prayer, cranked up the music and hoped that he could hear me. Lady Gaga belted out the chorus of 'I'll Never Love Again'. By the time the song had stopped, I couldn't bring myself to tuck him in. That final gesture was just too much. I bent over and kissed his loving face for the last time. "Ofa'anga folau a — smooth sailing, my love,' I whispered.

Only 35 people were allowed to be part of Ken's service because of Covid restrictions. We arrived at the chapel just before Ken. My sisters were already there fluffing about with their mats and tapa cloth to put Ken's casket on. Ken arrived and was transferred onto the prepared place in front of the chapel. He was 20 minutes early for the scheduled service, so my family did what they do best — sing. They sang Tongan hymns and some songs from our childhood. Considering they were small in number, the unaccompanied melody that poured out like a choir from the small chapel was unbelievable. My Australian family and friends were introduced to a small part of my culture. Even in death, Ken brought the two cultures and families together as his farewell gift.

Our love for each other was so strong that it gave me the strength to pay tribute to my darling heart. I took a deep breath as the celebrant introduced me to the small gathering. I stood in front and bowed to Ken, the white man I'd dared to love, who'd given me the world.

'How ironic that Ken might say that it took until now for me to finally bow to him. Never mind, darl. Better late than never.

'Tonga was a big part of Ken's life and I think it's only appropriate that I share a bit of that with you today. Ken arrived in Tonga in 1979, a 29-year-old and very handsome electrician.

'We got married in my little village of 200 people in Vava'u. Ken accepted me, my family and my humble beginnings. We sat on the floor to eat and Ken sat on the floor with us. We ate with our fingers; Ken ate with his fingers. Ken loved my family, as you can see, for every brother and sister I have in Australia is here with me today. Thank god for Covid, because I tell you what, I have seventeen brothers and sisters and they would all be here if allowed.

'I'd like to share a short story to sum up the man I love. We were holidaying in Plantation Island, Fiji. We went for a walk. There was a runway that ran from one end of the island to the other. To get to the other side, you had to go down into a ditch then across the runway. I didn't know that Fiji was infested with frogs. They were everywhere and I stood frozen and terrified, unable to move, unable to cross. Ken turned around and put me on his back and piggybacked me across to the other side. A black woman on a back of a white man. Unheard, unseen before.

'Ken saw no colour. Ken saw no status. Ken saw no difference in culture. He only saw me. And for that Ken, I love you with all my heart. You will always be the wind beneath my wings.'

Epilogue:
My wings have been clipped

I went back to Bunurong Memorial Park two weeks later to organize Ken's headstone. During our meeting, I asked the consultant, 'Where's Ken now?'

'In the storeroom.'

'Oh! In the dark, amongst strangers?'

The consultant looked confused when I blurted out against Ken's wishes, 'Can I take him home until you're ready?'

'Of course.' She left to collect Ken but when she returned, she had two plastic boxes. 'Two? Why?'

'Sometimes the ashes don't fit into one, so they put them into two containers.'

'Whoa! That's not good enough. I left him whole and I want him whole, not split up. This is disrespectful in my culture.'

On the drive home with Ken's ashes on the front seat, I couldn't believe the relief and comfort I felt taking him home. I'd advised the memorial park that I would source my own urn made from natural material and had ordered a handmade wooden one.

Finally, his beautiful hand-carved urn made from mango timber arrived. *How appropriate.* I chuckled at the thought that Ken was resting not under but in the mango tree at last. I thought he'd like his new home. I couldn't wait to put him all together in his new urn.

The Covid restrictions ramped up as Victoria went into hard lockdown. We were only allowed to travel within 5 kilometres of our home, and only for essential services. Bunurong Memorial Park was outside the limit and I couldn't get Ken's remains transferred. I looked at the beautiful timber urn in front of me. I knew I couldn't wait for the lockdown to be lifted. I had to put Ken's remains together and free him from the plastic boxes.

I slid open the timber urn and released Ken's remains into it. 'Darl, I'm sorry to disturb you but you can breathe now and rest beside me.' I cried as I laid the timber urn on his side of the bed. 'I hope you'll forgive me and be happy that your presence here at our home gives me comfort. I promise I'll put you to rest at our rock when I'm healed, then you can wait for me there.'

Sadly, we lost Ken's mum on 1 October 2020. I believe she never recovered from the loss of her firstborn.

The pandemic had been running amok and border closures around the world had been enforced. State borders in Australia were no exception. The biggest sufferers were the aviation and hospitality industries. On 3 October 2020, Virgin Australia announced the discontinuation of the international airlines. I was one of 250 pilots who were made redundant.

As if grieving for my Ken and his mum wasn't enough, I now had to grieve for my flying career also. How ironic that I lost both of my loves within three months.

In July 2021, I was offered a domestic flying position back with Virgin Australia but with one team member down, flying would never be the same again. Ken and I had been a team. Without him, flying no longer had a place in my heart. Perhaps, in due time I might heal and once again find the courage to return to the sky. Thankfully, I have the right to return to Virgin Australia within the next five years.

I don't fear death as I know Ken will be on the other side, watching, until my journey is completed, and he'll be once again ready to take me into his arms. Until then, I have to find a way to continue. Without the wind beneath my wings, I can't fly, but I shall walk.

Acknowledgements

It takes a whole village to raise an island girl. With warm heart, I would like to acknowledge my rich Tongan heritage that shaped me for the woman I am today. Thank you to my village people of Vava'u. Malo 'aupito.

I'm forever indebted to my late husband Ken McLeod; without you my love, there wouldn't be a story to tell. In 40 years of marriage you've taught me all there was in preparation to survive on my own. With heavy heart I say thank you. I know you would be watching from above with pride.

Elizabeth and Temaleti, my beautiful daughters, thank you for your support and your biased views: 'It's your story, Mum, through your eyes only. Own it. We're so proud of you.' Of course, you would say that and I love you for your bravery. To my grandchildren: Malakai, Eleanor, Leilani, Grayson, Orlando, Harlem and Loxy, the stars in my eyes, thank you for the reason ...

To Ken's family: Norm and Mona McLeod (Mum and Dad), Bruce and Brenda McLeod, Linda McLeod, thank you for welcoming me into the McLeod's clan and still continuing to love and support me on my own today.

I would have been lost without the help of my dear friends Lynette and Brian Earles. Your silent presence meant more than words could say. Thank you for the laughs and the tears over the years, Lynette. I needed you then and I need you more now.

A very special thanks to Ken's long-time friends: Keith and Maria Stephens, Paul and Pam Murphy for your unbiased love. Thank you for your encouragement in writing my story, accepting me into your lives and I know you have my back.

Lynne Stringer, thank you so much for your tireless efforts in helping me structure and assemble my first draft. Thank you for your sensitivity in cutting and filtering the huge manuscript. (I bet you didn't know I was Tongan when you accepted the challenge.) I appreciated your constructive feedback that made this book possible. Thank you for your encouragement and pushing me to have my story published.

A huge thank you to Anouska Jones and the collaborative team at Exisle for helping me navigate through this uncharted territory. I will always be grateful for the opportunity you've given me, of letting my voice be heard. Whakawhetai koe.

I would like to acknowledge Virgin Australia Airlines (a very white male-dominated airline) who gave me the opportunity of a lifetime. For an old island woman and of colour to be one of their airline pilots in those days was unheard of but I am humbled. With that life experience, it gives this book a whole new direction. Therefore, I hope that my story could be the bridge for the minority, especially young girls from underprivileged backgrounds, to cross over and reach their unreachable dreams. Thank you, Virgin Australia.

Finally, I would like to thank Australia, my adopted home, for all the comfort, love and safety it provides that I and my family take for granted today. I would like to acknowledge and pay respect to the past, present and future traditional custodians and elders of this nation.

INDEX

INDEX